Spiritual Exegesis and the Church
in the Theology of
HENRI DE LUBAC

Spiritual Exegesis and the Church in the Theology of HENRI DE LUBAC

SUSAN K. WOOD

WILLIAM B. EERDMANS PUBLISHING COMPANY
GRAND RAPIDS, MICHIGAN

T&T CLARK
EDINBURGH

© 1998 Wm. B. Eerdmans Publishing Co.
255 Jefferson Ave. S.E., Grand Rapids, Michigan 49503

Published jointly 1998 by
Wm. B. Eerdmans Publishing Co.
and by
T&T Clark Ltd
59 George Street
Edinburgh EH2 2LQ
Scotland

Printed in the United States of America

03 02 01 00 99 98   7 6 5 4 3 2 1

Library of Congress Cataloging-in-Publication Data

Wood, Susan K.
Spiritual exegesis and the church in the theology of Henri de Lubac / Susan K. Wood.
p.   cm.
Based on the author's thesis (doctoral) — Marquette University.
Includes bibliographical references and index.
ISBN 0-8028-4486-3 (pbk. : alk. paper)
1. Lubac, Henri de, 1896 — Contributions in hermeneutics.
2. Lubac, Henri de, 1896 — Contributions in doctrine of the church.
3. Bible — Hermeneutics.   4. Church — History of doctrines — 20th century.
5. Bible — Criticism, interpretation, etc. — History — 20th century.
6. Catholic Church — Doctrines — History — 20th century.
I. Title.
BS476.W66   1998
230'.2'092 — dc21   98-17360
CIP

British Library Cataloguing-in-Publication Data

A catalogue record for this book is available from the British Library
ISBN 0 567 08638 0

Contents

Contents

Preface

EVEN THOUGH THE DIALOGUE PARTNERS have changed, I find many similarities between the concerns which animated the movement in France in the 1940s known as the "new theology" and those which trouble the Church today. As outlined by Jean Daniélou's article "Les orientations présentes de la pensée religieuse" (1946), one of the main issues included a rupture between exegesis and systematic theology, resulting in a systematic theology divorced not only from scriptural studies but also from spirituality and the life of the Church. This rupture, owing to the increasing fragmentation and specialization of theological disciplines, continues to our own day. Today one finds not a few biblical exegetes who have difficulty in identifying themselves as theologians. From the other perspective, as valuable as the historical-critical method in biblical studies has been, the systematic theologian frequently has insufficient biblical training to incorporate biblical theology into systematic theology competently. For that matter, within the world of biblical scholarship there are discussions of what exactly constitutes biblical theology.[1] The historical-critical method has shown us that there is not "a" biblical theology, but a number of biblical theologies relevant to the Scriptures.

Henri de Lubac did not solve these problems for our contemporary theological situation, but his retrieval of the traditional hermeneutic with his study of patristic and medieval exegesis demonstrates a unity which exists when the Scriptures are read from a certain perspective. Interestingly enough, this work is historical and theological, not biblical. By this

---

1. Brevard Childs, in particular, tries to give a definitive answer with his attempt at canon criticism. See *Biblical Theology in Crisis* (Philadelphia: Westminster, 1970).

I mean that de Lubac is not directly engaged with a study of the biblical text: he does not undertake the work of biblical exegesis. However, the principles he derives from traditional hermeneutic provide him with the intellectual tools for thinking about history, the Eucharist, and the Church. Through a historical study of patristic and medieval exegesis we have a theology of history, a theology of symbol and sacrament (including not only the sacred species but also the sacred text), and a way of thinking about the Church's relationship both to Christ and to the Eucharist. Paradoxically, his work on spiritual exegesis is ultimately not so much about biblical exegesis and four different meanings of a text — the literal, tropological, allegorical and anagogical senses of Scripture — as it is about these relationships. These relationships remain operative in the daily life of the Church through its public prayer in the liturgy and in the individual appropriation of biblical texts in the *lectio divina*, divine reading, of Christians.

De Lubac does not advocate that we abandon the contemporary methods of biblical scholarship, what he calls "scientific exegesis." He does, however, wish to retrieve a unity which has been lost. This vision of unity constitutes a sort of mysticism in de Lubac's grasp of the sacred mysteries. For de Lubac, history is not merely a succession of linear events which stretch from the Old Testament to the New Testament and from there into the future. Rather, in his view type and antitype, past and future, are depth dimensions within each other. History is to be understood spiritually and spiritual realities are to be understood historically.[2] De Lubac's mysticism is a discovery of spiritual meaning in historical realities. It is thus a mysticism of the incarnate rather than an escape to something otherworldly or disembodied. Furthermore, it is not a solitary contemplation of God by an individual, but is social, found in the common destiny of all to be reunited in the unity of the whole Christ in his Mystical Body.

It would be a grave mistake to suppose that de Lubac had a number of separate theological interests, one being spiritual exegesis, another being the Church, and another being the Eucharist. In his mind they are all of a piece. It is the hope of the present study to demonstrate this unity through consideration of the four senses of Scripture. These are not simply four different approaches to a scriptural text, but ways of relating the text

2. Henri de Lubac, *Catholicism* (London: Burns, Oates & Washbourne, 1950), 83.

to the events in history, to an individual Christian, to Christ and Church, and ultimately to the final completion of all in the eschaton.

The renewed interest in Henri de Lubac is possible because his work is more accessible to English-speaking readers thanks to the translations being published by William B. Eerdmans in Grand Rapids, Michigan, and Ignatius Press in San Francisco. The availability of these translations is a valuable service to the Church and the theological community.

The present book is a shortened, more focused version of what began as a doctoral dissertation at Marquette University. I gratefully acknowledge the contribution of many people who made this project possible: my family who believed in me, my religious community, the Sisters of Charity of Leavenworth, for the time and resources to do doctoral study, and the Arthur J. Schmitt Foundation who assisted with their award of a Schmitt Fellowship for the academic year 1984-1985. Saint John's University in Collegeville, Minnesota, provided me with released time for research.

Many people who assisted along the way include the Rev. Joseph A. Murphy, S.J., William J. Kelly, S.J., Rev. Joseph T. Lienhard, S.J., and Dr. Patrick Carey. The library staff of Marquette University and Saint John's University provided valuable assistance. I thank, too, Tamara Stasik, my student assistant, who proofread the revisions.

I cannot adequately thank the Rev. Donald J. Keefe, S.J. As the director of the original dissertation, his prompt reading of my material, his probing questions, insightful criticism, supportive presence, and friendship were invaluable.

Finally, I am grateful to Henri cardinal de Lubac, S.J., the subject of this study, for having shared his scholarship, faith, and integrative vision of the Church. Through his many theological works he has been a true mentor.

Collegeville, Minn.   Susan K. Wood
July 1997

For my mother

with love and gratitude

CHAPTER ONE

De Lubac and the "New Theology"

DE LUBAC CLAIMS NEVER TO HAVE WRITTEN an ecclesiology, but an examination of his works reveals the Church to be a frequent theme. Perhaps Hans Urs von Balthasar offers the most accurate characterization of de Lubac's work when he describes it as having an organic unity rather than being a systematic presentation.[1] That is, many themes and issues are missing from what would be a systematic ecclesiology, yet there is an organic unity within his work on grace, exegesis, and ecclesiology. The thesis of this study is that the organic continuity identified by Hans Urs von Balthasar is largely due to de Lubac's immersion in the patristic and medieval practice of spiritual exegesis. The principles of this exegetical method provide an intellectual framework which enables him to discuss the relationship between such themes as Christ and the Church, Christ and salvation history, and the relationship between the Church and the Eucharist. While de Lubac is not himself engaged in a study of the biblical text and consequently does not practice spiritual exegesis as a method of biblical interpretation, the senses of Scripture constitute a theological method for correlating many of his major theological themes. A retrieval of the principles of patristic and medieval exegesis responds to the interests of theologians associated with the movement known as the "new theology."

---

1. Hans Urs von Balthasar, *The Theology of Henri de Lubac: An Overview* (San Francisco: Ignatius Press, 1991), 24.

1

Henri de Lubac's Life

Henri de Lubac was born in Cambrai (Nord), France, on February 20, 1896. As a young student, he studied with the Sisters of Saint Joseph, then with the Christian Brothers in Bourg-en-Besse and at the school of the Jesuits of Mongré. In 1912-1913 he studied law at the Catholic university in Lyon. Henri de Lubac entered the Society of Jesus in 1913. French laws hostile to religious communities had exiled the Jesuits in Lyon to England from 1901 to 1926. Thus de Lubac entered the novitiate at Saint Leonard's in Sussex. He was drafted into the French army in 1915, where he served until 1919; during this time he was wounded in action and received the Croix de Guerre. He then pursued philosophical and theological studies on the Isle of Jersey from 1920 to 1923, followed by a Jesuit regency at the college of the Jesuits of Mongré from 1923 to 1924. His advanced theological training, commenced in Hastings, was completed at Lyon-Fourvière, where he was ordained a priest August 23, 1927. Named Professor of Fundamental Theology in the School of Catholic Theology at Lyon in 1929, he added the history of religions to his responsibilities a year later. In 1935 he joined the faculty of the theologate at Fourvière, where he taught only occasional courses until 1940. Remarkably, given his influence in the Church and in the theological world, Henri de Lubac never received a doctorate in theology.

In 1940 he founded, with Jean Daniélou, the series *Sources chretiénnes* in order to make patristic and medieval texts accessible to a larger public. From 1941, while at Fourvière, he was an inspirational force behind the clandestine journal of the Resistance, *Cahiers du témoinage chretién,* along with Pierre Chaillet and Gaston Fessard. Among his several contributions to the *Cahiers* is a well-known article on anti-Semitism. From 1945 to 1950, de Lubac was editor of *Recherches de science religieuse.* Beginning in 1944, he actively collaborated in the collection *Théologie.* His reputation as a scholar was established by two contributions to this collection, *Surnaturel* (1946) and *Corpus Mysticum* (1949). He became a member of the Institut de France (Académie des sciences morales) in 1953, but a degree of suspicion concerning his work, evident since 1935, persisted in many quarters.

De Lubac's first major work, *Catholicism* (1938), contains in seminal form the major themes of his theological career. Subtitled "A Study of

Dogma in Relation to the Corporate Destiny of Mankind," it emphasizes the communal character of salvation and the solidarity of the human race in its common vocation. His controversial work on the supernatural destiny of the human person, *Surnaturel* (1946), challenges the interpretation of St. Thomas which holds the possibility of a purely natural order. De Lubac argues that there is only one destiny for an intellectual creature, the supernatural destiny of the Beatific Vision. *Corpus Mysticum* retrieves a eucharistic theology grounded in the symbolism of patristic exegesis by showing that the term *corpus mysticum* originally referred to the Eucharist rather than to the Church.

Such original and fresh examinations of the tradition in order to address the problems of the present were consonant with the spirit of a theological movement in France in the 1940s known as the "new theology," although de Lubac maintained the actual existence of such a "school" of theology to be a myth. Nevertheless, a number of theologians associated with Fourvière, including de Lubac, were thought by many to be implicated in the encyclical *Humani Generis* (1950). De Lubac left his teaching post in the School of Theology at Lyon as well as the residence at Fourvière and moved to Paris in 1950. His friend Hans Urs von Balthasar reported that "his books were banned, removed from the libraries of the Society of Jesus and impounded from the market." The specific books in question included *Surnaturel, Corpus Mysticum,* and *Connaissance de Dieu* as well as the volume from the journal *Recherches de science religieuse* containing his article, "Mystery of the Supernatural."[2] The first was out of print, and the second edition of the third was nearly so, but *Corpus Mysticum* had just been published. An interesting footnote to the affair is that in the course of being moved from one storage place to another, a number of copies of *Corpus Mysticum* disappeared and became the object of a small black market.

De Lubac, however, later said that during those years he was never questioned, and did not have a single discussion with Roman Catholic authorities, the papal curia, or the Society of Jesus about the main issues.

2. This event is also narrated in Henri de Lubac, *Mémoire sur l'occasion de mes écrits* (Namur: Culture et vérité, 1989), 75. The first two texts have never been translated into English. The third was reedited, not corrected, but augmented and published as *The Discovery of God,* trans. Alexander Dru (Grand Rapids: William B. Eerdmans, 1996). French original: *Sur les chemins de Dieu* (Paris: Aubier, 1956).

Nor was he ever told what he was accused of or asked to provide something equivalent to a "retraction" or declaration.[3]

Cardinal Gerlier demonstrated his support of de Lubac by refusing to name a successor to his chair and by naming him a member of his theological council. De Lubac's fidelity to and love of the church during this personally trying time found expression in his book *Méditation sur l'Eglise* (1953), a work all the more remarkable for the circumstances surrounding its publication. His portrait of the *vir ecclesiasticus,* the "man of the Church," contained in this work describes his own spirit and labors:

> In a true man of the Church the uncompromisingness of the faith and attachment to Tradition will not turn into hardness, contempt or lack of feeling. They will not destroy his friendliness, nor will they shut him up in a stronghold of purely negative attitudes. . . . He will not give way to the spirit of compromise. . . . He will take great care that some generalized idea does not gradually come to take the place of the Person of Christ. . . . His total and unconditional faith will not come down to the level of a sort of ecclesial nationalism. . . . He will hold himself apart from all coteries and all intrigue, maintaining a firm resistance against those passionate reactions from which theological circles are not always free, and his vigilance will not be a mania of suspicion. . . . He will not show himself hostile on principle to legitimate diversity.[4]

The reversal of his ten years of ostracism resolved slowly and gradually, culminating in the invitation from Pope John XXIII to be a consultant for the preparatory Theological Commission of the Second Vatican Council in 1960. Heinz Neufeld, however, chronicles the lingering suspicion of de Lubac on the part of some at the Council.[5] At the Council itself he was a *peritus* and was associated with the work on the documents *Dei Verbum, Lumen Gentium,* and *Gaudium et Spes.*

3. For de Lubac's account of these events, see *Mémoire sur l'occasion de mes écrits,* 61-80.

4. Henri de Lubac, *The Splendour of the Church,* trans. Michael Mason (New York: Sheed and Ward, 1956), 184-186.

5. Karl Heinz Neufeld, "In the Service of the Council: Bishops and Theologians at the Second Vatican Council (for Cardinal Henri de Lubac on His Ninetieth Birthday)," in *Vatican II: Assessment and Perspectives: 25 Years after 1962-1987),* vol. I, ed. Rene Latourelle (New York: Paulist Press, 1988), 74-105.

After the Council, in addition to being appointed to the International Theological Commission, de Lubac was a consultor for the Secretariat for Non-Christians as well as for the Secretariat for Non-Believers. On February 2, 1983, Pope John Paul II elevated Henri de Lubac to Cardinal in the Roman Catholic Church. De Lubac requested and received a dispensation from the requirement of being ordained a bishop, arguing that he could not perform the duties of a bishop properly at his age and therefore would not do justice to the episcopal office. De Lubac died in Paris on September 4, 1991.

A Theological Renewal

The theology of Henri de Lubac aims to "recover Christianity in its fullness and purity" by "returning to its sources, attempting once more to seize it within its periods of explosive vitality."[6] De Lubac's fundamental conviction is that in order for Christianity to be adaptable to a modern generation it must first discover its essence through a return to the originating creative thought of its doctrines and institutions. Such a theological program requires a solid historical foundation established upon the patristic and medieval giants, whose chief value, in turn, lies in their witness to the apostolic tradition. More proximately, many of the themes in de Lubac's theology can be traced to the inspiration of the Tübingen school, especially to J. A. Möhler, the philosophy of Maurice Blondel and Joseph Maréchal, and the thought of John Henry Newman.[7] It is beyond the scope of this study to trace these historical roots of de Lubac's theology. For the present, it suffices to direct our attention to the lively controversy in the 1940s surrounding de Lubac's efforts, which clarified the issues with which theologians were grappling during the two decades before the Second Vatican Council.

6. Henri de Lubac, *Paradoxes* (Paris: Livre français, 1946), 67-69.
7. These historical influences are treated in Austin J. Lindsay, "De Lubac's Images of the Church: A Study of Christianity in Dialogue" (Ph.D. dissertation, Catholic University of America, 1974).

The "New Theology"

Intellectual history situates de Lubac within a movement known as the "new theology." This title was first conferred on the work of a group of theologians associated with the Jesuit faculty at Fourvière who were particularly interested in Scripture and patristic literature as theological sources.[8] Since there was never a specifically delimited group of theologians who identified themselves as representing a "new theology," the identification of those associated with this movement varies from author to author. Fouilloux mentions Jean Daniélou, Henri de Lubac, Gaston Fessard, Henri Bouillard, M.-D. Chenu, and Pierre Teilhard de Chardin, although Chenu was a Dominican and not connected with the group at Fourvière.[9] Labourdette includes Hans Urs von Balthasar. Critics of the movement associated it with the thought of Maurice Blondel. The term "new theology" or *"la nouvelle théologie"* was first used by Msgr. Parente in the *Osservatore Romano,* February 1942, in reference to two Dominican theologians, M.-D. Chenu and L. Charlier. Reginald Garrigou-Lagrange then applied it to certain Jesuit theologians in 1946. De Lubac himself disliked this title because it contradicted the very impetus of the movement which was to renew theology by a return to its biblical and patristic sources. Congar would later refer to it as an "abusive" term.[10]

8. De Lubac taught only occasional courses at the Jesuit scholasticate at Fourvière. His primary teaching responsibilities were at the Catholic University at Lyon.

9. See M. Labourdette, M.-J. Nicolas et al., *Dialogue théologique* (Saint Maximim: Les Arcades, 1947), 99. This book collects several of the articles in the debate surrounding the "new theology."

10. Since it is beyond the scope of this book to trace the history of this movement, I am including only that part of the controversy bearing directly on an interpretation of Henri de Lubac. I refer the reader to T. M. Schoof, *A Survey of Catholic Theology 1800-1970* (New York: Paulist Newman Press, 1970), 157-227; Etienne Fouilloux, *Les catholiques et l'unité chrétienne du XIXᵉ au XXᵉ siècle: itinéraires européens d'expression française* (Paris: Le Centurion, 1982), 887-894; T. Deman, "Tentatives françaises pour un renouvellement de la theologie," *Revue de l'Université d'Ottawa,* Section spéciale 20 (1950): 129-167; A. Esteban Romero, "Nota bibliografica sobre la llamada 'Teologia nueva,'" *Revista Española Teologia* (1949): 303-318, 527-546.

The Goals of the "New Theology"

The general orientation of this "new theology" was sketched out in an article by Daniélou, "Les orientations présentes de la pensée religieuse."[11] In this article he noted the gulf which had opened up between theology and the pressing concerns of the day; he surveyed a progressive rupture between exegesis and systematic theology, with each discipline developing according to its own method, and a consequent aridity within systematic theology.[12] The "new" orientation aimed at a reunification of theology, including a return to Scripture, a return to the Fathers, and a liturgical revival. Much of the emphasis upon the biblical renewal, according to Daniélou, concerned an interpretation of the Old Testament that restored its character as prophecy and figure.[13] Such an interpretation of the Old Testament underscored its relation to the New Testament. The revival of patristic studies followed naturally in the wake of the biblical renewal since the work of the Fathers comprised a vast commentary on Scripture and incorporated just such a figurative interpretation of the Old Testament.

The liturgical renewal associated with this movement affirmed the mystery of a personal God and sought to use liturgy as a theological source. As a balance to a notion of the efficacy of liturgical action, the liturgical renewal reaffirmed the sign value of liturgy and sought to understand better the symbolic elements of liturgical worship.

Henri de Lubac contributed to the renewed interest in the patristic tradition in theology by founding with Jean Daniélou the series *Sources chrétiennes* in order to make the works of the Fathers available to a wider public. He also collaborated with the Jesuits of Lyon-Fourvière in the *Théologie* series: his contributions to it include such historical studies as *Corpus Mysticum: L'Eucharistie et l'Eglise au moyen-age; Histoire et Esprit:*

---

11. Jean Daniélou, "Les orientations présentes de la pensée religieuse," *Etudes* 249 (1946): 5-21. The anonymous collective response (see pp. 7-9) describes this as "An article of broad information with sometimes precipitous formulas." In particular, Daniélou's references to what Marxism can contribute to a sense of historicity, as well as to what existentialism can contribute to the dialogue between theology and contemporary thought, remains undeveloped and unnuanced. Another article of broad orientation on the same subject is Yves Congar's "Tendances actuelles de la pensée religieuse," *Monde nouveau* 4 (1948): 33-50.

12. Daniélou, "Orientations présentes," 7-8.

13. Ibid., 9.

L'intelligence de l'Ecriture d'après Origène; and his magisterial four-volume work, *Exégèse médiéval.*[14]

Since de Lubac's work emphasizes the distinctive theological and exegetical orientation of the Fathers, it is helpful to look further at what those theologians sympathetic to this orientation perceived to be the benefits of this "new theology." Daniélou noted several distinctive patristic contributions which scholastic theology had lost sight of. The first of these is the notion of history which he described as "étrangère au thomisme."[15] Christianity not only includes a matrix of doctrines, but represents a progressive "economy" of the saving action of God. Secondly, patristic theology envisages salvation in its collective dimension as the salvation of humanity rather than in its individual dimension. This is certainly emphasized in de Lubac's work. His book *Catholicism* is subtitled "The Social Aspects of Dogma." The introduction of this foundational work written in 1938, considered as the "program" of his later works, contrasts the social and individual dimensions of Christianity:

> We are accused of being individualists even in spite of ourselves, by the logic of our faith, whereas in reality Catholicism is essentially social. It is social in the deepest sense of the word: not merely in its applications in the field of natural institutions, but first and foremost itself, in the heart of its mystery, in the essence of its dogma. It is social in a sense which should have made the expression "social Catholicism" pleonastic.[16]

In his article, Daniélou noted that the return to the dogma of the Mystical Body supports such a patristic emphasis.

A third advantage noted by Daniélou, but perhaps better expressed by Louis Bouyer, is the contribution of patristic study to a more existential theology.[17] As Bouyer expressed it, the Fathers were not only nominal

14. De Lubac, *Corpus Mysticum: L'Eucharistie et l'Eglise au moyen age,* Coll. Théologie 3 (Paris: Aubier-Montaigne, 1944); *Histoire et Esprit: L'intelligence de l'Ecriture d'après Origène,* Coll. Théologie 16 (Paris: Aubier-Montaigne, 1950); *Exégèse médiévale: les quatre sens de l'Ecriture,* Coll. Théologie 41, pt. 1 and 2, 42, 59 (Paris: Aubier-Montaigne, 1959, 1961, 1964). *Exégèse médiévale* is hereafter designated simply as vol. I, II, III, or IV.

15. Daniélou, "Orientations présentes," 10.

16. De Lubac, *Catholicisme,* trans. Lancelot C. Sheppard (New York: Mentor Omega Book), xi.

17. Louis Bouyer, "La Renouveau des études patristiques," *La vie intellectuelle* (February 1947): 6-25.

"fathers" of a Christian civilization, but actually engendered the faith since their sanctity, for the most part, influenced their intellectual work in the Church. According to Bouyer, one of the most distinctive characteristics of the Fathers was their integrative vision. Scriptural commentary, spirituality, and liturgical tradition were all integrated in a view of the unity of the whole.[18] Since their theology was situated within a context of faith, their witness to the faith provided the existential dimension of their theology.

Although the controversy surrounding the "new theology" tended to set the proponents of scholasticism over against those wishing to return to patristic sources, Bouyer noted that the origins of scholasticism were in close and extensive contact with patristic thought, a fact eminently clear in the work of Thomas Aquinas.[19] Moreover, the scholastic tradition was but one intellectual tradition in the Middle Ages. The monasteries, particularly, used the Fathers not only as authorities, but as the inspiration for the form and orientation of the monastic theological questions.[20] Bouyer noted that the real rupture with patristic thought occurred only on the eve of the Renaissance and the Reformation. The Counter-Reformation, the silver age of scholasticism, witnessed "an arbitrarily simplified Thomism cut from its roots."[21] This resulted in a disproportion between the perceived importance of the dialectic apparatus of scholastic argument and of the scriptural and patristic base on which this dialectic rested. The first result of a retrieval of patristic theology would thus be a theology renewed at its foundation. Second, this renewed theology would unify knowledge and wisdom because purely speculative knowledge would be complemented by a kerygmatic theology which announced the Word of God. Third, the rationality of speculative knowledge would be balanced by a renewal of an appreciation of mystery within dogma.

Critics of the "New Theology"

One of the most outspoken critics of J. Daniélou and Henri de Lubac was M.-Michel Labourdette. In a critical review of both *Sources chrétiennes* and *Théologie,* in which he also cited Daniélou's article in *Etudes,* he noted the

18. Ibid., 9, 13.
19. Ibid., 15.
20. Ibid.
21. Ibid., 16.

parallel concerns of these collections and accused both series of being dominated by a prior theological intention which guided the commentaries and the choice of texts.[22] Labourdette lauded a theology conscious of its sources and its historical expressions,[23] and acknowledged that theology had become too theoretical and bookish, that questions were too often formulated according to traditional categories,[24] and that any understanding of a theological synthesis can profit greatly from a more precise knowledge of its historical and cultural milieu.[25] He sharply criticized, however, the general orientation of both series. Specifically, he stated that the renewed emphasis on the patristic tradition was accompanied by a depreciation of scholastic theology,[26] which in his opinion represented the "truly scientific state of Christian thought."[27]

Labourdette accurately identified the "new theology's" criticism of scholasticism. De Lubac's opinion that the scholastics had transformed a sacred history into an organized science remained constant. Twenty years later in his 1968 "commentaire du préambule et du chapitre I," he states that the scholastics "did not, however, abandon a consideration of history to the extent often claimed, but that it is necessary to recognize that in modern times, under the action of numerous and complex causes, the theology of the schools had finished by excessively divorcing itself not only from the mode of historical discourse, but from all attention to history, turning more and more to an a-temporal abstraction."[28]

22. M.-Michel Labourdette, "Etudes critiques," *Revue thomiste* 46 (1946): 353-371. Also printed in *Dialogue théologique* (Saint-Maximim: Las Arcades, 1947), 23-64. This volume contains reprints of the major articles of the debate, including the anonymous response to Labourdette's article with a counter-reply by Labourdette, "De la critique en théologie. Réplique." Daniélou did, in fact, contrast the new collection with the one directed by Hemmer and Lejay: "For this last, it was above all a question of publishing documents, testimonies of the faith of the ancients.

"The new collection thinks that there is more to ask of the Fathers. They are not only the witnesses of a past state of affairs; they are still the most current nourishment for people of today because we find there precisely a certain number of categories which are those of contemporary thought and which scholastic theology had lost." Daniélou, "Les orientations présentes," 10.

23. Labourdette, "Etudes critiques," 355.

24. Ibid.

25. Ibid., 363.

26. Ibid., 358.

27. Ibid.

28. De Lubac, "Commentaire du préambule et du chapitre I," Coll. Unam Sanctam 70 (Paris: Cerf, 1968), 186. Unless otherwise indicated, all translations are my own.

The historical emphasis raised the issue of the development of dogma, which many thought would render doctrine impermanent and relative.[29] For example, M.-J. Nicolas accuses de Lubac, in *Corpus Mysticum,* of historical relativism. Specifically, Nicolas criticizes de Lubac for having perceived the neglect of eucharistic symbolism as the necessary consequence of the scientific form of theology of the Middle Ages. Secondly, Nicholas criticizes him for considering this scientific form as the expression of an outmoded mentality that is perhaps less accessible to us and assuredly less traditional than the symbolic mentality of the Fathers.[30] Thirdly, Nicholas criticizes de Lubac in reference to his *Corpus Mysticum* and his "Introduction aux homelies d'Origène" in the series *Sources chrétiennes* for considering the introduction of dialectic, a method of thought at the root of scholastic theology, an impoverishment of theological reflection. Finally, he criticizes the return to symbolism, particularly in exegesis.[31]

The fear was that if every system of intellectual expression were to be judged by its relation to its historical situation, these judgments would become subjective and this subjectivity would replace impersonal truth.[32] Symbolism rather than analogy would then become the necessary category, for concepts would be judged by how well they expressed a "living" reality in a human person.[33] For example, Labourdette lamented the depreciation of intelligence, which would then be seen as only capable of attaining concepts — abstractions or logical categories empty of all pragmatic value. However, in another article, replying to the anonymous collective response which this first article

---

29. Labourdette, *Commentaire,* 356, 360, 362. For further material on historical and doctrinal relativism see Hans Urs von Balthasar, *Présence et pensée* (1942); Jean Daniélou, review of "Théologie et histoire de la spiritualité," in *Revue du moyen age Latin* (1945): 65; H. Bouillard, *Conversion et grâce chez Saint Thomas* (Paris: Aubier, 1964), 219-224; Henri de Lubac, *Corpus Mysticum* (1944), 365-367 and *Surnaturel* (1946), 5-6; G. Fessard, *Autorité et bien commun* (1944), 8; Daniélou, "Les orientations présentes," 14.

30. Nicholas's postscript to Labourdette's article "De la critique en théologie," in *Dialogue théologique,* by M. Labourdette, M.-J. Nicolas, et al., 139. A similar criticism occurs in his review of *Corpus Mysticum* in *Revue thomiste* 46 (1946): 384-388.

31. Labourdette, "Etudes critiques: la théologie et ses sources," *Revue thomiste* 46 (1946): 363. See Marcellino D'Ambrosio, "Henri de Lubac and the Critique of Scientific Exegesis," *Communio* (U.S.) 19 (Fall 1992): 365-388, as well as his dissertation, "Henri de Lubac and the Recovery of the Traditional Hermeneutic" (Ph.D. dissertation, Catholic University of America, 1991).

32. Labourdette, "Etudes critiques," *Revue thomiste* 46 (1946): 559-560.

33. Ibid.

elicited, Labourdette defended the possibility inherent within Thomism of accommodating a reflection on history: "We believe that Thomism is perfectly open to history and that the beginnings of that opening are not lacking even in the work of St. Thomas 'historically considered.' "[34] The depreciation of intelligence, however, would be the destruction of theology as a science.[35]

The articles by J. Daniélou and Labourdette represented to some extent the touchstones of each side of the controversy. In response to Labourdette's critique, Monsignor de Solages, rector of the Institut Catholique in Toulouse, and M.-J. Nicolas, provincial of the Dominicans of the Toulouse Province, publicly exchanged letters in the *Bulletin de littérature ecclésiastique*.[36] De Solages pointed out that Labourdette had denounced almost the entirety of the two collections, *Sources chrétiennes* and *Théologie,* then numbering eighteen volumes, while he had explicitly treated only the conclusion of Bouillard's *Conversion et grâce chez Saint Thomas d'Aquin* and Daniélou's introduction to his translation of Gregory of Nyssa's *Contemplation of the Life of Moses.* De Solages further noted the influence of Daniélou's article in *Etudes* on Labourdette's criticism of the two series. Both in Labourdette's article and in the subsequent responses to it, much emphasis was placed on Bouillard's work on Thomas Aquinas.[37]

The statement by Bouillard which gave most fuel to his critics was "A theology which would not be a theology of the present time would be

34. Labourdette, "De la critique en théologie," 121, 123, 124, n. 1 on 130, and 136.
35. Ibid., 363.
36. B. de Solages, "Autour d'une controverse," *Bulletin de litterature ecclésiastique* 48 (1947): 3-17.
37. This led to some interesting discussions on the role of analogy in theology, but since this does not directly touch on de Lubac's role in the controversy, I cannot develop this particular topic other than to indicate that this was a major theme in the discussion and to refer the reader to the article by J. Le Blond, "L'analogie de la verité, réflections d'un philosophe sur une controverse théologique," *Recherches de science religieuse* 34 (1947): 129-141. Labourdette and M.-J. Nicolas responded to this article in "L'analogie de la verité et l'unité de la science théologique," *Revue thomiste* 47 (1947): 417-466. Related articles include R. Garrigou-Lagrange, "Verité et immutabilité du dogme," *Angelicum* (1947): 124-139. Here Garrigou-Lagrange renews his opposition to the Blondelian notion of truth and the distinction proposed by Bouillard between "notions" which change with time and "affirmations" which remain stable and firm although expressed in diverse categories. Other articles by him include "Les notions consacrées par les Conciles," *Angelicum* (1947): 217-230; and "Necessité de revenir à la notion traditionnelle de verité," *Angelicum* (1948): 285-298. H. Bouillard replied to these articles in "Notions conciliaires et analogie de la verité," *Recherches de science religieuse* (1948): 251-270.

a false theology."[38] Garrigou-Lagrange in his article "La nouvelle théologie où va-t-elle?" ("Where Is the New Theology Going?") raised the cry that such a position jeopardizes the immutability of doctrine. He accused Blondel, Fessard, and Teilhard de Chardin of modernism. Concerning de Lubac, Garrigou-Lagrange stated that in *Surnaturel* (1946), de Lubac "is totally uninterested in the *pronunciata maiora* of the philosophical doctrine of St. Thomas," by which he meant the twenty-four thomistic theses approved in 1916 by the Sacred Congregation of Studies.[39] De Solages once again rose to the defense of the accused theologians in his article "Pour l'honneur de la théologie. Les contresens du Père Garrigou-Lagrange."[40] Regarding Garrigou-Lagrange's criticism of de Lubac, de Solages noted that it had ignored the thirty-page chapter in which de Lubac had explicated the thought of Saint Thomas.

A Collective Response

To what extent can one speak of a coherent movement known as the "new theology?" Daniélou disclaimed any role as a spokesman for such a movement, saying of his "Les orientationes présentes" that "the article in question was in no way in the spirit of a manifesto, but rather an article of general information on certain aspects of contemporary religious thought in France."[41] H. Bouillard denied the existence of a group whose members consciously employed a common theological goal:

38. "Une théologie qui ne serait pas actuelle serait une théologie fausse." H. Bouillard, *Conversion et grâce chez Saint Thomas d'Aquin. Etude historique,* Coll. Théologie 1 (Paris: Aubier-Montaigne, 1944), 219.

39. R. Garrigou-Lagrange, "La nouvelle théologie où va-t-elle?" *Angelicum* 23 (1946): 133. Pius X, with the *Motu Proprio* "Doctoris Angelici," published on June 29, 1914, prescribed that in all the schools of philosophy the principles and major propositions of Thomas Aquinas should be held. Twenty-four theses were submitted to the Sacred Congregation of Studies and approved by Pius X as containing the principles and major propositions of Thomas. *Acta apostolicae sedis* (August 1914). An English translation and commentary of these theses can be found in Peter Lumbreras, "The Twenty-Four Fundamental Theses of Official Catholic Philosophy," *The Homiletic and Pastoral Review* 23 (1923): 588-598, 1040, 1053.

40. De Solanges, "Auteur d'une controverse," 68-84.

41. J. Daniélou, p. 1 of a text of 20 pages, typed, both sides, with the signatures of Bouillard, de Lubac, Fessard, Daniélou, and Teilhard de Chardin. *Papiers Congar.* Cited by Fouilloux, *Les catholiques et l'unité chrétienne du XIXe au XXe siècle,* 889.

Why group under the title of "new theology" citations gathered from the most diverse works into anonymous sheets whose origin no one knows? Each author is responsible for his own statements, not those of someone else. One would commit an injustice by desiring to force someone's thought into a system created from all the pieces by the very person who criticizes that system.[42]

Such disclaimers notwithstanding, the issue is not so easily solved. A group of theologians did indeed publish a response to Labourdette's criticism. Unfortunately, the response was anonymous, and its very anonymity served to substantiate the thesis of a "new theology." Garrigou-Lagrange in a letter to Congar commented:

> I nowhere stated . . . that the various authors of whom I spoke had a common "system." . . . If something were able to give substance to this impression, would it not be the very manner of their response where, while claiming that they are different, they undertook together *in solidum* the defense of all that I had accused each one of them?[43]

The anonymous response had expressed the desire that Labourdette criticize specific texts rather than spread suspicion on a whole series. It also questioned the method used in his criticism, that of commenting on the articles or books of one author in reference to those of another without a thorough analysis of any. This again raised the question as to how homogeneous the group really was; as de Solages noted, it included theologians, a philosopher, and a scientist. This diversity in and of itself made such a method of criticism even more dubious than if all the works involved were by theologians. It is regrettable, however, that the anonymous response was itself guilty of much of what it criticized in its critics. As has been noted, its very anonymity made it representative of a group and thus substantiated claims of a certain homogeneity within that group. It, too, evidenced a reluctance to name specific books and authors. For example, the note regarding Nicolas's critique (p. 401) is an obvious reference to de Lubac's *Corpus Mysticum* although the book is never mentioned by name.

---

42. H. Bouillard, p. 8 of a text of 20 typed pages. Cited in Fouilloux, *Les catholiques*, 889.

43. Garrigou-Lagrange in a letter to Congar, 8 November 1949, cited by Fouilloux, *Les catholiques*, 891.

Most of the public discussion came to a halt in 1950 with the publication of *Humani Generis* on August 12, 1950, by Pope Pius XII. This encyclical reiterated the importance of scholasticism, cited the dangers of existentialism, denounced the concept of progressive evolution, and condemned, as compromising the gratuity of the supernatural order, the position that God could not create intellectual beings without at the same time ordering and calling them to the beatific vision.[44] No theologians were mentioned by name in the encyclical, but those associated with the "new theology" were clearly implicated.

In an interview in 1985 de Lubac commented that neither Pius XII nor any other legitimate authority of the Church ever took any action against him.[45] His superior general, however, without the formality of a written order, asked him to interrupt his teaching. At his request, de Lubac informed Cardinal Gerlier, the chancellor of the theological schools at Lyon, of this decision. For several years de Lubac was officially "on leave." The provincial catalogues of the Society of Jesus indicate that he resumed teaching in Lyon in 1954.

Regarding the encyclical *Humani Generis,* de Lubac noted that it was very different from what some had hoped for, disappointing those who were looking for a stronger censure of the "new theology." As for his own case, de Lubac commented:

> One can, if one chooses, find two allusions to me in *Humani Generis.* Pius XII mentions in passing his fear lest dangerous doctrines should be spread secretly. I have no reason to take that as referring to me. Rather, I have good reasons for thinking that for the Pope, at that date, the fear did *not* concern me. The second allusion is in connection with the supernatural: Far from containing any rebuke in my regard, the passage borrows a sentence from me to express the true doctrine. And it is no accident that it avoids all mention of that "pure nature" which so many established theologians wanted to canonize and accused me of not sufficiently appreciating.[46]

44. Claudia Carlen, ed., "Humani Generis," *The Papal Encyclicals 1939-1958,* 175-184. A bibliography on *Humani Generis* appears on pp. 183-184. See also M.-Michel Labourdette, "Les enseignements de l'encyclique," *Revue thomiste* 50 (1950): 32-55; Gustave Weigel, "The Historical Background of the Encyclical *Humani Generis,*" *Theological Studies* 12 (1951): 208-230.

45. Henri de Lubac, *De Lubac: A Theologian Speaks* (Los Angeles: Circle Publishing Co., 1985), 4; *Mémoire,* 72.

46. De Lubac, *De Lubac: A Theologian Speaks,* 4.

In this same interview de Lubac denied the existence of a "School of Fourvière" or a "new theology" of which he supposedly was the leader.[47] To at least some extent, however, this is a matter of definition and interpretation. While it is true that there was no "school" in an organized sense, the controversy as well as the anonymous response indicates that there was a "spirit" or undefined "movement" to renew theology by a return to traditional sources. The conflict with Boyer, Labourdette, and Garrigou-Lagrange represented a real difference in theological perspectives. While there is a certain irony in calling a theology based on a retrieval of patristic and medieval sources "new," such a shift away from the perspectives of neo-scholasticism did require some kind of designation.

Later assessments of the encyclical tend to concur with de Lubac's judgment. For example, Avery Dulles comments that the most important elements of the encyclical may prove to be its concessions rather than its affirmations: "while asserting the capacity of human reason to establish the preambles of faith, including the existence of God, the pope recognized the indispensability of moral dispositions and the important role of knowledge 'by connaturality.' " While defending the validity of scholastic theology, he praised the biblical movement, and noted that "theology grows barren when it does not constantly nourish itself from the original sources." He further notes that the encyclical urged theologians to devote careful study to new problems raised by our modern culture.[48] Dulles thus concludes that although *Humani Generis* may be called a conservative document, it is not reactionary or repressive; it has, however, suffered from a sometimes excessively rigid interpretation.

The Fundamental Issue: Relativism

The final value of the controversy, however, in spite of the inexactitudes and the sweeping generalizations, was to focus the fundamental issues. The question was whether a return to historical sources would lead to doctrinal relativism. The anonymous response did address this issue by making an unequivocal statement clarifying the position of its authors. They affirmed

47. Ibid., 3.
48. Avery Dulles, in *Revelation Theology: A History* (New York: Seabury Press, 1969), 153-154.

that it was evident from what they had written that "truth remains immutable across the centuries and our intelligence is not cut off from the absolute."[49] Second, they drew some distinctions which facilitated the discussion.

First, relativism takes two forms which need to be distinguished — historical relativism and doctrinal relativism. Thomism, as one moment of theological synthesis, does not and cannot exhaust all the intellectual nourishment contained in the preceding centuries, however scientific it may be. As a theological synthesis proposed at a given moment in history, it is not to be confused with doctrine. Furthermore, Thomism does not annihilate any more than it exhausts what has preceded it, since a systematization does not necessarily include the more concrete elements of the earlier tradition. Thus the authors affirmed that "the more one exalts Saint Thomas, the less one has to fear that a direct return to those sources that he himself used is a mistake."[50] On the contrary, that is all the more reason to return to those sources.

The second distinction concerns doctrinal relativism and the difference between an "anti-intellectual" and "anti-intellectualist" position. The first is against intelligence, while the second is against the tendency to reduce the Christian revelation to a system of ideas when it is first and foremost the manifestation of a Person, the Truth of a Person.[51] Such a concept of revelation always exceeds conceptual expression. The authors rejected an identification of a system with the truth or, even more, the notion of truth as a system, naming such an identification an intellectualist deformation.[52]

Spiritual Exegesis and the "New Theology"

A lively interest in the spiritual interpretation of Scripture coincided with the movement designated as the "new theology." The connection was more than coincidental, however, since spiritual exegesis, in addition to being the object of study of several of the theologians associated with the "new

49. Henri de Lubac, *La foi chrétienne* (Paris: Aubier, 1970), 391.
50. Ibid., 395.
51. Ibid., 396.
52. Ibid., 398.

theology" (especially Daniélou and de Lubac), also responds to many of their concerns.[53] Five points of correspondence between spiritual exegesis and the "new theology" are especially noteworthy.

First, the context and *locus* of this interpretation is the Church since in the traditional concept of exegesis, Scripture is always "in fide catholica tractata,"[54] that is, interpreted within the Catholic faith. The concept of tradition as bearer of the faith is very important. The spiritual interpretation of Scripture has been associated with the earliest strands of this tradition since St. Paul first used the word "allegory" in its Christian context.[55] The Fathers of the Church, privileged witnesses to this tradition, practiced the spiritual interpretation of Scripture. De Lubac takes care to emphasize the continuity of the tradition in the Church which has used spiritual exegesis and to examine critically historical works which put in doubt the continuity of that tradition.[56]

Second, this type of exegesis avoids extrinsicism and historicism. In extrinsicism, one moves directly from historical evidence to an assertion of faith in such a way that historical evidence becomes a demonstrable proof of faith. In historicism, there is a sharp distinction between the material and supernatural worlds. Biblical exegesis under the influence of historicism does not approach Scripture as a privileged expression of faith, but rather interprets it as any other historical document. Historicism denies that dogmas have any correspondence with the realities that they attempt to express.

The errors of both extrinsicism and historicism were articulated by Blondel, who perceived them as false solutions to the problem posed by

---

53. See, e.g., Jean Daniélou, *From Shadows to Reality: Studies in the Biblical Typology of the Fathers* (London and Westminster: ET 1960); *Origen*, trans. Walter Mitchell (New York: Sheed and Ward, 1955); "Les divers sens de l'Ecriture dans la tradition chrétienne primitive," *Analecta lovaniensia biblica et orientalia*, ser. II, fasc. 6 (Bruges-Paris: Desclée de Brouwer, 1948).

54. De Lubac, *Exégèse médiévale*, I, 59, citing Augustine, *De Genesi ad Litteram* 1.xii (PL 34.484).

55. Gal. 4:24.

56. In de Lubac's opinion, Joachim Fiore's exegesis lies outside the continuity of this tradition. *Exégèse médiévale*, II, 437ff. De Lubac's work differs from that of Beryl Smalley, *The Study of the Bible in the Middle Ages* (New York: Philosophical Library, 1952), in that Smalley stresses discontinuity in the exegetical tradition in the figure of Andrew of St. Victor where de Lubac stresses the continuity in this tradition exemplified by Hugh of St. Victor. De Lubac's references to B. Smalley's work are indexed in *Exégèse médiévale*, IV, 548.

a faith based on historical events which reciprocally guarantees those events a doctrinal interpretation.[57] The problem consists in this, that the content of the faith itself constitutes a historical reality, but is not under the jurisdiction of the historian's judgment. For example, Christianity is grounded in the historical event of the Incarnation, but the fact of God having become a human person cannot be proven by the secular historian. Blondel looked for a principle of explanation which would account for this double movement from historical event to dogma, and from dogma to interpretation of historical event. If this double movement is not held together in a unity, either history is considered to be entirely dependent on dogma, or dogma is seen to be entirely subordinate to history. Blondel sought to examine the proper authority of each and the manner in which dogma and history mutually condition each other.

In examining this problem, Blondel considered two solutions which he judged to be both incomplete and incompatible. The first, which he called extrinsicism he described as the separation of historical event from dogma. This separation occurs where the events serve as signs which, when subjected to elementary logic, lead to the conclusion of the divine character of the event. Three elements lead to this conclusion: the senses perceive a miraculous event, the event is judged to be of divine origin through ratiocination, and the supernatural is defined according to what is received in a revelation authenticated by the miraculously divine. Blondel notes that these three elements remain exterior to each other and are joined only by reason, resulting in an intellectual edifice founded uniquely on an empirical authentication.[58] This results in a relation of the sign to the thing signified, of events to dogma, and of our thought and our life to the truths proposed outside of us, which Blondel judges to be extrinsic.

57. Maurice Blondel, "Histoire et dogme. Les lacunes philosophiques de l'exégèse moderne," in *Les premiers écrits de M. Blondel* (Paris: Presses Universitaires de France, 1956), 149-228. First published in *Quinzaine* 56 (16 January 1904): 145-167; (1 February): 349-373; (16 February): 435-458. This article applies Blondel's philosophy of action to the biblical question. Although no names are mentioned in this article, Gayraud is representative of extrinsicism and Loisy of historicism. For an article sympathetic to this position see M. B. Allo, " 'Extrinsicisme' et 'historicisme,' " *Revue thomiste* 12 (September-October 1904): 437-465. For information on the historical context, pertinent bibliography, and a discussion and criticism of Blondel's position see Yves Congar, *Tradition and Traditions*, Part Two, trans. Thomas Rainborough (London: Burns and Oates, 1966), 359-368. French original: *La Tradition et les traditions: essai théologique* (1963).
58. Blondel, "Histoire et dogme," 157.

19

The problem with extrinsicism is that from the point of view of the proof or demonstration, what is important is the fact that God has acted and spoken, not what he said and did through human instruments, since the historical or natural aspects of events are excluded from the argumentation on which the authority of the Bible is founded. This leads to an absolutism uninterested in the internal criticism of texts or the work of the historian.[59] For example, the narratives of miracles in the New Testament would be cited as evidence of Christ's divinity, but would be divorced from any discussion of literary genre.

Blondel called the other unsatisfactory solution historicism. Historicism admits only the empirical data of events and fails to appeal to a principle outside of those events for their interpretation. Such a historical science cannot account for the spiritual reality which historical phenomena neither represent nor exhaust.[60] In historicism historical science takes the place of historical reality. Historical science, grounded in a phenomenological method, insufficiently expresses the substantial reality which transcends phenomenological observation.

Blondel looked for an intermediary between history and dogma which would facilitate their synthesis without compromising their independence. He found this intermediary in tradition — which includes historical events, the effort of reason, and the accumulated experiences of faithful action. He saw tradition as providing the human element in the act of faith which prevents a pure fideism. It is important to note that Blondel conceives of tradition from the point of view of a "philosophy of action." It is thus a "living synthesis" rather than a clearly defined object which is handed down and which never changes.

In his application of his philosophy of action to the biblical question, Blondel did not discuss the spiritual interpretation of Scripture. De Lubac, however, in his *Exégèse médiévale,* is conscious of the potential of this type of exegesis to respond to the problems articulated by Blondel.[61] De Lubac points out that the problem of the relationship between history as science and history as reality, otherwise stated as the relationship between history and dogma, was formerly discussed as the relationship between history and allegory. He questions, with Blondel, whether the objectivity of science

---

59. Ibid., 158.
60. Ibid., 168.
61. De Lubac cites this essay in *Exégèse médiévale,* III, 366.

really permits one to understand what one studies since such objectivity does not solve the problem of how to determine the vantage point from which to criticize or interpret the historical or literal senses.

De Lubac does not elaborate any further on the relationship between the spiritual interpretation of Scripture and the problems of extrinsicism and historicism as articulated by Blondel or the relationship between the role of tradition in this type of exegesis and Blondel's solution. However, from the perspective of Blondel's essay, the spiritual interpretation of Scripture can be seen to avoid such an extrinsicism and historicism because the spiritual senses are grounded in the literal or historical sense. Thus they cannot be separated from the historical any more than dogma can be separated from history. At the same time, the spiritual interpretation of Scripture provides the critical and interpretative vantage point from which to interpret historical phenomena — Christ and his Church. Finally, the spiritual interpretation of Scripture is governed by faith in Christ and this faith is not individualistic, but nurtured and transmitted in the tradition of the Church. This type of exegesis consequently responds to Maurice Blondel's proposal that the solution to extrinsicism and historicism lies in tradition.

Third, spiritual exegesis affirms the unity of theology and spirituality. De Lubac dates the dissociation of spirituality, exegesis, and theology from that period, after Hugh of St. Victor, when history and allegory separated.[62] History evolved into a positivistic science, leaving doctrinal questions to the theologian. Exegetes distanced themselves from the larger vision which gave intelligibility to their history and confined themselves to multiform details and the immediate significance of texts. This historical and literal exegesis ceased to interpret phenomena as elements within a divine plan of salvation.

At the same time, allegory developed in two different directions. In the first, allegory as the doctrinal sense of Scripture, became more rational, abstract, and speculative, giving birth to the great summas of the high Middle Ages. The *quaestiones* and the theological reasoning which developed at this time displaced theological speculation from its exegetical and historical foundation. De Lubac comments that if there is more of a historical sense in the *Summa Theologiae* of St. Thomas than in the work of many theologians who came after him, it is because there is more Scripture in his work.

---

62. *Exégèse médiévale*, III, 418-435.

In the other direction, allegory interpreted mystically developed into a highly individualistic spirituality, less scriptural and less theological, dominated by sentiment and imagination.[63] This spirituality was highly interior in a restrictive sense and detached from its ecclesial dimensions.[64]

The spiritual interpretation of Scripture, by contrast, permits a synthesis of the individual and the communal. The tropological sense of Scripture considers the individual in relation to the mystery of Christ, while the anagogical sense, itself a synthesis of the tropological and the allegorical senses, envisions the consummation of each individual and the Church at the end of time in the whole Christ, the ultimate fulfillment of all history and allegory.

Fourth, spiritual exegesis is inseparable from the liturgy which is structured to comment on the mysteries of Christ by a meditation upon the Old Testament texts within a dynamic of promise and fulfillment. De Lubac's treatment of the Eucharist in the eighth chapter of *Corpus Mysticum* develops the connection between exegesis and the liturgy. Louis Bouyer likewise develops the connection between spiritual exegesis and the liturgy where he comments:

> Spiritual exegesis, which is supposed by the whole liturgy, is an exegesis dominated by two principles. The first principle is that the Bible is the Word of God, not a dead word, imprisoned in the past, but a living word addressed immediately to the man of today taking part in the celebration of the liturgy. The second principle is that the Old Testament is illumined by the New, just as the New only discloses its profundity once it is illumined by the Old. We must be still more specific: the bond between the two is determined by allegory in the precise sense given to that term by antiquity.[65]

Bouyer's first principle, that the Bible is a living word addressed to the person of today, further supports the union between theology, exegesis, and liturgical spirituality.

Fifth, and finally, spiritual exegesis is consistent with the concept of

---

63. Ibid., III, 423.
64. Ibid., III, 424.
65. See Louis Bouyer, "Liturgie et exégèse spirituelle," *La Maison-Dieu* 7 (1946): 27-50. Citation translated by Walter J. Burghardt, "On Early Christian Exegesis," *Theological Studies* 11 (1950): 78.

Christ as both the object and the mediator of revelation. This Christological emphasis figures strongly in the work of the theologians of the "new theology," particularly Teilhard de Chardin and Henri de Lubac. The unifying element holding the senses of Scripture in interrelation is faith in the revelation contained in the Christ event. In this exegesis the revelation is not primarily the written document, but the Christ event which is prior to the document:

> Indeed, what we today call the Old and New Testaments is not primarily a book. It is a twofold event, a twofold "covenant," a twofold dispensation which unfolds its development through the ages, and which is fixed, one might suppose, by no written account.[66]

It is clear that the spiritual interpretation of Scripture is at least one possible answer to the concerns articulated by those theologians identified with the "new theology," concerns for the role of the Church as the context and *locus* of the interpretation of Scripture, for the problem of historicism and extrinsicism, for the unification of theology and spirituality, for the relationship between exegesis and liturgy, and for the Christological foundation of revelation.

The value of this spiritual exegesis is that while it provides an interpretation of history which confers meaning on historical realities from a faith perspective, it also grounds spiritual realities historically. These two poles provide the continual historical check and balance which differentiates the spiritual interpretation of Scripture from non-Christian allegory. The social character of Christianity finds its basis both in this

---

66. Here I rely on the translation offered by Lancelot C. Sheppard, although his English is much more static than the French. What is here translated "development" is the French "péripéties," which refers to a sudden change of situation in a dramatic action or a narrative. These changes not only unfold, but they also respond or react to one another. The narration of all this is supposedly never fixed by any written account. Thus the French evokes the dynamism of salvation history and the newness effected by Christ. The French text: ". . . ce que nous appelons aujourd'hui l'Ancien et le Nouveau Testaments, n'est pas, en soi, un ouvrage. C'est un double événement, une double 'Alliance', une double 'disposition' dont les péripéties se déroulent et se répondent au cours des âges, et dont on pourrait concevoir que le récit n'ait jamais été fixé par écrit," *Catholicisme: Les aspects sociaux du dogme*, 4th ed. (Paris: Cerf, 1947), 137. Translated by Lancelot C. Sheppard, *Catholicism* (New York: Mentor-Omega Books, 1964), 95. This same idea is expressed in *Exégèse médiévale*, IV, 290.

historical nature of revelation and in the fact that history mediates salvation. In de Lubac's theology, grace is concretely embodied in the world because revelation has, in Christ, taken a historical form. The Church, as social institution, is a social embodiment of this grace because of its inherent relationship to Christ. The demonstration of this, however, rests, first, on the historical character of the revelation and the Church's relation to this history and, second, on the Church's relationship to Christ. The principles of spiritual exegesis as understood by de Lubac offer an intellectual framework for considering both the historical and Christological character of the Church.

De Lubac does not call for a return to the spiritual interpretation of Scripture as it was practiced in the Middle Ages. He acknowledges that, as unfortunate as the separation between historical studies and theological studies, between theology and spirituality, has been, the specialization within theology was necessary and inevitable if history and allegory were to continue to develop.[67] Allegory had always been subject to excesses and during the Middle Ages had finally hardened while tropological interpretation had become insipid. Nevertheless, the spiritual interpretation of Scripture does offer principles which can reunite theology and spirituality, theology and exegesis. Such exegesis attempts to correlate the mysteries of the Christian faith and at the same time allows for both an individual and a communal appropriation of these mysteries.

67. *Exégèse médiévale*, III, 423.

CHAPTER TWO

The Spiritual Interpretation
of Scripture

SPIRITUAL EXEGESIS GENERALLY IDENTIFIES four senses of Scripture: the literal, allegorical, tropological, and anagogical senses. The literal or historical sense is the sense directly conveyed by the words of the text. It refers to the historical events related in the text such as the exodus or the sacrifice of Isaac, or to the text itself, as, for example, the laws. The allegorical sense interprets the literal sense in terms of Christ and the Church. The tropological sense applies the literal sense to an individual, and the anagogical sense is the eschatological meaning of the text. For example, according to the literal or historical sense Jerusalem is a specific Middle Eastern city. It refers, however, to Christ or the Church according to its allegorical sense, to an individual Christian according to its tropological sense, and to the eschatological kingdom (New Jerusalem) according to its anagogical sense.

Among de Lubac's major studies of such exegesis are *Histoire et Esprit,* a study of Origen's use of Scripture, and *Exégèse médiévale,* a four-volume study of medieval exegesis. De Lubac's immersion in and familiarity with this patristic exegesis is consequently amply documented.[1] The present

---

1. Henri de Lubac, *Exégèse médiévale: les quatre sens de l'Ecriture,* Coll. Théologie 41, Part I; 41, Part II; 59, Part I; 59, Part II (Paris: Aubier-Montaigne, 1959, 1961, 1964), hereafter designated as *Exégèse médiévale* I, II, III, or IV; *Histoire et Esprit: L'intelligence de l'Ecriture d'après Origène* (Paris: Aubier, 1950). De Lubac also treats this topic in "Allégorie hellénique et allégorie chrétienne," *Recherches de Science Religieuse* 47 (1959): 5-43; "Sens Spirituel," *Recherches de Science Religieuse* 36 (1949): 523-576; " 'Typologie' et 'Allé-gorisme'," *Recherches de Science Religieuse* 34 (1947): 180-226; his Introduction to *Homélies sur l'Exode,* by Origen, trans. P. Fortier, Coll. *Sources chrétiennes,* vol. 16 (Paris: Cerf, 1946),

study of de Lubac's ecclesiology shows that spiritual exegesis provides the theological foundation and the principles which integrate many of de Lubac's theological themes. As Hans Urs von Balthasar remarks, the doctrine of the senses of Scripture is not simply "a curiosity of the history of theology" but "an instrument permitting the discovery of the profound interconnections within the history of salvation."[2] Assuming that de Lubac's interest in spiritual exegesis results from his conviction that theological renewal is accomplished through a return to the sources, we may conclude that his interest in this type of exegesis is at least partly motivated by his belief that it responds to contemporary theological concerns. This study will show that while the allegorical sense is critical, since it interprets the text in terms of Christ and the Church, the anagogical sense, that is, the eschatological emphasis within spiritual exegesis, represents the completion of the allegorical sense and as such provides the key to understanding de Lubac's ecclesiology, particularly in its social dimension. Furthermore, the principles of spiritual exegesis provide an intellectual framework for understanding how the Eucharist is at one and the same time the historical body of Christ, the sacramental body, and the ecclesial body.

Since the primary interest of this study is in the principles governing the spiritual interpretation of Scripture and their relation to de Lubac's ecclesiology, it does not attempt to evaluate de Lubac's analysis of the historical development of this type of exegesis nor to reproduce the rich detail that his exegetical studies afford.[3]

7-75; his Introduction to *Homélies sur la Genèse* by Origen, 2nd ed., trans. Louis Doutreleau, Coll. Sources chrétiennes, vol. 7a (Paris: Cerf, 1976), 9-12; and "The Interpretation of Scripture," in *Catholicism* (New York: Longmans, Green and Co., 1950), 83-103.

2. Hans Urs von Balthasar, *Le Cardinal de Lubac: l'homme et son œuvre* (Paris: Lethielleux, 1983), 100.

3. Thus it is not the task of this study to evaluate de Lubac's assessment of Origen's work. The purpose here is rather to discover the exegetical principles which de Lubac believes to be fundamental to the spiritual interpretation of Scripture. However, there is some scholarly debate as to whether the spiritual interpretation of Origen is always founded on the literal sense, as de Lubac suggests. R. P. C. Hanson, *Allegory and Event* (London: SCM Press, 1959), is de Lubac's most vocal critic in this regard. John L. McKenzie in "A Chapter in the History of Spiritual Exegesis: de Lubac's *Histoire et Esprit*," *Theological Studies* 12 (1951): 376, also doubts whether de Lubac's assertion can be sustained. On the other hand, Walter J. Burghardt states that "we cannot ignore the declaration of de Lubac that 'when you come right down to it, he [Origen] denies the letter in cases far less numerous than he himself seems to say, and almost always in trifling points and nothing more' (Early Christian Exegesis," *Theological Studies* 11 [1950]: 110, citing de Lubac, *Sources chrétiennes*, VII, 44).

The Principles of the Spiritual Interpretation of Scripture

In the history of exegesis the delineation of the senses of Scripture varies. Some commentators, following Origen and Jerome, list three senses: a historical, moral, and mystical sense.[4] The historical sense refers to the events related or to the literal content of the text, as, for example, the laws. The moral sense is the application of these events or texts to an individual's conduct. This application may or may not be related to the Christ event. If the moral sense is not considered in reference to Christ, it refers to a "natural morality" rather than a morality which takes Christ as the model and norm of morality. The mystical sense relates the events or text of the historical sense to Christ, the Church, or some aspect of Christian faith.

Those writers using the quadripartite delineation preferred by Cassian and Augustine refer to the literal sense, the tropological sense, the allegorical sense, and the anagogical sense. Here the literal sense is the historical sense. The tropological sense is the moral application of the historical sense. The allegorical sense conforms to the mystical sense of the tripartite delineation since it refers the historical sense to the mystery of Christ and the Church. The anagogical sense is an eschatological sense applicable to both the individual and the community. These four senses are those named in a couplet dating from the Middle Ages to which de Lubac refers throughout his study:

> Littera gesta docet, quid credas allegoria
> Moralis quid agas, quo tendas anagogia.

> ("The literal sense teaches what took place,
> the allegorical sense what you ought to believe,
> the moral sense what you ought to do,
> the anagogical sense what you must strive for.")[5]

---

4. Henri de Lubac, *Histoire et Esprit: L'intelligence de L'Ecriture d'après Origène* (Paris: Aubier, 1950), 139. Also "Le 'quadruple sens' de l'Ecriture," in *Mélanges Offerts au R. P. Ferdinand Cavallera*, doyen de la Faculté de Théologie de Toulouse à l'occasion de la quarantième année de son professorat à l'Institut Catholique (Toulouse: Bibliothèque de l'Institut Catholique, 1948), 348ff.

5. *Exégèse médiévale*, I, 23ff. Robert E. McNally in "Medieval Exegesis," *Theological Studies* 22 (1961): 447, notes that this distich originated with the Dominican Augustine of Dacia (d. 1282). See *Rotulus pugillaris*, c. 1: "De introductoriis scientiae theologicae," ed. P. A. Walz, O.P., *Angelicum* 6 (1929): 252. The couplet actually concludes: "quid speres anagogia."

The quadripartite sense was first used by Clement of Alexandria, although de Lubac notes that he is probably not the originator of the hermeneutical doctrine which is the subject of *Exégèse médiévale.* This position he reserves for Origen, the test being whether the levels of meaning in question apply to the same scriptural text. For both Clement and Augustine, he argues, it is rather a question of several kinds of texts, each demanding a particular kind of explanation.[6] Although de Lubac appears to insist on the application of the four senses to the same text, he notes that "since St. Augustine one distinguishes, either in narrative or prophecies, three categories of texts: certain passages are purely historical; others, notwithstanding their historical form, are purely allegorical; finally others are historical and allegorical at the same time." This apparent inconsistency arises from an equivocation in the use of the word "historical." Since de Lubac identifies the historical meaning with the literal meaning and says that in certain cases a figurative meaning may be considered a historical meaning, it is difficult to see how, without further qualification, he can agree with St. Augustine here that some passages are purely allegorical.

It is important to note that de Lubac's terminology does not reflect the uniform usage of the patristic or medieval period; such uniformity did not in fact exist. De Lubac notes that the names of the four senses vary, and indicates that Augustine, for example, in *De Genesi ad Litteram,* refers to the historical, allegorical, analogical, and aetiological senses.[7] Walter J. Burghardt notes "the terminological anarchy" within the early writers, a confusion still evident as recently as the Eleventh General Meeting of the Catholic Biblical Association of America in 1948, where Patrick Cummins cited 15 terms used by biblical scholars in reference to the senses of Scripture, without fixed acceptation.[8]

Within a quadripartite delineation, the tropological sense is sometimes placed before the allegorical sense and sometimes after it. This difference in position is significant. When in the second position, as in some of Cassian's texts, the tropological sense reflects a moral interpretation of the historical event without reference to Christ and the Church, a moral interpretation founded on nature that is therefore not specifically Christian

---

6. *Exégèse médiévale,* IV, 95.

7. C. II, n. 5; c. II, no. 6; PL 34.222.

8. "On Early Christian Exegesis," 83, 112. See Patrick Cummins, "Semantic Terminology," *Catholic Biblical Quarterly* 1 (1949): 9-13.

but equally applicable to nonbelievers. When the tropological sense follows the allegorical sense, however, the moral interpretation is always understood with reference to Christ and the Church.[9]

The difference between the tripartite and the quadripartite delineation is not, in itself, very significant because the quadripartite delineation simply divides the allegorical (or mystical) sense into two senses — the allegorical and the anagogical. The position of the tropological sense, however, has considerable significance.[10] The different orders do not have their origins in two different systems; both come from Origen.[11] In Origen's tripartite schema, the moral sense, although placed before the allegorical or mystical sense, is often an evangelical sense, meaning that it carries an explicitly Christian interpretation, an indication that usage was far from uniform.[12] De Lubac prefers to interpret the tropological sense as an evangelical sense so that it is then related to an allegorical interpretation.

The tripartite formula recalls the trichotomy: body, soul, spirit.[13]

9. Cassian and Eucharius, a fifth-century bishop of Lyon and contemporary of Cassian, used the first schema — although Cassian did invert the two (*Exégèse médiévale,* I, 192). Gregory the Great used the second.

10. *Exégèse médiévale,* I, 211. However, elsewhere de Lubac states that "neither the number nor especially the order appears to be indifferent." "Le 'quadruple sens' de l'Ecriture," 354-355. De Lubac concludes his discussion of the symbolism of numbers with the observation that the quadripartite formula expresses solidarity while the triple formula adopts a spiritual rhythm (*Exégèse médiévale,* IV, 40). This observation parallels his comments in other places that the quadripartite is the more doctrinal formula and the tripartite is more mystical.

11. *Exégèse médiévale,* I, 211; *Histoire et Esprit,* 145-146.

12. *Histoire et Esprit,* 147. This represents an inconsistency with the principles just enumerated. There are two possible reasons: either this is an indication that the early practice of Christian allegory was neither entirely consistent nor rigidly codified, or the inconsistency represents an interference between Origen's inheritance from Philo, the tropological sense, and his Christian use of it.

13. This tripartite division of the senses of Scripture (historical, mystical, moral) corresponding to the three parts of a person (body, soul, spirit) reflects Origen's anthropology. See Henri Crouzel, "L'anthropologie d'Origène: de l'arché au telos," in *Arché e Telos: L'Anthropologia di Origene e di Gregorio di Nissa,* Analisi Colloquio Milano, 17-19 Maggio, 1979 (Milano: Vita E. Pensiero, 1981), 36-57. Such a division is often attributed to Philo's influence (so J. Daniélou, *Origen* [New York: Sheed and Ward, 1955], 188). However, Crouzel here argues that even though both Philo and Origen adopt a tripartite division, the two are quite different since Philo's concerns only the soul and Origen's concerns the entire person. De Lubac argues for Origen's independence and originality in *Histoire et Esprit,* 152ff.

Considered by de Lubac to be the more practical and subjective of the two, this formula presupposes that the literal understanding of Scripture is completed in contemplation and, conversely, that mystical knowledge seizes the Mystery signified by Scripture.[14] The quadripartite formula, on the other hand, is fundamentally a development of a two-term formula consisting of the literal meaning and spiritual interpretation.[15] It is founded on the continuity between the Old and New Testaments and is the more doctrinally and objectively oriented of the two formulas. In contrast to the more mystical and contemplative interest of the tripartite formula, that of the quadripartite formula tends to be more Christological, ecclesial, and sacramental.[16] Since the more frequent formula in the history of exegesis, particularly since the twelfth century, is the "fourfold sense,"[17] and since de Lubac himself focuses on the "four senses" in his elaboration of spiritual interpretation,[18] this is the formula addressed in the present study as well.

This, however, is done with the awareness that these four senses do not constitute a monolithic exegetical system in either the patristic era or in the Middle Ages. Both the names attributed to the spiritual senses and the manner in which they were described varied. De Lubac notes this variation at the same time that he attempts to demonstrate that a certain continuity and unity persisted in spite of the differences. In doing this he situates his comments within the structure afforded by the quadripartite division and makes generalizations regarding the characteristics of those four senses. Since the purpose here is not to recreate the exegesis of the patristic or medieval period but to study the theology of Henri de Lubac, we will examine those generalizations with the awareness that they do not ordinarily reflect individual variations.

14. *Exégèse médiévale,* I, 634-637.

15. Jean Daniélou in "Les divers sens de l'Ecriture dans la tradition chrétienne primitive," *Analecta lovaniensia biblica et orientalia,* ser. II., fasc. 6 (Bruges-Paris: Desclée de Brouwer, 1948): 119-126, argues that there are only two senses: the literal sense and the typological sense, the sense which interprets the persons, events, and institutions of the Old Testament in terms of Christ.

16. *Exégèse médiévale,* I, 203.

17. Ibid., I, 158.

18. Ibid., II, chap. IX.

The Literal Sense

The literal or historical sense is applicable both to a historical event and a literary text. De Lubac states that an etymology permits such an equivalence between history and letter.[19] According to this equivalence, history essentially becomes narration. However, it is important to note that narration is not here equivalent to fables or fictions — accounts of those things which might happen — but rather to chronicles and annals — the record of events that do happen. De Lubac notes that the medievals did not distinguish between history and historiography, but tended to reserve "chronicle" for the narration of the past and to use "history" for the narration of contemporary events.[20] The medieval chronicler envisioned his work as "explaining history and inserting the events into a superior order or as composing a discourse on universal history."[21] Examples of such projects include the *Chronicle* of Eusebius and Augustine's *City of God*. "History" refers thus both to the event narrated and the narration of the event.

One consequence of this correlation of "history" and "letter" is that Scripture, the narration, first communicates events to us. De Lubac cites Scotus: "The letter is the deed which sacred history narrates."[22] Scripture is neither an exposition of abstract doctrine, nor a collection of myths, nor a manual of interiority, but the narration of a series of events which really happened.[23] It is essential that these events really happened since revelation not only took place within time and history but has, itself, a historical form.[24] Thus de Lubac comments that when we profess our faith, we profess that a series of events really happened, that God really intervened in history and chose for himself a people. To focus on minute details within these events, however, would be to misconstrue de Lubac. His vision is obviously fastened on the main outline of salvation history rather than the minutiae which occupied many of the writers practicing spiritual exegesis, including Origen.

---

19. Ibid., II, 426.
20. Ibid., II, 427.
21. Ibid., II, 428.
22. "Littera est factum, quod sancta narrat historica." *In Jo.*, Fr. 2 (PL 122.320B). See also Augustine, *De doctrina Christiana* 1, III, c. xxviii, no. 4. Cited in *Exégèse médiévale*, II, 429.
23. *Exégèse médiévale*, II, 429.
24. Ibid.

Throughout de Lubac's study of the spiritual interpretation of Scripture, the literal sense is emphasized insofar as it historically grounds subsequent spiritual interpretation. De Lubac, following his interpretation of Origen, insists on the historical foundation of spiritual exegesis. An essential principle for the relation between spiritual exegesis and theology will be that theological argumentation and reflection can only proceed from the literal meaning, and theological proofs cannot be based on the allegorical sense.[25] Such a principle respects the historical character of Christianity and distinguishes Christian allegory from nonhistorical allegory.

Although an understanding of the literal sense is essential to de Lubac's theology since it historically grounds the other senses, no other sense is as subject to equivocation. The first complication is that it can refer to a figurative text as well as to an empirical historical event. The literal sense of Scripture does not require that every passage recount a literal historical event. Both Origen and Hugh of St. Victor, as well as many others, noted that there are a number of passages that are to be understood figuratively rather than literally.[26] The Song of Songs and the beginning of the book of Genesis were often cited as requiring something other than a strictly literal historical interpretation. However, this does not mean that the figurative interpretation ceases to be a historical interpretation. In the ancient terminology the figurative meaning of a text was still a historical sense, not to be confused with the spiritual sense.

The consideration of the figurative as a literal sense permits one to distinguish literary genres and thus the literary intention of the author. The spiritual interpretation requires this information since this literary intention reveals in what manner the literal sense is to be interpreted.[27] The literary genre, then, helps determine the literal sense. If, for example, the genre is history, the literal sense is the historical fact which is narrated. On the other hand, if the genre is myth as in the case of the creation myth in Genesis, the literal sense is the primary truth communicated by the

---

25. Ibid., IV, 382.

26. Ibid., II, 448. This equivocation is not original to de Lubac. Walter J. Burghardt, "Early Christian Exegesis," *Theological Studies* 11 (1950): 83, notes that the confusion between the allegorical or typical sense and what was called either the figurative literal sense or the metaphorical sense was more or less perpetuated until the time of St. Thomas.

27. *Exégèse médiévale*, II, 482.

myth, e.g., the goodness of creation, God as creator, etc.[28] Consequently, when a text such as Genesis 1–3 is to be understood in a figurative sense, this figurative sense is neither historical in the sense of empirical, nor figurative in the sense of fabulous, but is an historical interpretation grasped in faith. One might argue, however, that this is also precisely what allegory is. The difference would appear to reside in the fact that the figurative meaning of Genesis is not an interpretation restricted to Christian faith. Allegory, on the other hand, is necessarily an interpretation from the perspective of the Christ event.

This leads to a second problem regarding the literal sense. De Lubac identifies the literal sense with the historical sense of Scripture. The historical or literal meaning can refer to the empirical historical event, but the allegorical meaning is also historical insofar as history is the interpreted event and the principle of this interpretation is the Christ event, an event which is historical. It is therefore mistaken to suppose that the literal sense is historical and the other senses are ahistorical. These other senses are also historical inasmuch as their Christocentrism grounds the objective actuality of history from the Christian perspective.

28. De Lubac refers to the thought of A. M. Dubarle (*Le péché originel dans l'Ecriture* [1958], 51-55, 70) as demonstrative of the historical character of Genesis: "Genesis does not teach atemporal religious truths in the manner of a parable. It reports 'real fact.' The narrative of the first sin does not simply have the purpose of making us understand the nature, process, and results over the course of time of every sin committed. Its literary form is apparently that of myth, but the content and orientation of mythical thought had been profoundly modified by the historical faith of Israel. One does not, however, seek 'the concrete detail of events,' but 'only their significance in the drama of salvation'." *Exégèse médiévale*, IV, 166. De Lubac did not find this distinction between the literal metaphorical sense and the proper literal sense in Origen since Origen never made the distinction, but instead included the metaphorical sense under the spiritual sense. See John L. McKenzie, "A Chapter in the History of Spiritual Exegesis: De Lubac's *Histoire et Esprit*," *Theological Studies* 12 (1951): 365-381. Raymond E. Brown attributes the realization that metaphor belongs to the literal sense to Jerome in *The Sensus Plenior of Sacred Scripture* (Baltimore: St. Mary's University, 1955), 52.

In a similar vein, de Lubac alludes to Karl Barth's distinction between myth and saga, the former a fictional narrative of atemporal realities, fundamentally impersonal and monist, which expresses the principles, whether natural or spiritual, constitutive of the cosmos. The latter is "a prophetic and poetic description of a historical reality, concrete, of a singular event, situated in space and time, but which by nature escapes the verification of the historian." *Dogmatik*, vol. III, I, 405-10. See Henri Bouillard, *Karl Barth*, vol. II, ch. IV, cited by de Lubac, *Exégèse médiévale*, IV, 68. De Lubac notes that Barth's definition of myth differs from that of both Paul Ricoeur and Rudolf Bultmann.

A third problem regarding de Lubac's use of the literal sense is whether it refers to secular history or to the Old Testament. There appears to be no clear solution to this equivocation within de Lubac's theology since he does not take into account the fact that the Old Testament is itself an interpretation of positivistic phenomena from a perspective of faith. The literal sense can thus refer both to the positivistic phenomena of secular history as well as to the events of the Old Testament as interpreted by the Jews. Where de Lubac contrasts the literal with the allegorical sense within a dialectic of the two Testaments, he equates the literal sense with a Jewish interpretation of the Old Testament.

For the medievals, the "letter" which kills is not the historical reality, but the Judaic interpretation of the Scriptures.[29] When de Lubac associates the literal sense with the Jews, it is important to remember that his perspective is always that of *Christian* faith and that he sets the literal sense off against the allegorical or Christian interpretation of historical phenomena. However, from another perspective it is somewhat misleading to deprive the Jews of any but a literal sense of the Old Testament since they, too, give historical phenomena a religious interpretation. In this sense the literal narrative is itself an interpretation, even a "spiritual" one.

It would be a serious mistake to interpret de Lubac's failure to acknowledge the Jewish spiritual interpretation of the Scriptures as a form of anti-Semitism. His study of the word *perfidia* as applied to the Jews attempts to soften its potentially injurious character when he says:

> A great number of texts where it is a question of *perfidia* are too involved in polemics not to more darkly color this concept than would be the case were it in the calmness and precision of purely dogmatic thought. Let us also note that its application is more collective than individual and that its collective application refers more to the leaders of the people at the time of Jesus than to the whole of the Jewish nation and that it defines a type rather than a real individual.[30]

He finally notes that the reprobation resulting from the appellation *perfidia* is limited to the domain of faith and concerns only relations with God, not human relations.[31] He argues that the qualifier is applied objectively

29. *Exégèse médiévale*, II, 439.
30. Ibid., III, 153-181.
31. Ibid., III, 169-170.

to someone — Jew, apostate, or pagan — who rejects the spiritual interpretation of Scripture. He thus argues against its use to injure an individual or a people. De Lubac's position as here expressed does not solve the theological problem of the literal sense and Jewish belief, but it does clarify the fact that this position is not an instance of anti-Semitism. Also noteworthy in this regard is de Lubac's work during World War II to oppose anti-Semitism in France.[32]

In their insistence upon the spiritual interpretation of the *littera,* Christians do not disvalue history but interpret it differently than Jews do. The opposition letter/spirit is not, then, an opposition between history and spiritual interpretation, but an opposition between two states of historical faith, two economies.[33] Both senses are necessary, for if one rejects allegory in order to hold the literal sense, the result is a judaization of Scripture. On the other hand, if one rejects the literal sense to hold the allegorical sense, one eliminates the foundation of the Scriptures.[34] The literal meaning, however, in and of itself, remains a truncated meaning and is the "letter which kills" unless related to Christ and his Church.

Exegesis does not end with the historical or literal sense. The historical sense of Scripture presupposes a viewpoint other than that of a simple narrator. A principle of discernment governs the explication of the events, a principle which belongs to another sphere than that of the positivistic phenomena narrated and which transcends the mere recitation of phenomena. This principle refers events to final causes which the empirical events themselves cannot furnish and which illumine them.[35] De Lubac concludes that such a total interpretation of history can only be theological since only faith can securely anticipate the future, provide a definitive principle of discernment, and refer discrete events to final causes.[36]

---

32. See Henri de Lubac, *At the Service of the Church: Henri de Lubac Reflects on the Circumstances That Occasioned His Writings,* trans. Anne Elizabeth Englund (San Francisco: Ignatius Press, Communio Books, 1993), 48-55; Renée Bédarida, *Les armes de l'Esprit: témoinage chrétienne (1941-1944)* (Paris: Les Editions Ouvrières, 1977), 118-119, 125, 286; Jacques Prévotat, "Quatre jésuites devant le totalitarisme nazi [G. Fessard, J. Lebreton, H. de Lubac, and H. du Passage]" in *Spiritualitém théologie, et résistance,* ed. P. Bolle and J. Godel (1987), 98-120; Joseph Komonchak, "Theology and Culture at Mid-century: The Example of Henri de Lubac," *Theological Studies* 51 (1990): 579-602.

33. *Exégèse médiévale,* II, 445.

34. Ibid., IV, 451.

35. Ibid., II, 469.

36. Ibid., II, 470.

For the ancients, who had a sense of biblical history, the principle of discernment and final cause is the Mystery of Christ.[37] Thus the principle of spiritual understanding of the literal or historical sense is Christian faith. The Mystery of Christ grounds the objective meaning of history and thus gives it value. The spiritual interpretation of the Old Testament according to the four senses treats the events recounted there not as events containing their meaning in themselves, but as prefigurations.[38] It is true that unbelievers may question the principle of intelligibility used by the believer to give meaning to the history of ancient Israel. Furthermore, from the perspective of faith one may question how this principle may be applied, but de Lubac notes that if one wishes to find a meaning, a value, a unity in history, one must refer to some principle or reality which the empirical event as such does not provide. Thus it is necessary to pass from the literal sense to the allegorical sense.

The Allegorical Sense

For de Lubac the first and fundamental principle of the allegorical sense of Scripture is that it is not situated, properly speaking, in the text, but in the events themselves.[39] That is, the allegory is not in history as narrative, but in history as event. One can say that it is in the narrative, but it is so only insofar as the narrative recounts a real event. The text serves only to lead to the historical realities which constitute the figure. Thus "figure" here is different from a "figure of speech," which resides in the text, not in an historical event. The historical character of figure also distinguishes Christian allegory from the Hellenistic allegory of someone such as Philo.[40]

De Lubac's use of the term "allegory" as the spiritual interpretation

37. Ibid.

38. Ibid., II, 471.

39. Ibid., II, 493. This is how the allegorical sense differs from what was later called the *sensus plenior,* which was based not on the historical event, but on the text. See Brown, *The Sensus Plenior of Sacred Scripture,* 92.

40. De Lubac takes considerable care to distinguish Origen's use of allegory from that of Philo. See *Histoire et Esprit,* 150-166; *Exégèse médiévale,* I, 204-207; as well as de Lubac's introduction to *Homélies sur l'Exode,* trans. P. Fortier, *Sources chrétiennes,* vol. 16 (Paris: Cerf, 1946), 15ff.

of historical events sets it apart from a contemporary tendency to want to abandon "allegory" in favor of "typology." According to this distinction allegorical exegesis treats the text as a mere symbol, or allegory, of spiritual truths, with the literal or historical sense playing a relatively minor role. In typological exegesis, on the other hand, the events and persons of the old Testament are "types" which anticipate and prefigure events and personages of the New Testament.[41] Such a distinction consequently sees allegory as nonhistorical and typology as historical. For de Lubac, however, Christian allegory is grounded in historical event. He considers the term "allegory" the more dynamic, expressing the living relationship between figure and reality. "Typology," on the other hand, he sees as a more static recognition of a historical fact, event, or person which prefigures a future reality. De Lubac further criticizes the use of "typology" over "allegory" because the "figurative" or "metaphorical" sense can be considered part of the literal sense when *figura* is the translation of *typos*.[42]

According to de Lubac, the word "allegory" was used for the first time in a Christian context by St. Paul.[43] In the broadest sense of the term, the allegorical sense of Scripture has been understood as referring to the mysteries of Christ and the Church as prefigured in Scripture. Thus de Lubac states that the allegorical sense was the dogmatic sense par excellence rooted in history.[44] Far from compromising the historical foundation of the faith, the allegorical sense assures the essentially historical character of the faith since it does not seek its referent apart from the literal or historical meaning, but within it, much as the Father is not found behind the Son, but in the Son.[45] Here de Lubac closely approaches a sacramental view of history. As Christ is the sacrament of the Father, so in an analogous way the allegorical meaning is the sacrament

---

41. This distinction is found in J. N. D. Kelly, *Early Christian Doctrine* (New York: Harper and Row, 1978), 70-71; and Boniface Ramsey, *Beginning to Read the Fathers* (New York: Paulist Press, 1985), 30-31. Jean Daniélou in "Les divers sens de l'Ecriture dans la tradition chrétienne primitive," *Analecta lovaniensa biblica et orientalia,* ser. II, fasc. 6 (Bruges-Paris: Desclée de Brouwer, 1948), 119-126, speaks of two senses, the literal sense and the typological sense.

42. Henri de Lubac, " 'Typologie' et 'Allégorisme,' " *Recherches de science religieuse* 34 (1947): 180-226.

43. De Lubac, *Histoire et Esprit,* 22-23.

44. Ibid., 384.

45. Ibid.

of the historical meaning. The historical meaning is encompassed within the allegorical meaning.

De Lubac summarizes the relationship between the historical event and the biblical narration by saying that Scripture is doubly the Word of God since in it God speaks to us in words of what he has already spoken to us in deeds.[46] Consequently, biblical allegory is essentially *allegoria facti et dicti,* allegory of deed and word.[47] The relationship here is one of correlation rather than identity. That is, narrative communicates events to us. Thus the allegory of the written text communicates an allegory present within an historical event; it is more than a figure of speech or literary device.

The second principle of the allegorical sense is that the object of allegory is properly Christ and the Church. As has been noted, Christ is the principal and final cause providing the reference for the interpretation of historical events. The Church is included in the allegorical sense by virtue of the mystery of the union of Christ and his Church. In this regard de Lubac cites Gregory: "Christ and the Church are one person"; and Augustine: "if two in one flesh, why not two in one voice."[48] Further citing Augustine, he continues: "There is nothing in sacred Scripture which does not pertain to the Church."[49] The Church in union with Christ comprises the total Christ, head united with members.[50]

---

46. *Exégèse médiévale,* II, 497.

47. Ibid.

48. "Christus et Ecclesia, una persona est." "Si duo in carne una, cur non duo in voce una." Ibid., II, 502.

49. "Nihil est in divina Scriptura quod non pertineat ad Ecclesiam." Ibid., II, 504.

50. This statement obviously needs clarification and nuancing in order to distinguish between Christ and the Church. De Lubac approves of R. P. C. Hanson's comment that "the essential reality is not the historical life of Christ, not some timeless philosophical interpretation of Christ's significance, but the life of the Church in the present world" (*Allegory and Event* [London: SCM, 1959], 287). However, in response to Hanson's question whether the Church is really a higher stage after the Incarnation, de Lubac says: "There is never an opposition . . . between the fact of the Incarnation and the mystery of the Church. The more one gives importance to the Church the more one exalts the grandeur of Christ. The whole mystery of the Church, its whole life, depends on the fact of the Incarnation. When the author [Hanson] speaks of 'the historical life of Christ' he uses an equivocal formula: it is indeed clear that the exterior events have passed, but the point is that they were something more than that, they had an interior dimension and the efficacious mystery of which they were the carrier continues to exist and to bear fruit" (*Exégèse médiévale,* II, 511, n. 7). This "interior dimension" recalls the entire dynamic of the spiritual interpretation of Scripture. Ultimately this relationship between Christ and his Church must be seen in its eschatological dimension.

The third principle of the allegorical sense is that the object of allegory in reference to the Old Testament is a reality in the future. Once again, this principle underlines the historical character of Christian allegory. Not only is allegory primarily rooted in historical events rather than narrative, but the allegorical referent is also historical as opposed to a disembodied meaning or idea. Christ and Church are historical realities.

Fourth, the structure of allegory is fundamentally sacramental. That is, the content or signification of both the historical event and the future historical reality of Christ and the Church to which the allegorical meaning refers exceed what is observable within history. Just as what is observable within history does not limit the mystery it embodies, so too, Christian allegory is not limited to the historical dimension.[51] That is, allegory points not only to future historical realities, but to future mysteries which, belonging to the fulfillment of history, surpass history. Thus the concept of *mysterium,* that which is hidden within, is proper to both the past historical event and the future reality it prefigures. De Lubac notes that to misunderstand this is to make the allegorical meaning another literal meaning, constituting a denial of the interiority of the Christian mystery.[52]

This allegorical structure of the scriptural word of God parallels the relation between the humanity and divinity of the Incarnate Word of God. The letter is his flesh and the spirit is his divinity.[53] De Lubac states that there is more than an analogy between the object of allegory and the divinity of the Word of God. Rather than being analogous, these two are coincidental; the central object of allegory is in fact the divinity of the Word.[54] This union of the human and the divine which de Lubac sees as the allegorical structure of Scripture is also the key to his ecclesiology. This is an instance where de Lubac's underlying analogy of the hypostatic union results in an apparent disjunction of the divinity and humanity of Jesus. The central object of allegory rather is the Christ, incarnate, both human and divine in his historical mediation. This is consistent with the rest of de Lubac's thought that the allegorical sense is grounded in the literal and historical sense. Consequently, the central object of allegory has to be more than the divinity of the Word, but rather the Incarnate Word — in spite

---

51. *Exégèse médiévale,* II, 507.
52. Ibid., II, 512.
53. Ibid., II, 523.
54. Ibid., II, 524. De Lubac borrows here from Origen. See *Histoire et Esprit,* 93.

of his analogy between letter and spirit, on the one hand, and humanity and divinity, on the other.

This, of course, situates the spiritual interpretation of Scripture entirely within the context of faith. In fact, de Lubac defines Christian faith as "allegorica doctrina," doctrinal allegory, and asks what allegory is if not the mystical doctrine of the mysteries.[55] This relation between faith and allegory is therefore one of reciprocal causality.[56] In one and the same act Christ is recognized through prophecy, and prophecy is understood by means of Christ. Faith precedes understanding, and an understanding of the faith is concretized in an understanding of Scripture.[57] Consequently, de Lubac views the passage from history to allegory, from the letter to mystery, from shadow to truth as a passage to spiritual understanding, a conversion by faith.[58]

The context for the present discussion of allegory has been the Old Testament. The question then arises whether the New Testament can be allegorized, that is, whether there are "prophetic types," "spiritual meanings," or "allegories" in the New Testament as well as the Old Testament. First, if the two Testaments are considered as a single *corpus* or book, the first Testament makes up the history, or letter, and the second comprises the allegory or spirit of the former.[59] Since the New Testament is defined as the allegory of the Old it cannot be allegorized. An allegory cannot in turn be converted into another letter in the same way that the allegorical interpretation of Scripture cannot be mistakenly understood as a second-level literal interpretation.

Second, Jesus Christ is the definitive and absolute revelation of God. We have nothing more to receive or to hope for beyond what has been received in Jesus Christ. The New Testament does not refer to another mystery or spiritual meaning beyond itself, but presents the mystery of Christ to the believer. This, however, does not negate the fact that even

---

55. *Exégèse médiévale,* II, 525.

56. Ibid., II, 526.

57. Ibid., II, 534. For this principle, de Lubac relies on Augustine, who, according to de Lubac, only arrived at an understanding of the faith through the discovery of the mysteries of Christ under the letter of the Old Testament. He associates faith with the letter and understanding with the allegorical sense, that is, the reference of the Old Testament to the New Testament.

58. Ibid., II, 536.

59. Ibid., IV, 107.

though the New Testament is the spiritual meaning or allegory of the Old Testament, it, too, has a literal meaning since the Christ event is an event in history. However, in this case, the literal meaning is itself spiritual.[60] That is, there is an identification between the historical and the spiritual.[61]

Does this mean that history and allegory are absorbed into one another? De Lubac denies such an absorption on the basis that the Church is the pleroma of Christ.[62] Christ is a figure of the Church, and his redemptive acts are figures, "sacraments" of our salvation. It sounds at best contradictory, at worst blasphemous, to say that Christ should be a sign of the Church, for it would seem that the Church should point to Christ. However, it is false to interpret this in such a way that the Church is considered to be greater than Christ in that Christ is the figure and the Church is the completion. Such an interpretation divorces the Church from Christ, the body from its Head. Christ remains greater than the Church as the Head is superior to the "mystical body." Second, since the Church finds its fullness only in union with Christ, it can never be considered apart from him. What is at stake here is the mystery that the Incarnation of Jesus Christ, the union of humanity and divinity, prefigures the union to which we are all called in Christ. However, in this instance it is the figure that is the dominant reality, not only active and efficacious, but assimilating.[63]

De Lubac's response, then, to the question whether history and allegory are absorbed into one another is negative, since the body of Christ achieves its fullness only in the eschaton. They have not yet been united in the "Mystery."[64] The figure still points to a union not yet complete. De Lubac concludes that there is no allegorical meaning to be found beyond the New Testament. The appropriation of the Mystery in the life of the Christian and its final consummation are more properly tropological and anagogical applications than second-level allegories.[65]

---

60. Ibid., IV, 114.
61. To some extent the same danger of equivocation is present here, as was mentioned in connection with the historical/literal understood as empirical or understood as historical, but not empirical.
62. *Exégèse médiévale*, IV, 114.
63. Ibid., IV, 113.
64. Ibid., IV, 120.
65. Ibid., IV, 121.

The Tropological Sense

The tropological sense of Scripture is that sense which is the application of a scriptural text to the moral life. De Lubac explains that a trope, in the broadest sense of the word, is a figure of speech, a turn of language by which one "turns" an expression to designate something other than its natural meaning. Thus *tropologia* came to suggest the idea of moral conversion.[66]

Where the allegorical sense contributes to the development of dogma, the tropological sense contributes to a Christian anthropology and spirituality.[67] As noted earlier, the position of the tropological sense is significant. De Lubac cites Honorius, who said that the first tropological sense, that is, the one preceding the allegorical sense, unites the soul to the spirit and this union results in good work.[68] The second, where the tropological sense follows the allegorical sense, unites the soul to Christ through charity. The first is "natural," and the second is "mystical."[69] The tropological sense is related to the allegorical sense in that what is achieved in the mystery of Christ is realized and completed in the soul.[70] The revelation of who God is is therefore always a revelation of who God is for us.[71] This recalls the relationship between theology and economy in *La foi chrétienne* and is a striking instance of the inner coherence between the structure of the spiritual interpretation of Scripture and de Lubac's later contemporary theologizing.

---

66. For de Lubac's comments on conversion see *L'Ecriture dans la Tradition* (Paris: Aubier-Montaigne, 1966), 36ff.; "Sens spirituel," *Recherches de science religieuse* (1949): 557.

67. De Lubac, "Sens spirituel," 555.

68. *Exégèse médiévale,* II, 554.

69. This distinction appears to create a dualism between nature and grace analogous to the distinction between natural virtue and supernatural virtue; it is difficult to reconcile with de Lubac's later statement that "there are not two different orders, but only one, that of the covenant, which had creation for its first act; and Christ is its Alpha and Omega, its beginning and its end; and this order is supernatural." *A Brief Catechesis on Nature and Grace,* trans. Richard Arnadez, F.S.C. (San Francisco: Ignatius Press, 1984), 190; French original: *Petit catéchèse sur nature et grâce* (Paris: Communio, 1980), 135. However, in this early treatment in *Exégèse médiévale,* de Lubac approaches the problem from a historical viewpoint, noting the different uses of the tropological sense in the medieval tradition; he does not engage the systematic questions they raise.

70. *Exégèse médiévale,* II, 557.

71. Ibid.

The Christian soul to which this tropological sense refers is not a particular human being, or souls in general, or human nature abstractly considered, but Christian people.[72] Thus the tropological sense presupposes not only the mystery of Christ, but also the Church, since the Church only exists in Christian souls and souls are Christian only in the Church.[73] We can summarize the relationship between the tropological and the allegorical senses by noting that the allegorical sense refers to the Church as the body of Christian people in communion with their Head, while the tropological sense refers to the individual members of that body as participants in that communion.

De Lubac considers a person within a social context, not only in union with Christ, but with other Christians. What applies to the Church applies to the Christian and vice versa. Each individual person is a microcosm of the Church and is able to be united to the Word of God because the Church is united with Christ.[74] For example, Mary's perfection is one means by which she can be considered as a type of the Church. As the one most closely united to her Lord, she most perfectly represents the union between the Church and its Lord. Even though the individual is always considered within a social context, the locus of spirituality is always the individual in relationship with Christ. De Lubac states that "everything which is accomplished in the Church has no other end."[75] Redemptive action finds its terminus in the individual although the individual is always considered a member of the total Christ. De Lubac cites Augustine, who writes that everything that Christ accomplished in his life, death, and resurrection is the "sacrament of the interior man."[76] Thus Christian life is a configuration to the mystery of Christ.

Even though the allegorical sense is related to faith and the tropological sense to charity,[77] and although the allegorical sense reveals the meaning of Scripture while the tropological sense reveals the human person to himself or herself, it would be a mistake to view the tropological sense as divorced from the allegorical sense. While the tropological sense considers the mystery as appropriated by an individual person, this is never

72. Ibid., II, 558.
73. Ibid., II, 558-559.
74. Ibid., II, 560.
75. Ibid., II, 563.
76. Ibid., II, 565.
77. Ibid., II, 568.

an individualistic appropriation — because of the social character of life in the Church and the solidarity which unites each person in Christ.[78]

The Anagogical Sense

In the exegesis of the Fathers, the anagogical sense is the eschatological sense of Scripture which looks forward to the consummation of everything in Christ at his final coming. When the spiritual senses of Scripture are viewed in relation to the several comings of Christ, the allegorical sense represents the first coming of Christ in the Incarnation since this sense interprets the historical event in reference to Christ and his Church. The tropological sense refers to Christ's coming to each individual. The anagogical sense is reserved for Christ's triumphant return at the end of time.

To view the anagogical sense wholly in terms of the return of Christ is somewhat misleading, however, since such an interpretation considers only the objective anagogical sense. De Lubac notes that there are two anagogical senses, one an objective and doctrinal sense, the other a subjective and contemplative sense. The first is defined by its object, and the second by the manner of apprehending the object. The first is eschatological; the second is mystical.[79] In spite of the differences, however, these two orientations of the anagogical sense are not in opposition. The doctrinal and the mystical are held together in the anagogical sense, because only in its individual members can the body of Christ achieve the work of the Father at the end of time.[80] Consequently, the anagogical sense of Scripture constitutes the perfection of the allegorical and tropological senses by achieving the synthesis of the doctrinal and communal emphasis of the first and the moral and individual emphasis of the second.[81]

The significance of the anagogical sense for ecclesiology consists in part in the eschatological identification of the Church of heaven with the Church of earth. An understanding of the anagogical sense prohibits any

78. Ibid., II, 586.
79. Ibid., II, 624.
80. Ibid., II, 631.
81. Ibid., II, 632.

Platonic dichotomization of the Church in de Lubac's ecclesiology. In his ecclesiology, as in his spiritual exegesis, the question arises whether historical realities of the New Testament or of our present time are figures or types of noncorporeal realities, whether Platonic ideas or speculative truths. However, were this the case, the relation between the Old Testament and the New Testament, the New Testament and a spiritual world, would be extrinsic. Such an extrinsic relation would constitute an escape from the historical into the atemporal. On the contrary, de Lubac sees the relation between the two as being neither a historical progression, which would represent a type of historical evolution, nor a purely vertical symbolism.[82] Regarding a mere historical progression, he argues that although history passes and preparation is fulfilled, the figure remains: the eschaton fulfills, but does not nullify, the historical figure.

On the other hand, a pure vertical symbolism suggests a certain Platonism. De Lubac admits the Platonic flavor of many of the expressions of the Fathers in regard to the anagogical sense and comments that "one would be mistaken in considering every trace of Platonism in the thought of the Fathers as undesirable."[83] However, de Lubac states that spiritual exegesis escapes Platonism because the future to which the anagogical sense refers is not a Platonic idea, but Reality itself.[84] For de Lubac, unlike Plato, the idea is not reality. Neither is the spiritual meaning signified by the anagogical sense another kind of literal meaning. Historical events are not simply figures of other historical events and so on indefinitely; the corporeal and the historical are rather figures of the spiritual and the intelligible — which are not extrinsic to, but a dimension within, the historical and the corporeal.[85] This relationship between the historical and the spiritual is well expressed by de Lubac where he states:

> There is a spiritual force in history; by reason of their finality, the facts themselves have an inner significance; they are already, in time, charged with eternity. On the other hand, the reality typified in the Old and even the New Testament is not only spiritual, but is also incarnate. It is not only eternal, but it is historical as well. For the Word was made flesh and sets his tabernacle among us. The spiritual meaning, then, is

82. Ibid., II, 631.
83. De Lubac, *Histoire et Esprit*, 287.
84. De Lubac, *Exégèse médiévale*, II, 631.
85. De Lubac, *Histoire et Esprit*, 284.

everywhere, not only or especially in a book, but first and foremost in reality itself.[86]

Finally, the relations within Christian anagogy differ from those relations supporting Platonic exemplarism because the reality to which Christian anagogy refers does not precede its figure, but rather is its future.[87] As transcendent and preexistent, Christ is prior to his figures, but he appears after them historically in his Incarnation, posterior in time, anterior in eternity. Similarly, the anagogical sense points to a perfection and completion not yet achieved. Salvation is in the future, and the final meaning of Scripture is relative to that salvation.[88] All the spiritual senses of Scripture relate the historical event to the mystery of Christ, but it is the anagogical sense which finds its referent in the eschatological plenitude of Christ.[89]

A second reason the anagogical sense is important for ecclesiology is that it looks forward to the completion of the whole Christ in the eschaton. As such, the anagogical sense represents the fulfillment of the allegorical sense. Christ, the "meaning" or the "anti-type" of the Old Testament figures, does not point to another spiritual meaning or mystery beyond himself; nevertheless, there is a definite sense in which Christ becomes a "figure" of the fullness of union between head and members which will only be achieved at the end time. In the most profound sense, this is what it means for the Church to be the body of Christ. The foundations of this doctrine in de Lubac's ecclesiology may be found in 1 Corinthians 12, but the anagogical sense of Scripture expresses the doctrinal conclusions drawn from this text at the same time that it reads it in light of the doctrine of the Incarnation, the union of humanity and divinity in Christ in the hypostatic union. This becomes more evident in the next chapter where a comparison is be made between the Church/Eucharist correlation and spiritual exegesis.

---

86. De Lubac, *Catholicisme,* 136.
87. Ibid., 139-142.
88. De Lubac, *Histoire et Esprit,* 291.
89. De Lubac refers to the Church as the plenitude of Christ in *Exégèse médiévale,* II, 650. See also *L'Ecriture dans la Tradition,* 260.

A Hermeneutic of the Two Testaments

The theology of the spiritual interpretation of Scripture presupposes an intrinsic relationship between the two Testaments. The Christ event is the hermeneutical principle which unifies the four senses of Scripture and which creates the unity between the Old and New Testaments. Furthermore, just as revelation is not primarily the written document but the Christ event which is prior to the document, so, too, the two "Testaments" are not essentially two books, but two "Economies," two "Dispensations," two "Covenants" which have given birth to two peoples, Israel and the new Israel, the Church.[90]

To conceive the relationship between these two Testaments as merely one of promise and fulfillment, however, would be to exteriorize their relationship. The same principle which unites the literal meaning of Scripture to the allegorical, tropological, and anagogical meanings unites the two Testaments. Just as the historical and the corporeal are figures of the spiritual and the intelligible which are not, themselves, extrinsic to, but a dimension within, the historical and the corporeal, so too the Old Testament does not merely promise the New, but is transformed by it. According to de Lubac:

> The Christian tradition knows two senses of Scripture; their most general name is the literal sense and the spiritual sense ("pneumatic") and their relationship is like that between Old and the New Testament; more precisely and in the strict sense of the word, they are the Old and New Testament.[91]

Thus the spiritual sense is much more than an interpretation; it is a way of expressing the relationship between the historical and the spiritual, the Old and New Testaments.

De Lubac expresses this relationship, one of continuity and discontinuity, in terms of what he calls the Christian dialectic. On the one hand, he contrasts the relationship between the two Testaments to the point of making them contradictory, and on the other hand he unites them to the point of blending them into one.[92] The relationship between the two is

---

90. *Exégèse médiévale,* I, 309.
91. Ibid., I, 305.
92. For de Lubac's discussion of paradox see *Exégèse médiévale,* III, 128-152. Here he describes the dialectical movement as that movement, starting with history, which gives

not merely a historical evolution by which the Old Testament flows into the New, nor a changed intellectual perspective which reinterprets the Old Testament. The Old Testament is not just annulled by the New, nor is the New simply added on to the Old. There is historical continuity since the Old prepares for the New, and discontinuity because the Old Testament is transformed by the New. De Lubac states that the Christian understanding of the Scriptures

> implies the occurrence of a spiritual revolution and it results from a dialectical movement in which the signs are reversed. Hence the perpetual transition from continuity or succession to antithesis, then from antithesis to harmony.[93]

The result of this dialectic is that the Testaments are included in each other.[94]

The Christ event has transformed the Old Testament in such a way that for the believer, the Old Testament only continues to exist in its relation with the New Testament.[95] The Old Testament thus described is entirely different from the Hebrew Bible even though both may comprise the same texts. For the Christian the Old Testament is defined by its relationship to the New — a relationship established only in faith.

The spiritual interpretation of Scripture is thus grounded in history and yet, at the same time, is the product of faith. De Lubac seeks to avoid both illuminism and scientism. He considers it as much an illusion to imagine that we can attain the meaning of the Old Testament by means of symbolic transpositions as to imagine we can do so by purely human science, particularly by those methods of religious history designed to establish proofs.[96] The spiritual understanding of Scripture requires both faith, the gift of the Spirit, and learning, the fruit of scientific exegesis. The gift of the Spirit gives us discernment which allows us to read the Scriptures in the context of faith, and scientific exegesis establishes the

---

rise to two assertions, the two covenants or Testaments, and which alone makes it possible to understand their relationship.

93. *Exégèse médiévale*, III, 144.

94. De Lubac often cites Augustine: "Novum testamentum in Vetere latebat: Vetus nunc in Novo patet." *Questiones in Heptateuchum*, Lib. 1, q. 73 (PL 34.623).

95. *Exégèse médiévale*, I, 310.

96. *Ecriture dans la Tradition*, 199.

empirical historical meaning. Thus de Lubac argues for the union of faith and scientific knowledge at the same time as he rejects an appeal to one at the expense of the other.

It is important to remember that in light of the relationship between text and event, not only is the sacred text transformed by the Christ event, but so is history itself. De Lubac emphasizes that the dialectical movement of the two Testaments operates within the tissue of historical reality before being present in the spirit of the believer. As de Lubac says, "The Summit of history, the Christ Event, presupposed history and its radiance trans-figured history."[97] Consequently, the relationship between the Testaments entails not merely a transfiguration in the interpretation of sacred texts, but a transfiguration within history itself.

Limitations and Criteria of Allegorical Interpretation

Perhaps a central problem in the spiritual interpretation of Scripture is that such exegesis seems to be subject to fancy and lacking any controls. De Lubac names two criteria governing such exegesis which place the myriad details in perspective. Such criteria are particularly important in view of the statement that "everything in the Bible is figure."[98]

The first test of authenticity for Christian allegory is divine revela-tion. It comes to us in two ways: first, by a formal indication in Scripture that an event recounted in the Old Testament is allegorized in a New Testament text; second, by the unanimous agreement of the Church Fathers in regard to a specific interpretation.[99] The basic criteria are thus Scripture and Tradition. De Lubac observes that in general Protestants accept the first criterion and reject the second, thus accounting for a difference in the interpretation of Catholics and Protestants.

The presupposition is that Scripture forms a whole and has a mean-ing when viewed in its entirety. The Church possesses as an innate and unfailing charism a certain intuition of this whole which guides its inter-

---

97. According to de Lubac, Origen's achievement was the demonstration of this relationship between Christ and history. In this sense, he states that "there is no more 'historical' thought than Origen's." *Ecriture dans la Tradition,* 217.

98. *Exégèse médiévale,* IV, 60.

99. Ibid., IV, 69.

pretation of the individual parts. This is why union with the Church is so important. De Lubac defines the heretic as one who has broken union with the Church and consequently also has lost unity with Scripture.[100] Union with the Church and correct interpretation of Scripture are in tandem.

In addition to the twofold doctrinal criteria, there are other principles which help control the use of allegory. The first is the principle of the analogy of faith.[101] De Lubac applies this to the spiritual interpretation of Scripture by defining it as the explication of one scriptural text by another. Behind such a principle is again the presupposition of the unity and totality of Scripture which results in a compenetration of all its parts, not in its literal meaning but in its final meaning. The spiritual interpretation of Scripture is limited because there are not a number of different meanings, but one meaning. The one object of Scripture is Christ, the radical criterion, and the unity of this object unifies the various meanings.[102] The principle of the analogy of faith results in a type of exegesis that is synthetic rather than analytic.

Second, de Lubac distinguishes between *allegoria facti* and *allegoria dicti* or *verbi*. Only the first applies to Scripture in view of the fact that the biblical narrative is in the closest relation to historical events. In contrast, *allegoria verbi* is applicable to any narrative. This distinction is the same as that which Scotus makes between mystery and symbol. Mysteries are those things which are handed on according to the allegory of both deed and word. That is, allegory concerns historical events which are narrated. In contrast, symbols are *allegoria dicti* only and have no historical basis.[103]

Third, de Lubac distinguishes between *allegoria innate,* an inherent allegory, and *allegoria illate,* an inferred allegory. Once again biblical allegory admits only the first. Allegory is not an association invented by an imaginative biblical commentator, but is inherent to the historical event as expressed in the biblical narrative.

100. Ibid., IV, 91.

101. Ibid., IV, 90. See also *The Spendour of the Church,* trans. Michael Mason (New York: Sheed and Ward, 1956), 276. French original: *Méditations sur l'Eglise,* Coll. Théologie 27 (Paris: Montaigne, 1953).

102. *Exégèse médiévale,* IV, 81.

103. Scotus, *In Jo.,* Fr. 3 (PL 122.144-145). Cited by de Lubac in *Exégèse médiévale,* II, 497-498. This distinction is also mentioned in "Introduction," *Homélies sur la Genèse* (Paris: Editions du Cerf, 1976), 10.

Conclusion

This synthetic exposition of the principles of spiritual exegesis has shown these principles to be interrelated. They are neither successive nor progressive "methods" of reading a biblical text that can be separated one from the other, but rather demonstrate a compenetration of meanings within the historical events which ground the biblical text. The spiritual senses of Scripture provide a theology of history from the perspective of its Christological center that reaches into the past and illumines it in reference to Christ at the same time that it strains toward the future fulfillment and union of letter and spirit, which is to say, the union of humanity and divinity into the "whole Christ." The real symbolism inherent in this form of exegesis can properly be called sacramental as well as mystical. The sacramental and mystical character of this type of exegesis will become more evident in the next chapter, which shows the relationship between the Church and the Eucharist in de Lubac's examination of the history of the term *corpus mysticum*.

CHAPTER THREE

The Eucharist/Church Correlation and Spiritual Exegesis

THE LITERATURE ON DE LUBAC does not generally relate his work on the Eucharist and the Church to his work on the spiritual interpretation of Scripture. Indeed, his consideration of spiritual exegesis is typically examined in isolation from his other themes.[1] The historical period prior to the middle of the twelfth century, the period during which the term *corpus mysticum* was applied to the Eucharist, coincides with the period when spiritual exegesis was the habitual manner of approaching the Scriptures. From this historical perspective one can expect a correlation between the two themes. This chapter, by situating the Church/Eucharist correlation within the principles of spiritual exegesis, intends a new contribution to the literature on de Lubac at the same time that it supports a systematic

---

1. Herbert Schnackers, in *Kirche als Sakrament und Mutter*, Regensburger Studien zur Theologie, vol. 22 (Frankfurt am Main: Peter Lang, 1979), discusses the relationship between the Church and Scripture in six pages, citing *Exégèse médiévale* twice. Eugen Maier, in *Einung der Welt in Gott* (Einsiedeln: Johannes Verlag, 1983), comes closer in that he discusses history, a category borrowed from de Lubac's writing on spiritual exegesis, as an essential dimension of that which is catholic. In another chapter he discusses the mystical body as the insertion of humankind into the catholic unity of the mystery. He does not, however, relate the two ideas according to the various senses of Scripture. Marcellino D'Ambrosio's work, "Henri de Lubac and the Recovery of the Traditional Hermenuetic" (Ph.D. dissertation, The Catholic University of America, 1993), presents an extensive study of de Lubac's recovery of spiritual exegesis, but does not relate it to his theology of the Church or to the Eucharist. Paul McPartlan's study of the Eucharist, *The Eucharist Makes the Church: Henri de Lubac and John Zizioulas in Dialogue* (Edinburgh: T & T Clark, 1993), does not relate this to spiritual exegesis.

reading of de Lubac's work by showing the interrelation of three major themes in his theology — Scripture, Eucharist, and Church.

Henri de Lubac wrote *Corpus Mysticum* (1944) before he wrote *Exégèse médiévale* (1958). Although both are historical studies, it is evident that each treats the past not as a historical curiosity but as part of a living tradition that retains its theological importance for the present. Although de Lubac draws no direct connection between the two projects as histories, there exists a definite theological connection. In *Corpus Mysticum* de Lubac traces the term *corpus mysticum* from its use to designate the eucharistic body to its use, from the middle of the twelfth century, to designate the ecclesial body. The importance of the shift is not merely linguistic; with this change the perception of the original unity between the body of Christ born of Mary, the eucharistic body, and the ecclesial body was lost.

The purpose of this present study is not to retrace the history of this linguistic change, but to examine the intellectual framework which expresses the unity of the historical, sacramental, and ecclesial bodies. The principles of the spiritual interpretation of Scripture provide this framework. The task here is to examine the original meaning of the terms used in reference to the Eucharist and the church in reference to the spiritual interpretation of Scripture.

Clarifications

Before examining the relationship between spiritual exegesis and the Church/Eucharist correlation, some clarifications are necessary. First, de Lubac sees the Eucharist as related to the Church as cause is related to effect, means to end, sign to reality.[2] Each of these three ways of expressing the relationship can be examined from a different perspective. For example, the relation cause/effect can be developed from the biblical text in 1 Corinthians 10:17. Partaking of one loaf causes the unity of the ecclesial body. The relation means/end can be and was developed in the scholastic period by relating the *res et sacramentum* to the *res tantum*. Here the Eucharist is the means to the end of the unity of the ecclesial body, as is evident in the invocation of the Holy Spirit after the memorial prayer within the eucharistic prayer: "Grant that we, who are nourished by his

2. *Corpus Mysticum: L'Eucharistie et l'Eglise au moyen age* (Paris: Aubier, 1948), 24.

body and blood, may be filled with his Holy Spirit, and become one body, one spirit in Christ."[3]

The relation sign/reality, however, must be viewed with reference to the principles of spiritual exegesis if the sign and reality are not to be severed — as they were by Berengarius. If the relationship between the sign and the reality it signifies becomes extrinsic, either, like Berengarius, one no longer affirms that the Eucharist is the body of Christ or one no longer affirms that the Eucharist also signifies the ecclesial body. Consequently, it is the sign/reality relation that is the focus of the present study.

The second point of clarification is that for de Lubac, as well as for the early medieval authors he studies who wrote prior to Berengarius, the realism of the eucharistic presence is never called into question. It is an anachronism to consider them "dynamists" or "symbolists" in the modern restrictive sense.[4] At various points in history the emphasis in eucharistic teaching varied. The scholastic period, for example, largely as a result of the eucharistic controversy involving Berengarius, emphasized the real presence. In the context of spiritual exegesis, however, the focus is the efficacy of the sacrament viewed as union with Christ achieved across the sign of the sacrament rather than the efficacious confection of the real presence, although this is never called into question.[5] Here the unity of the body received in communion is a sign of the union of the ecclesial body. The emphasis is never on an individual's union with Christ in communion, but the union effected among individuals in Christ.[6] Consequently, the sign, that is, the eucharistic body, becomes the figure of the Church.[7] In this context the "figure" functions as the effective sign, that is, sacramental cause of the Church. Later scholastic terminology would refer to this as the *res et sacramentum*, looking to the *res sacramenti* which is the union of Christ and the Church.[8] De Lubac takes the *res et sacramentum* and the *res sacramenti* as given simultaneously in the

3. Eucharistic Prayer III.
4. *Corpus Mysticum*, 25.
5. Ibid., 24.
6. Ibid., 24, 26.
7. Ibid., 27.
8. According to this terminology, the *res sacramentum* is the outward rite of the sacrament, including the sign of the sacrament. In the case of the Eucharist, this is the bread and wine. The *res et sacramentum* is the inner reality of a sacrament — the Real Presence, in the case of the Eucharist. The *res sacramenti* is the ultimate purpose of the sacrament. For the Eucharist, this is the unity of the Church and the indwelling of Christ in the soul of the communicant.

totus Christus and speaks of this *totus* as the *res,* the effect or the reality, of either the Eucharist or the Church. In other words, the Eucharist is the effective sign of both Christ and his union with his members in the Church, this union identified as the *totus Christus.*

The third point of clarification is that the unity of the eucharistic body and the ecclesial body is never an extrinsic unity because the ecclesial body is not another body than the body of Christ, but the *totus Christus,* the fullness of Christ.[9] It is essential to note here that the *totus Christus* represents the end of the mystery and therefore represents the Church in its eschatological dimension. De Lubac notes that from the perspective of totality and unity there is no need for epithets to distinguish one body from another.[10] In this sense the Church is seen as a continuation of the Incarnation.

Contemporary theology has sharply criticized a view of the Church as a continuation of the Incarnation. Many theologians fear that this kind of theology attributes to the Church a power of grace that belongs to Christ alone. For example, Congar notes the Second Vatican Council's hesitation in identifying the Church too closely with Christ:

> At the very moment when for the first time in history the Church defined, or rather declared and described itself, it wanted to avoid an ecclesiocentrism of such a sort that would end by transferring to a very human reality an interest and ultimately the worship due to God and his Christ.[11]

Karl Rahner voices another caution concerning the way the relationship between Christ and his Church should be perceived:

> As with Christ the distinction between his Godhead and his humanity remains without confusion though they are inseparable. Sign and reality, manifest historical form and Holy Spirit are not the same in the Church, but as in Christ, are not separable any more either.[12]

Still other theologians associate the image of the Church with a Christo-

---

9. *Corpus Mysticum,* 34.
10. Ibid.
11. Yves Congar, *Un peuple messianique* (Paris: Editions du Cerf, 1975), 73.
12. Karl Rahner, *Studies in Modern Theology* (London: Burns & Oates, 1964), 201.

monism in Western theology needing a corrective pneumatology.[13] Finally, the Catholic notion of the Church as a continuation of the Incarnation is one of the major differences between Roman Catholic ecclesiology and Protestant ecclesiology.[14]

These are significant criticisms. Therefore, it is necessary to discover whether such criticisms are not founded on a simplistic notion of the Church as the body of Christ which in fact fails to account for nuances present in such a doctrine when informed by the principles of spiritual exegesis. Specifically, such criticisms may be founded on a view of the Church as a society rather than sacrament. Further, they may fail to account for the fact that even though the Church is a present sacramental reality, the *totus Christus* is complete only eschatologically.

A fourth and decisive point of clarification which guards against an improper identification of Christ and his Church is that the final unity of head and members which constitutes the *totus Christus* is not a collective unity, but a unity accomplished by Christ in one flesh.[15] This marital model preserves the distinction between Christ and Church at the same time as it emphasizes their unity. *Caro,* in addition to being the word used in the marital image (*una caro,* one flesh), is a eucharistic term in the Johannine tradition.[16] The association of the two words synthesizes the marital and the eucharistic images. However, de Lubac states that the Pauline metaphors of the union of Christ and his Church in a single flesh and the union of the member of Christ in a single body do not overlap. The double symbolism of the eucharistic species, joined to the natural opposition of meaning between *caro* (flesh) and *corpus* (body), maintains a separation between the eucharistic tradition of St. Paul and that of St.

---

13. So Jürgen Moltmann, *The Church in the Power of the Spirit* (New York: Harper and Row, 1977), 202.

14. Bishop J. A. T. Robinson reflects this attitude when he says: "Have as high a doctrine of the Ministry as you like as long as your doctrine of the Church is higher; and have as high a doctrine of the Church as you like, as long as your doctrine of the kingdom is higher." "Forward," *The Church in the Thought of Bishop John Robinson* by Richard McBrien (Philadelphia: The Westminster Press, 1966), viii. Jürgen Moltmann notes that the Protestant inclination to resolve ecclesiology into Christology corresponds to the opposite inclination on the Catholic side (*The Church in the Power of the Spirit*, 72).

15. *Corpus Mysticum*, 101.

16. John 6:51, 54.

John. However, even if there is no strict overlapping in de Lubac's synthesis, there are at least resonances.

De Lubac associates the marital model based on the image of *una caro,* one flesh, with the Pauline image of *unum corpus,* one body, in the Eucharist through the identification of *virtus* and *res.* However, in this development of the identification of *virtus* and *res,* he relies not on the Ephesian marital imagery of *caro,* but the Johannine eucharistic use of the term. According to de Lubac's exposition, *virtus* is the effect of the sacrament, the spiritual efficacy of the sacrament, considered in its nourishing aspect, that is, as the Bread of Life.[17] The *res,* on the other hand, is the objective and social unity of the Church formed by the union of many members.[18] Thus the *virtus* emphasizes the Johannine concept of the Eucharist as the source of eternal life, while the *res* emphasizes the Pauline concept of the body. Both the *virtus* and the *res* are effected by partaking of the body and blood of Christ. The union of the two terms results in the realization that "the spiritual life is a social unity,"[19] with the consequence that spiritual life becomes the incorporation of the members in the body of Christ.

"Communion" is not primarily an object received, nor primarily an action between an individual and Christ, but incorporation into Christ's ecclesial body. This is further emphasized by the fact that in a number of medieval texts examined by de Lubac, the subject who receives the sacrament is not the individual member, but the Church. Other texts, remarking on Augustine's commentary on John, note that the food and drink, the flesh and blood of Christ, is the society of the saints. Here the Church is seen as perfectly joined to Christ. The two *res sacramenti* are united, with the result that eternal life is found in participation both in the sacramental body of Christ and in the society of the Church.[20]

The terminology and images are fluid, synthetic rather than analytic. The result is a synthetic rather than an analytic doctrine of the Eucharist

17. *Corpus Mysticum,* 191.

18. Ibid.

19. Ibid., 203.

20. The Augustine text is found in *In. Joannem,* tract. 26, c. 6, n. 17 (PL 35.1614). Authors using this text are cited by de Lubac, *Corpus Mysticum,* n. 51, p. 198. Werner Elert, in *Eucharist and Church Fellowship in the First Four Centuries,* trans. N. E. Nagel (St. Louis: Concordia Publishing House, 1966), also proposes that *communio sanctorum* can refer to the saints or to the communion "in holy things" which is the Eucharist.

which incorporates marital imagery, bread of life imagery, head and members imagery, and the identification of the Eucharist as participation both in Christ and in the ecclesial body. De Lubac describes this whole as a plenitude of thought not belonging to the order of merely rational discourse, but capable of expression only through elliptical and paradoxical expressions.[21] Although this synthetic vision unites doctrines to the point where distinctions between Christ and his Church seem blurred, with the result that the Church can seem to be accorded a dignity proper to Christ alone, there are distinctions which maintain the differences. We have seen that the marital imagery of "one flesh" precludes the absorption of Christ into the body of the Church at the same time that it expresses the unity of the two bodies. More importantly, in the context of the present thesis the distinction between the various senses of Scripture is maintained alongside an assertion of the unity of worshipers in the Church, and the unity of Christ with the Church. Since the spiritual senses are always based on the historical literal sense, the reality of Christ's real presence in the Eucharist is presupposed in the anagogical completion of the "whole Christ."

Memorial, Presence, Anticipation

The key to the connection between spiritual exegesis and the Church/Eucharist correlation is that both the Eucharist and Christ correspond to the allegorical sense of Scripture. The allegorical sense of Scripture looks back to the literal sense and interprets the figures of the Old Testament in terms of Christ. Allegory also looks forward to its ultimate eschatological fulfillment. For example, Christ as the allegorical meaning of Old Testament prophecy is in turn a figure of the "whole Christ" which will be fulfilled in the eschaton. Similarly, the Eucharist is prefigured by the old forms of sacrifice in the Old Testament and itself prefigures the anagogical union of all people in Christ. Thus both Christ and his sacramental presence, the Eucharist, are in a relationship of memorial, presence, and anticipation to a past, present, and future which can be correlated within the categories of spiritual exegesis.

De Lubac notes that the term *corpus mysticum,* in its early medieval

---

21. *Corpus Mysticum,* 199.

usage, is susceptible of three interpretations. In the first, it is considered as a term for a mystical action — as the body which is mystically hidden in the symbol of bread.[22] This is the sacramental eucharistic body, and this interpretation emphasizes the presence of Christ in the Eucharist.

In the second, *corpus mysticum* can be considered the beginning of a process of mystical signification in what de Lubac calls a "scriptural zone."[23] This second interpretation considers the Eucharist as sacrifice. The sacrifices of the Old Testament prefigure Christ's sacrifice in the New Testament. The Eucharist as the unbloody representation of Christ's sacrifice has the same relationship to the sacrifices of the Old Law and the Patriarchs as does Christ. This interpretation of *corpus mysticum* consequently situates the Eucharist in the context of the symmetrical opposition of prophecy and memory, *praesentio* and *repraesentio*, which is also the relationship between the Old and New Testaments.[24] As de Lubac notes:

> To speak of the Old and New Testament is to speak of the sacraments which in some way define them; to speak of the relations between them is to speak of the relations between their respective sacraments, and, reciprocally, one would not know how to consider the sacraments without entering, in a more or less explicit fashion, upon a consideration of the Testaments to which they are attached.[25]

Here de Lubac associates the eucharistic unity of history and the Christic unity of history.

Precisely because of this close relationship between sacraments and Scripture, de Lubac holds that in order to understand certain eucharistic terms, one must refer to what he calls the "scriptural zone" — the theories elaborated in the first Christian centuries concerning Scripture and its understanding. He thus draws a direct connection between eucharistic terminology and spiritual exegesis. De Lubac comments on a certain reciprocity between the doctrine of the Eucharist and exegesis:

> Just as the reflection of the Fathers on the eucharistic mystery is inseparable from their reflection on the entire Christian economy whose

22. Ibid., 67-70.
23. Ibid., 70.
24. Ibid., 75ff.
25. Ibid., 77. The reference is to Augustine, *De spiritu et littera,* c. 8, n. 14.

revelation they found in Scripture, so does their reflection on Scripture greatly exceed the boundaries of an exegesis: their reflection wants to seize in spirit the totality of the work of God in the world.[26]

The second interpretation of *corpus mysticum* consequently envisions the Eucharist within this wider perspective and emphasizes over against the former stress on real presence the historical, dynamic, and sacrificial character of the Eucharist within its scriptural context — not simply as defined by the institution narratives, but within the entire Christian economy.

The third interpretation of *corpus mysticum* does not consider the Eucharist in reference to the past but in reference to the future, and views it as a simultaneous process of signification and efficacy.[27] Just as the anagogical sense represents a synthesis of the literal and allegorical senses, so does this third interpretation of the Eucharist unite the first two — those referring, respectively, to the Eucharist as presence and the Eucharist as sacrifice. Just as the anagogical sense envisages the Church as the pleroma of Christ, so does this third interpretation of the Eucharist view the Eucharist as building up the Church. The Eucharist causes the Church and looks forward to its completion at the end of time. As the anagogical sense is the scriptural sense related to the theological virtue of hope, so is the Eucharist the sacrament of hope. The Eucharist is the *vignus,* pledge, of the bond of charity which will unite all the members of the Church to each other in Christ.

Finally, where the first interpretation of *corpus mysticum* emphasizes Christ's presence with us and the second emphasizes the sacrificial character of the Eucharist, the third interpretation emphasizes the Eucharist as signifying us as we will be in the future completion of the body of Christ. In this third interpretation the Eucharist is a type of the Church in a manner analogous to that in which Christ is seen to be a figure of the Church. Both interpretations have an eschatological orientation.

De Lubac's contribution to eucharistic theology becomes evident when the eucharistic relationship of memorial, presence, and anticipation are correlated with scholastic terminology. The *res tantum,* considered as the eucharistic rite, corresponds to the idea of memorial and its association with the literal sense of Scripture. The *res et sacramentum,* considered as

26. *Corpus Mysticum,* 78.
27. Ibid.

the actualization of the New Covenant which makes present both Christ and the Church, corresponds to the allegorical sense of Scripture. The *res tantum,* the ecclesial unity effected by the Eucharist, corresponds to the notion of anticipation and the anagogical sense of Scripture. These correlations, however, are only analogous — largely because the scholastic terminology lost its historical setting and emphasizes the real presence rather than the matrix of relationships described by spiritual exegesis. One major difference is that the unity designated by the *res tantum* and effected by sacramental participation in Christ's body and blood is really present at that moment and is therefore not only eschatological. Its ultimate completion, however, is coincidental with the "whole Christ" whose fulfillment is eschatological.

De Lubac's retrieval of an earlier tradition reveals a richer eucharistic theology than is represented by the scholastic formulations. First, rather than isolating a doctrine of the real presence, it places the Eucharist within the historical dialectic of the two Testaments. This heightened historical emphasis underlines the sacrificial character of the Eucharist. Second, by associating the Church with the *res et sacramentum* instead of associating it with the *res tantum* as an effect of the *res et sacramentum,* it emphasizes the sacramental character of the Church. In other words, the outward rite signifies and effects the real body and blood of Christ. Communion with the sacramental Christ in turn signifies and effects the union of Christ with his Church, for it is by partaking of the one bread that we become one body, namely the body of Christ which is his Church. This union of Christ and his Church in the New Covenant is an effective sign of that final union of the whole Christ in the eschaton. Within spiritual exegesis, then, the "figure" or "type" functions as a sacrament which both reveals and conceals a spiritual reality. Consequently we can conclude that the spiritual interpretation of Scripture is in fact a sacramental theology, but one which situates sacraments within the entire historical economy of salvation.

De Lubac's demonstration of how the meaning of certain eucharistic terms related to this scriptural context changed when they ceased to designate the sacramental body of Christ is a further indication of the correlation between eucharistic theology and spiritual exegesis. Terms such as "mystical" and "spiritual" lost their scriptural ground and connotation at the same time that they began to refer to the Church rather than to the sacramental body of Christ. De Lubac emphasizes that the essential perspective of these terms is not the Eucharist as a presence or an object, but the Eucharist as an action and a sacrifice.[28] Thus the adequate theological consideration of the Eucharist greatly exceeds the theological interest of the relation between Christ considered "in himself" and the "sacramental species." This terminology is another indication that the entire eucharistic complex includes action as well as presence, sacrifice as well as sacrament.[29]

Shifts in Terminology

"Mystical," "spiritual," and "true" are three terms which shifted in meaning as *corpus mysticum* shifted from designating the Eucharist to designating the Church. In their original meaning, they express the relationship between a spiritual understanding of Scripture and the literal sense. In their most recent meaning, they lose their scriptural foundation at the same time the Church loses its eucharistic foundation.

The word "mystical" qualified two words used in reference to the Eucharist, *caro* and *corpus, corpus* being used to designate the Church or the Eucharist in its explicit relation to the Church.[30] The qualifier *mystica* used with *caro* served to distinguish the eucharistic body from the body of Christ born of the virgin.[31] However, toward the middle of the eleventh century and for reasons which de Lubac associates with the scandal caused by Berengarius, *corpus,* in its eucharistic connotation, began to replace the term *sacramentum corporis.*[32] Since *mysterium* was also associated with the term *sacramentum mysterium corporis,* the words *mystica* and *mysterium* ceased to be used in reference to the Eucharist as *corpus* replaced *caro* or *sacramentum corporis.*

De Lubac finds that before being named *corpus mysticum* the Church was named *caro mystica* and notes the eucharistic origin of this term. Peter Lombard was the first to use *caro mystica* to distinguish between the *sacramentum-et-res,* which he called *caro propria,* and the *res-et-non-*

28. Ibid.
29. Ibid., 79.
30. Ibid., 94.
31. Ibid., 90-94.
32. Ibid., 95.

sacramentum, sometimes called the *res tantum,* which he named *caro mystica.* Then *corpus mysticum* was used in reference to the *Christus integer,* head in union with members, considered as the "mystical man" which we understand as being the Church. Thus the term *corpus mysticum* had a eucharistic origin, and its first use in reference to the Church retained these eucharistic connotations. Furthermore, its use in connection with the Church referred to the eschatological concept of the completed Christ.

Regarding the scriptural context of *mysticum,* the first point to note is that *mysticum* is not an attribute of nature.[33] The Church is not "the" mystical body, but "a" body which is mystical, or, as it was designated in the thirteenth century, a body which is spiritual. In either case, the qualifier served to distinguish Christ's body, the Church, from Christ's historical body. De Lubac notes that *corpus mysticum* is founded on an analogy of the body, not primarily Christ's body or the sacramental species, but the general concept of body. As such, the expression is a commentary on the passages in 1 Corinthians 12 or the Epistle to the Romans where Paul speaks of the head and members of Christ, rather than a commentary on 1 Corinthians 10 or 11.

The expression *corpus mysticum* lost its eucharistic connotation when the Church was considered apart from its sacramental context. As a result of the influence of Aristotle's *Politics* the Church was thought of as a visible reality or as a human society.[34] In such a context, the unity of the body with the head was no longer understood sacramentally, scripturally, or eschatologically, but was modeled on a society with its leader, whether he be pope or emperor.[35] A concept of Church as "mystical body" changed to that of "visible body." Later, under the "symbolist" influence of Wyclif, Hus, Luther, and Calvin, the mystical body of Christ became completely dissociated from the visible Church.[36] The dissociation was so complete, and the distance from the original meaning of *corpus mysticum* so great, that a number of the Fathers of the First Vatican Council were surprised when it was proposed that the Church first be defined as *corpus mysticum.*[37] Pius XII's encyclical *Mystici*

33. Ibid., 121.
34. Ibid., 129.
35. Ibid., 130.
36. Ibid.
37. Ibid., 132.

corporis, 29 June 1943, finally laid to rest many of the fears associated with the term.

The second term associated with the Eucharist is "spiritual." The same antithesis between flesh and spirit which had dominated speculations concerning Scripture now dominated speculations concerning the Eucharist.[38] The opposition flesh/spirit translates into the opposition reality/symbol. "Spiritually" was applied to the Eucharist in contrast to "carnally" in order to speak of the presence of Christ while avoiding a materialism due to the peculiarly Augustinian problem of localization. The problem made it difficult to understand how the Eucharist could be the body of Christ if the body of Christ were sitting at the right hand of the Father. In this context, however, even though the body of Christ is spiritual and invisible, it is nonetheless substantially present.[39] However, when Berengarius contrasted corporeal eating with spiritual eating, and the object of the first was the bread and wine, this affected eucharistic terminology. It became difficult to explain how Christ, although not a corporeal nourishment, was nevertheless the object of corporeal eating.[40] The affirmation of a corporeal eating led to the affirmation of a corporeal presence.[41] One could no longer speak of a "spiritual body" with a "corporeal presence" without contradicting oneself.[42] "Spiritual presence" was similarly to be avoided.[43] "Spiritually" had come to be seen not only as the opposite of "carnally" and "sensually," but also the opposite of "naturally" and "substantially."[44] In short, "spiritually" was interpreted as "figuratively" as opposed to "really."[45]

The final result was that the first two of the "three" bodies, that is, the historical and sacramental bodies, were identified with each other while the third, the ecclesial body, was detached from the historical and the sacramental.[46] This resulted in a theory of the double body, the historical-sacramental body and the ecclesial body. The first was called the *corpus verum* and the

38. Ibid., 181.
39. Ibid., 168.
40. Ibid., 173.
41. Ibid., 176.
42. Ibid., 174.
43. Ibid., 179.
44. Ibid., 182.
45. Ibid.
46. Ibid., 184.

second *corpus mysticum*. The "spiritual flesh" of the Eucharist was no longer considered the very reality of the Eucharist, but the effect of the Eucharist.[47]

The third term associated with the Eucharist to undergo a shift in meaning was *verum* or *veritas*. In its original association with the Eucharist it signified a plenitude of perfection. De Lubac draws this analogy: "What the body was to the shadow, what the spirit was to the letter, truth is to the figure."[48] This "truth" or plenitude was no less than the plenitude of Christ consisting in the Church.[49]

In his discussion of *veritas,* de Lubac draws an explicit parallel between the Eucharist and the New Testament. Noting that the New Testament can be seen either as the definitive truth following the preparations and figures of the Old Testament, or as the intermediary state between the shadows and figures of the past and the full light of eternity,[50] so the Eucharist, as well as being a memorial, anticipates the eschatological completion of the body of Christ.[51] In their original meaning, what was typical or mystical was the Eucharist, that which was celebrated mystically, the *corpus mysticum*.[52] The "truth" which was to be discovered within the rite through spiritual understanding was the ecclesial body.[53] This parallel use of *veritas* and *corpus* came to be joined in such expressions as *corpus veritatis* and *veritas corporis*.[54] Subsequent changes finally led to the latter being interpreted as the truth of the unity between the matter offered, bread and wine, and the body and blood of Christ.[55] This change, associated with the fact that corpus was identified with *substantia,* resulted in *veritas* losing its association with the contrast *in figura/in veritate* founded in the scriptural relation between the Old Testament sacrifices prefiguring the Eucharist and the fullness of truth of which the Eucharist is the image.[56]

47. Ibid., 187-188.

48. Ibid., 212.

49. Ibid.

50. Ibid., 218.

51. Geoffrey Wainwright emphasizes the eschatological dimension of the Eucharist in *Eucharist and Eschatology* (New York: Oxford University Press, 1981).

52. *Corpus Mysticum*, 229.

53. Ibid.

54. Ibid., 234.

55. Ibid., 236.

56. The fact that the Eucharist is identified as figure or image does not undermine the reality of the real presence any more than the reality of Christ is undercut when he is viewed as image of the Father. Ibid., 223-225, 353.

Veritas eventually became identified with the reality of the body and blood whose substance was on the altar under the appearance of bread and wine rather than the completion of the Eucharist in the Church.[57]

De Lubac concludes that an apologetic for the real presence replaced an understanding of the faith in a broader context. He further concludes that the change in the meaning of the terminology leads to a misunderstanding of the ancient texts[58] and a neglect of the ecclesial symbolism.[59] Such a development did not attend to the fact that the "true body" is itself a sacrament, a sacrament of the *Christus integer,* the body of Christ in its eschatological completion. *Figura* no longer referred to the sacramental body of Christ, but to the appearances of bread and wine.[60]

Within the dynamic of memorial, presence, and anticipation, there is a double sacramentality. In the first, the bread and wine become the sacrament of Christ's sacramental eucharistic presence. In the second, Christ's sacramental presence under the species of bread and wine becomes the sacrament of final completion of all in Christ. Or, stated another way, the memorial becomes the sacrament of the presence, and the presence becomes the sacrament of the anticipation. When the meaning of the ecclesial body became divorced from the historical and sacramental bodies, a strong theology of real presence, the first level of sacramentality, remained. However, the second level of sacramentality, where the Eucharist signifies the eschatological union of the Church with Christ, was lost. It is true that this final union was retained as the effect of the sacrament, but this effect was seen as the effect of the grace of the sacrament, not as the sacramental referent of the Eucharist.

The parallel with exegesis is apparent. A carnal interpretation of the Eucharist divorces the Church from its eucharistic origins and is the equivalent of an exegesis where the historical sense is divorced from the

---

57. Ibid., 244-245.

58. Ibid., 247.

59. Ibid., 249.

60. Ibid., 252. A historical question not fully explored by de Lubac is whether the separation of exegesis, theology, and spirituality at the time of the great summas, which represented a move from a synthetic to an analytic theology, paralleled the change from a view of the Eucharist from the perspective of spiritual exegesis centered on sign and reality to the dialectic of substance and accident. De Lubac notes the effect of the Berengarian controversy on the change in emphasis in eucharistic doctrine, but does not correlate the change with the larger shift in theological perspectives occurring around the same time.

anagogical sense. Just as the spiritual sense of Scripture does not eliminate the literal sense or add something else to it, but rather gives it its fullness and reveals its depths, so does the ecclesial sense of the Eucharist depend on the real presence at the same time it reveals its larger signification.[61] The key to de Lubac's understanding of the Church/Eucharist correlation is the anagogical dimension of the spiritual interpretation of Scripture.[62] Within such a context "mystical," far from being a denial of the "real" or the "true," becomes the ultimate reality or truth spiritually present within the "figure." In terms of the Church/Eucharist correlation, the Church in union with Christ is the truth signified by the Eucharist when considered not merely in terms of the sacramental species, but the entire liturgical rite within the historical matrix of memory, presence, and anticipation.

Conclusion

This chapter has examined the Eucharist/Church correlation presented in de Lubac's study of the term *corpus mysticum*. It has emphasized the connection between prescholastic eucharistic theology and the spiritual interpretation of Scripture. Specifically, in their original eucharistic context the terms *veritas, mysticum,* and *spiritualiter* refer to a reality within the *sacramentum* that preserves the concreteness or event-character of the eucharistic presence at the same time that it emphasizes the sign value of the sacrament within the dynamic of the two Covenants afforded by the scriptural context. The Eucharist/Church correlation is most closely associated with the anagogical sense when the Eucharist is considered as equivalent to the allegorical sense of Scripture and the Church is seen as the fulfillment of the union of Head and body in the *totus Christus*.

It is evident that de Lubac integrates his theological consideration of the Church, the Eucharist, and exegesis. De Lubac's study of spiritual exegesis concludes that Jesus Christ is the center of history in the sense that his Incarnation is the event by which history is interpreted. With the Incarnation history is not merely fulfilled, but transformed. That is, in the

---

61. *The Splendour of the Church,* trans. Michael Mason (New York: Sheed and Ward, 1955), 112. French original: *Méditation sur l'Eglise,* Coll. Théologie 27 (Paris: Aubier, 1953).

62. *Corpus Mysticum,* 263.

light of the Incarnation, history is interpreted according to a norm not previously available. At the same time, however, the past is now seen to have always been Christocentric and so appears illumined by Christ rather than transformed. In this sense, to speak of the transformation effected by Christ is to keep in mind the dialectic between the Old and New Testaments so that transformation or discontinuity is never viewed apart from a certain continuity which endures. This transformation permits de Lubac, in union with a long tradition to which his historical work bears witness, to speak of history in terms of two dispensations, two covenants, two Testaments. Jesus Christ entered history and in entering history represents in his person the actual meaning of history as it is freely appropriated in faith. In order for this to be so, it was necessary for Jesus Christ to be intrinsically present to history. In saying this, we are saying that Jesus Christ is able to mediate historically between God and human beings because he is both God and human being. That is, Christ, present as event within history, is that by which history is reinterpreted. Jesus Christ mediates by virtue of his historical immanence within history, not merely as an eschatological reality toward which history is tending. Once this is accepted, some further reflection indicates the necessity that the principle of historical interpretation continue to be immanent within history.

De Lubac's study of the term *corpus mysticum,* having placed the Eucharist within the relationships of the spiritual interpretation of Scripture, makes it clear that Christ's continued historical presence is achieved eucharistically. Recalling the three interpretations of *corpus mysticum* — as bodily eucharistic presence, as fulfillment of the sacrifices of the Old Law, and as figure of the Church — it is evident that de Lubac suggests a eucharistic unity of history which is identically the Christic unity of history. That is, if the Eucharist reflects the unity within history expressed in the dialectic between the two Testaments, it is because the Eucharist is the sacramental presence of the risen Christ within history and therefore participates in the same relationship of type/anti-type as Christ does within that dialectic.

Given this matrix which constitutes de Lubac's vision of the interrelation between history, liturgy, and exegesis, it is not surprising that in his view the Church is situated as the very heart of that interrelation. Some indications of this have already been given where the Church was seen as the anti-type of the Eucharist, as the *Christus totus* — the members of Christ joined to their head, who is Christ. This, of course, presupposes the most inclusive interpretation of the Eucharist within the unity of the Testaments as well as within the unity of the sacramental Christ and the sacramental Church. A consideration of the Eucharist limited to a static "presence" would be utterly insufficient. The designation of the Eucharist and the Church as the body of Christ entails a certain identification of the Church with Christ which requires further study. It is important to see what evidence de Lubac gives of maintaining the discontinuity between Christ and the Church while speaking of the Church in a manner which seems to stress their continuity.

CHAPTER FOUR

The Christological Center of de Lubac's Ecclesiology

IN DE LUBAC'S THEOLOGY the Church receives its identity from its relation to Christ. Among the images that express this relationship is that of the members of the body of Christ joined to their head, who is Christ, in the formation of the "total Christ." In *Exégèse médiévale* the Church is considered the fullness of Christ in relation to the anagogical sense of Scripture. For example, de Lubac cites Origen: "for, it is in each one of the members of his mystical body that Christ completes the work of the Father at the end of time."[1] This relationship, however, is probably more evident in *Corpus Mysticum* in de Lubac's treatment of the Church as the antitype of Christ and the Eucharist, for it is here that the Church as *corpus* is most closely related to the anagogical sense of Scripture.

A second image, less developed in de Lubac's study of the spiritual interpretation of Scripture, is that of the *una caro,* the one flesh, which is based on a relationship of the Church to Christ described in spousal or marital imagery.[2] The image of head and members constitutes an organic model, while the marital image constitutes a covenantal model.[3] In some

---

1. Origin, *In Jo.* 1. XIII, c. xxxvi.

2. See *Corpus Mysticum: L'Eucharistie et l'Eglise au moyen age* (Paris: Aubier, 1948), 189-209.

3. De Lubac explicitly describes the Church as an organism: "the Church, composed of men, was not made by the hands of men. She is not an organization. She is a living organism, what Saint Irenaeus called 'the ancient organism of the church.' 'The source of her life and her unity does not arise from the desire to live in common on the part of the individuals she gathers together; it is she who communicates it to them.' " *The Motherhood*

texts the organic model of head and members, when analogously compared to the union of humanity and divinity in the hypostatic union, considers the Church as a continuation of the Incarnation and risks absorbing the Church into Christ. The manner in which the Church/Christ relationship is expressed is thus very important since a variety of theological conclusions follow from the model chosen.[4]

Consequently, even though de Lubac's study of spiritual exegesis and of the term *corpus mysticum* has already led us to certain conclusions regarding the Church's relationship to Christ, it is now necessary to examine this relationship more closely in terms of three images of the Church in the thought of Henri de Lubac: the Church as a continuation of the Incarnation, the Church as the Bride of Christ, and the Church as the sacrament of Christ.

Part I: The Church and the Mystical Body of Christ

The Encyclical Mystici Corporis

The history of the literature in which the Church is identified in some fashion with the Mystical Body of Christ is long and beyond the scope of this study to review.[5] However, to place de Lubac's work in its immediate historical context it is necessary to note that in the course of de Lubac's lifetime the Church documents have differed in the manner in which they describe this relationship. Pius XII's encyclical *Mystici Corporis,* published

---

of the Church, trans. Sr. Sergia Englund, O.C.D. (San Francisco: Ignatius Press, 1982), 15; French original: *Les églises particulières dans l'Eglise universelle,* followed by *La maternité de l'Eglise* and *Une inverview recueillie par G. Jarczyk* (Paris: Aubier-Montaigne, 1971). The reference to Irenaeus is *Adversus Haereses,* 1, 4, c. 33, n. 8. The second quotation on the source of the Church's unity is from Yves de Montcheuil commenting on Möhler in Pierre Chaillet, *L'Eglise est une, hommage à Möhler* (Bloud and Gay, 1939), 237.

4. Here "model" is not to be understood in the context of Avery Dulles's "models" of the Church. De Lubac does not conceptually separate manners of referring to the Church into discrete models. However, for purposes of analysis here I have isolated what I consider to be three ways in which de Lubac refers to the Church.

5. Emile Mersch provides such a history in *Le Corps Mystique du Christ* (1933); English translation: *The Whole Christ: The Historical Development of the Doctrine of the Mystical Body in Scripture and Tradition,* trans. John R. Kelly (Milwaukee: The Bruce Publishing Co., 1938).

in 1943, identifies the Church with the Mystical Body of Christ without nuance where it states: "If we would define and describe this true Church of Jesus Christ — which is the One, Holy, Catholic, Apostolic Roman Church — we shall find nothing more noble, more sublime or more divine than the expression 'the Mystical Body of Jesus Christ. . . .' "[6] This identification occurred in a historical context in which there was a danger of separating the invisible communion of grace from the visible Church. Yves Congar, for example, views the accomplishment of this encyclical as the union of the thought of St. Thomas on the invisible union in grace and Bellarmine's emphasis on the Church as a visible society.[7] Consequently, this encyclical views the Church as a visible social body, the body founded by Christ who is its head and animated by the Spirit. The Mystical Body is thus identified with the historical and visible ecclesial institution which is the Church.

In *Mystici Corporis,* members of the visible Church, and therefore of the Mystical Body, are so by virtue of identification: they "have been baptized and profess the true faith, and have not been so unfortunate as to separate themselves from the unity of the body, or been excluded by legitimate authority for grave faults committed."[8] Those who do not belong to the visible body of the Catholic Church have a "certain relationship with the Mystical Body" by an "unconscious desire and longing."[9] This desire is the *votum ecclesiae,* desire for the Church.[10] Grillmeier notes

6. *Mystici Corporis,* I, 13. A bibliography on the encyclical can be found in Claudia Carlen, ed., *The Papal Encyclicals 1939-1958* (Wilmington, N.C.: McGrath Publishing Co., 1981), 62-63.

7. Yves Congar, *Le Concile de Vatican II,* Coll. Théologie Historique 71 (Paris: Beauchesne, 1984), 154.

8. *Mystici Corporis,* para. 22 in the translation in *The Papal Encyclicals,* ed. Claudia Carlen (Denzinger 3802).

9. Ibid., 103. "inscio quodam desiderio ac voto ad mysticum Redemptoris corpus ordinentur."

10. A. Grillmeier briefly sketches the history of this term in "Chapter II: The People of God" in *Commentary on the Documents of Vatican II,* ed. Herbert Vorgrimler (New York: Herder and Herder, 1967), 168-175. The origin of this term lies in the patristic affirmations of the baptism of desire and baptism of blood. In the council of Trent the notion appears as the *votum sacramenti,* particularly in regard to baptism (Denzinger 796, 1524, 898, 1677). R. Bellarmine, F. Suarez and the theologians of Vatican I used the term *votum ecclesiae,* which was subsequently used in *Mystici Corporis* and in the letter of the Holy Office to Archbishop Cushing of Boston in the case of Fr. L. Feeney, S.J. (Denzinger 3870). The text of the Holy Office letter can be found in *American Ecclesiastical Review* 127

that the doctrine of the *votum sacramenti* or *votum ecclesiae* formed the bridge between the reality that most people are outside the Church and the doctrine of the universal salvific will of God and the necessity of the Church for salvation.[11] He lists the following difficulties with this concept:

1. Is not an "unconscious desire" so "invisible" that it cannot be a substitute for belonging to the Church, when such membership is a necessary means of salvation?

2. The *votum* of unbaptized non-Catholics is not differentiated from that of baptized Christians.

3. There could be an explicit or implicit *votum* in good faith "against" membership of the Catholic Church as it is in the concrete, but the *votum* need not exclude a true obedience to God in the depths of conscience and readiness to accept his guidance.[31] In the concept of the *votum* as hitherto envisaged, only the relationship of the individual non-Catholic to the Church was dealt with. Their Churches or communities were not considered as elements of divine guidance to salvation. Justice was not done to the fact that there is a valid and fruitful baptism outside the Catholic Church, and that this baptism constitutes a certain link with the church (cf. *CIC,* Canon 87 and *Denzinger-Schoenmetzer,* paras. 2566-70), as do other sacraments and the preaching of the Word.

---

31. See U. Valeske, *Votum Ecclesiae* (1962), p. VIII.[12]

The concept of the *votum ecclesiae* ensured that the formula "extra ecclesiam nulla salus" (no salvation outside the Church) was never interpreted in a narrowly restrictive manner. However, in *Mystici Corporis* there is nothing between full membership in the Church and a relationship to the Church by means of the *votum*. The problem posed by the strict identification of the Roman Catholic Church with the

---

(October 1952): 307. The official English translation is on pp. 311-315. For a commentary see Joseph Fenton, "The Holy Office Letter on the Necessity of the Catholic Church," *American Ecclesiastical Review* 127 (July-December 1952): 450-461. De Lubac uses the phrase *voto saltem ac desiderio* in *Catholicism: A Study of Dogma in Relation to the Corporate Destiny of Mankind,* trans. Lancelot C. Sheppard (New York: Mentor and Omega Books, 1964), 126. French original: *Catholicisme: Les aspects sociaux du dogme* (Paris: Edition du Cerf, 1983; original edition, 1938).

11. Grillmeier, "People of God," in *Commentary on the Documents of Vatican II,* 171.

12. Ibid.

Mystical Body, on the one hand, and the inadequacy of the theology of the *votum ecclesiae,* on the other hand, necessitated a new presentation by the Second Vatican Council of the relationship of non-Catholics with the Church.

The Second Vatican Council

The preparatory commission of the Second Vatican Council reaffirmed the identification of the Church with the Mystical Body of Christ.[13] Chapter I was entitled "The Nature of the Militant Church." No. 6 carried the subtitle "The Church Society Is the Mystical Body of Christ," while that of no. 7 was "The Roman Catholic Church Is the Mystical Body of Christ." Congar notes that the same subject was designated as both the Church and the Body of Christ in a relationship comparable to the *sacramentum* and *res* in the sacraments.[14] The documents promulgated by the Council affirm the unity of the Mystical Body and the Church. Although they do not mention the adjective "Roman," this is not in itself significant because *Lumen Gentium* identifies the Church as "governed by the successor of Peter and the bishops who are in communion with him." *Lumen Gentium,* however, does not state that only Catholics are members of the Mystical Body. Instead, it states that the Church of Christ and the apostles *subsistit in* (subsists in) the Catholic Church "although numerous elements of sanctification and truth are found outside its visible organism" (no. 8). Congar concludes that there is not a strict, in the sense of exclusive, identity between the Church, the Body of Christ, and the Catholic Church.[15]

When *Mystici Corporis* is compared to *Lumen Gentium,* one finds that the latter retains the essential elements of the former when these are considered to be the identification of the Mystical Body of Christ with Christ's visible Church. The main difference, however, is that *Mystici Corporis* identifies this Church with the Roman Catholic Church while *Lumen Gentium,* in using *subsistit in* (subsists in) rather than *est* (is), may

13. The text is available in French in *Documents secrets du Concil. Première Session,* ed. C. Falconi (Monaco: Editions du Rocher, 1965).

14. Congar, *Concile de Vatican II,* 157.

15. Ibid., 160.

not affirm such a strict identity.[16] It avoids the term "member" and speaks instead of "incorporation."[17] It describes those who accept all other means of salvation given to the Church together with her entire organization as fully incorporated into the Church. Others, not fully incorporated, but who have faith and are baptized are joined in some real way to the Catholic Church in the Holy Spirit. Non-Christians may also achieve salvation, but the principle of their incorporation is not specified. Congar notes that in affirming the relationship of non-Catholics to the Church, *Lumen Gentium* does not qualify this possibility with such terms as *reapse* (actually), *voto* (by desire), and *ordinati ad* (ordained to).[18] The document allows for different degrees of incorporation into Christ's body which is the Church.

These degrees of incorporation account for various elements contributory to membership in or relationship to the Church. Such elements include the possession of visible human nature which inserts all people into the incarnational order of salvation, supernatural faith, justification in charity and sanctifying grace, and baptism as a visible basis of membership.[19] Although *Lumen Gentium* represents an advance in the magisterial teaching on the universal call to salvation, on the necessity of incorporation into the Church for salvation, and on varying degrees of incorporation in the Church, much theological work remains to be done on this topic.

The Eucharist and the Mystical Body

In de Lubac's thought the Church as the Mystical Body is indissolubly united with the Eucharist. Thus he comments:

> The Church, like the Eucharist, is a mystery of unity — the same mystery. . . . Both are the body of Christ — the same body. If we are to be faithful to the teaching of Scripture, as Tradition interprets it, and wish not to lose anything of its essential riches, we must be careful not

16. "This Church, constituted and organized as a society in the present world, subsists in the Catholic Church, which is governed by the successor of Peter and by the bishops in communion with him." *Lumen Gentium*, I, 8.

17. Ibid., II, 14.

18. Congar, *Concile de Vatican II*, 161.

19. Ibid., 173.

to make the smallest break between the Mystical Body and the Eucharist. It is even more important that we should not see the ecclesial symbolism of the Eucharist as a mere "secondary sense" or . . . as "a moral and accessory meaning."[20]

As indicated in Chapter Three above, the "mystical" identification between Christ and his Church, as with the Eucharist and the Church, is grounded in the same principles as underlie the spiritual interpretation of Scripture. Christ and the Eucharist are figures of the Church; the Church is the body mystically signified by Christ and the Eucharist. Here it cannot be overly stressed that the terms "figures" and "mystically signified" are to be understood technically within the context of the spiritual interpretation of Scripture with all that implies in terms of the historicity and reality of that which "figures" and "mystically" signify. "Figure" and "mystical" do not mean "unreal" or "immaterial," and "mystical" is related to *"mysterion,"* the mystery of salvation, rather than to "mysticism."

Both the Eucharist and Christ are the cause of the Church, not nominally or extrinsically, but intrinsically, for within the context of spiritual exegesis Christ and the Eucharist are eschatologically fulfilled or completed in the Church. The sacramental causation is intrinsic in the sense that the source of the Church is to be found in its relation to Christ and the Eucharist. However, this dependence will need careful statement in order to distinguish between union and identity. The *totus Christus* is always the Church in *union* with Christ. That de Lubac does thus distinguish between union and identity is evident in his use of the terms "head" and "members" to describe the *totus Christus.* The members are not the head.

The figurative relationship between the Eucharist and the Church has probably been more commonly accepted than that between Christ and the Church because the one body which is the Church results from faithfully partaking of the one Bread. In eating one Bread they, the partakers, become one body. Nevertheless, de Lubac's work with spiritual exegesis enables him to assert a similar relationship between Christ and the Church:

---

20. De Lubac, *The Splendour of the Church,* trans. Michael Mason (New York: Sheed and Ward, 1956), 110. French original: *Méditation sur l'Eglise,* Coll. Théologie 27, 2nd edition revised and augmented (Paris: Aubier-Montaigne, 1953).

The Mystical Body is the Body *par excellence,* that with the greatest degree of reality and truth; it is the definitive body, and in relation to it the individual body of Christ Himself may be called a figurative body, without any detraction from its reality.[3]

---

3. The teaching of Origen (richer from the viewpoint of ecclesiology than has often been thought) is already clear on this point: see *In. Matt.,* bk. ii, 14 (p. 58 in Klostermann's edition): *In Joannem,* bk. ii, 35 (pp. 209-10 in Preuschen's edition), etc. Cf. my *Histoire et Esprit,* ch. viii, pp. 255-63.[21]

In this text from *The Splendour of the Church* we see an application of the exegetical use of the eucharistic term *"verum"* which de Lubac develops in *Corpus Mysticum.* Here *"verum"* does not refer to the real presence of Christ in the Eucharist, but to the Church which is mystically signified by Christ. In a similar manner, "mystical" is equated with "real." That which is most real is that which is mystically signified. That which is most real is that which is represented *in figura.* The reality is the totality into which the Logos is incarnate. The notion is rooted in Origen, as de Lubac notes, and is linked to Origen's view that the "marriage" of the Logos to humanity is *the* reality which Christ figures and in some way realizes in his hypostatic union.

This view is highly Platonic and requires careful qualification if the Incarnation itself is not to be devalued. However, there are indications that even though de Lubac's thought here is heavily influenced by Origen, he does rely on principles which safeguard the value of the historical event of the Incarnation as well as the Eucharist. These principles are grounded in spiritual exegesis, specifically the historicity of the literal sense and the intrinsic relation between the figure and that which is figured, which de Lubac argues is fundamental to Origen's own exegesis.[22] The key is that the relation within allegory between the figure and that which is figured is intrinsic rather than extrinsic. Therefore the figure is not negated, disvalued, or superseded by that which is figured. In this instance, Christ's historical presence and the reality of the eucharistic presence are guarantees of the "mystical" reality of the Church in the same way that the literal sense grounds its spiritual meaning:

---

21. Ibid., 92.

22. De Lubac argues for these very principles in Origen's eucharistic theology in *Histoire et Esprit,* 358.

It is the same with the Eucharist as it is with the spiritual sense of Scripture, which does not eliminate the literal sense or add something else to it, but rather rounds it out and gives it fullness, revealing its depths and bringing out its objective extension. Through this "spiritual breaking" the "mystery of the Bread" is opened up, and we come to understand its ecclesial sense.[4]

---

4. See the texts given in *Corpus Mysticum,* pp. 82-83.[23]

Thus, although Hanson argues that in Origen's system the Incarnation is subordinate to a higher reality and thus ultimately ceases to be important,[24] for de Lubac the spiritual sense does not eliminate the literal meaning, but reveals its inner depth of meaning.

This means that neither the Eucharist nor Christ is superseded by the Church, but that the meaning of the Church is both contained within the Eucharist and Christ, and, reciprocally, is an objective extension of both. The person of Christ the eucharistic real presence, the unity of the Testaments, and the theological interpretation of history — all find their depth of meaning in their ecclesial signification. In de Lubac's theology, the Church, equated with the Mystical Body and in union with Christ, represents the end point, the eschatological completion, of the economy of salvation. The systematic basis for this theological vision is the presupposition of the unity of the human race, the belief in Christ as the focal point of history, and the dialectic of history operative in spiritual exegesis. The Church in union with Christ represents the restoration of unity, the culmination of human history, in short, the definitive body prefigured by Christ and the Eucharist.

The Mystical Body and Catholicity

Even though the material on the Eucharist and spiritual exegesis largely determines de Lubac's understanding of the Mystical Body, a more contemporary and dogmatic rather than historical treatment of this topic is found in *Catholicism* (1947), *The Splendour of the Church* (1953), and *The*

---

23. De Lubac, *The Splendour of the Church,* 92.

24. Richard Patrick Crosland Hanson, *Allegory and Event* (London: SCM Press, 1959), 284.

79

Church: Paradox and Mystery (1967).[25] A sequential study of these three works reveals a nuancing in de Lubac's position on the relationship between the Roman Catholic Church and the Mystical Body which parallels the shift occurring between *Mystici Corporis* and the Second Vatican Council.

In the introduction of *Catholicism* de Lubac comments:

> This is not a work on the *Catholica*. Consequently here will be found no treatise on the Church or on the Mystical Body — although these pages refer continually to both, and particularly to the question of their identity.[26]

Here it is clear that de Lubac identifies the Church with the Mystical Body. For our understanding of de Lubac's ecclesiology, however, the important issue is not his identification of the Mystical Body with the Church, but how widely or narrowly he conceives of the Church. In *Catholicism* de Lubac identifies the Mystical Body, at least potentially, with the whole of the human race:

> Thus the unity of the Mystical Body of Christ, a supernatural unity, supposes a previous natural unity of the human race. So the Fathers of the Church, in their treatment of grace and salvation, kept constantly before them this Body of Christ, and in dealing with the creation were not content only to mention the formation of individuals, the first man and the first woman, but delighted to contemplate God creating humanity as a whole.[27]

25. De Lubac, *The Church: Paradox and Mystery,* trans. James R. Dunne (New York: Ecclesia Press, 1969); French original: *Paradoxe et mystère de l'Eglise* (Paris: Aubier-Montaigne, 1967). In the text I have cited dates of the French edition since the purpose is to indicate the relative development of de Lubac's thought.

26. De Lubac, *Catholicism,* xi.

27. Ibid., 3. De Lubac notes that these views may find their roots not so much in the Platonic doctrine of essential being, but in the Stoic conception of universal being. However, the same theme is taken up in *Lumen Gentium,* II, 13: "All men are called to this catholic unity which prefigures and promotes universal peace. And in different ways to it belong or are related the Catholic faithful, others who believe in Christ, and finally all mankind called by God's grace to salvation." Aloys Grillmeier notes that "the presuppositions of this unity are the unity of the human race by virtue of creation, and the decree of God to heal the divisions of sin and its consequent alienation, by gathering men once more into one in Christ and giving them life from the one Spirit." "Chapter II: The People of God," in *Commentary on the Documents of Vatican II,* 167.

The principle of unity of the totality of humanity is the divine image in which all are created and which does not differ from one individual to another.[28] This image constitutes a participation in God and is fundamentally Christological and historical since it is founded on the existential fact that all human beings are created with a supernatural finality, with an orientation toward beatitude. Thus the unity of the body results from its orientation to and participation in God. In this context sin is defined as the separation of an individual from the unity of the body.[29] In this regard de Lubac refers to Maximus the Confessor's description of original sin as a separation or an individualization. Conversely, redemption is the recovery of lost unity, not only of humanity with God, but also of the unity of human beings among themselves.[30] Nevertheless, a certain incongruity is present in both de Lubac's presupposition of a natural unity of the human race and his statement that the principle of this unity is the divine image, an image which constitutes a participation in God, within each individual. First, such an image, presupposing more than the possession of intellect and will, must be graced and therefore immediately precludes a "natural" unity. Second, this places the unity of humanity at some distance from Christ since it is prior to Christ (unless the preexistence of Jesus Christ is granted as the condition of possibility of this unity). In other words, a prior unity of the human race as created in the divine image can only be a graced unity which in turn is only possible by virtue of Jesus Christ, the focus and origin of all grace. This is not to argue that no such prior unity existed, but to indicate that the theological implications of such a unity have been inadequately explored.

We have seen that de Lubac identifies the whole of humanity with the Mystical Body. Now it remains for us to see how this is related to the Church. He specifically states that everything he has said in this work applies equally to the visible Church and to the invisible body of Christ and that any separation in this regard runs counter to the facts of history.[31] De Lubac calls the Church "Jesus Christ spread abroad and communicated."[32] Yet several pages further he states:

28. De Lubac, *Catholicism*, 4.
29. Ibid., 8.
30. Ibid.
31. Ibid., 23.
32. Ibid., 17.

The Church, without being exactly co-extensive with the Mystical Body, is not adequately distinct from it. For this reason it is natural that between her and it — as within the Mystical Body itself between the head and the members — there should arise a kind of exchange of idioms: "*Corpus Christi quod est ecclesia.*"[33]

These statements can only be reconciled if they are read eschatologically. The Church is only co-extensive with the Mystical Body of Christ at the end of time. De Lubac is conscious of this when he describes the Church as "that mysterious structure which will become fully a reality only at the end time: no longer is she a means to unite humanity in God, but she is herself the end, that is to say, that union in its consummation."[34] The Church cannot be separated from the Mystical Body before this end time and the relationship between the two can be described as one of participation, but they are not coextensive until that end time. Nevertheless, de Lubac considers the relationship to be so close that he does hold the possibility of a communication of idioms between the Mystical Body and the Church.

The evidence from *Catholicism* seems to indicate that in this work de Lubac identifies the Mystical Body with the Church, but that he also has a concept of catholicity which identifies the church, at least potentially, with the whole human race.[35] In *The Splendour of the Church* he explicitly supports *Mystici Corporis*:

Today the adjective "mystical" is usually added to "body of Christ." This does of course serve to emphasize that it is truly the whole Church indivisibly, which is a mystery. And although it is not in itself Pauline, it does sum up in a most satisfactory manner the thought of St. Paul, who related the Church and the "mystery" so closely as to come near to making the one the content of the other.[4] Thus we may say, borrowing the very words of the encyclical *Mystici Corporis Christi*: "To describe

33. Ibid., 27-28. This citation is an instance where de Lubac puts Christ within the Mystical Body and asserts a communication of idioms between the head and the members, with the result that there is an organic rather than covenantal relationship between members and head.

34. Ibid., 26-27.

35. For a discussion of the concept of catholicity in de Lubac's works see Eugen Maier, *Einigung der Welt in Gott: Das Katholische bei Henri de Lubac* (Einsiedeln: Johannes Verlag, 1983).

this Church of Christ — which is the Holy, Catholic, Apostolic, Roman church — there is no name more noble, none more excellent, none more divine than the "Mystical Body of Jesus Christ."[5]

4. Col. i.24-9. This is noted by d'Herbigny, among others (*Theologia de Ecclesia*, vol. i, pp. 97-98). Cf. H. Diechmann, *De Ecclesia*, 1925, vol. i, p. 329; P. Demann, O.P., "Quel est le Mystére d'Israël?", CS, 1952, pp. 11-15, etc.; L. Cerfaux, *Théologie de l'Eglise*, pp. 304-5: "Later the expression 'Mystical Body' was to be employed and well employed, to describe this body. . . ."

5. *Mystici Christi.* Cf. also previously Pius XI in the encyclicals *Mortalium Animos* (1928), *Caritate Christi* (1932) and *Ad Catholici Sacerdotii* (1935): . . . hanc non modo in unum Jesu Christi corpus potestatem assecutus est sacerdos, sed in mysticum etiam ejus corpus, quod est Ecclesia, excelsam amplissimamque auctoritatem (A.A.S., 1936, p. 12). On the thought of St. Thomas, which sets up a close relationship between the interior of the Church and her hierarchical organization, see Congar, *Esquisses*, p. 80; "Structure du Sacerdoce Chrétien," *La Maison Dieu* 27 (1951).[36]

In this text de Lubac not only identifies the Mystical Body with the visible Church, but he identifies the visible Church with the Roman Catholic Church.

In *The Church: Paradox and Mystery* (1967) de Lubac continues the theme of the Church as the body of Christ and a continuation of the Incarnation:

She [the Church] is for us. . . . "Jesus Christ diffused and communicated." She is "the Incarnation continued." She is . . . "the presence of Christ on earth, the *Christus praesens,* she speaks with the authority of Christ living and present in her.[37]

36. De Lubac, *The Splendour of the Church,* 86; *Méditation sur l'Eglise,* 106.

37. De Lubac, *The Church: Paradox and Mystery,* 24. The concept of the Church as a prolongation of the Incarnation in a strict sense is a theme in Romanticism. J. A. Möhler, in *Symbolism* (New York: The Catholic Publication House, n.d.), 253-254, writes: "Thus the visible Church, from the point of view here taken, is the Son of God himself, everlastingly manifesting Himself among men in a human form, perpetually renovated, and eternally young — the permanent Incarnation of the same, as in Holy Writ, even the faithful are called 'the body of Christ'. He it is who, concealed under earthly and human forms, works in the Church, and this is wherefore she has a divine and a human part in an undivided mode, so that the divine cannot be separated from the human nor the human from the divine. Hence these two parts change their predicates." German original: *Symbolik* (1895). The Church is also described by Emile Mersch as a continuation of the Incarnation in his well-known *The Theology of the Mystical Body,* trans. Cyril Vollert (St. Louis: B. Herder Book Co., 1952), 479-486; French original: *La théologie du corps mystique,*

However, even though *The Church: Paradox and Mystery* continues these themes from his earlier works, it attenuates them, as does *Lumen Gentium*. For example, de Lubac is aware of the difficulties of the image: "The image of the Church as a body is ambivalent, making, as it does, a single organism of Jesus Christ and his Church, but signifying at the same time the subjection of the members to the head."[38] Furthermore, in a rare instance where de Lubac does speak of the kingdom of God, he notes that "it is as impossible to simply identify the two (however that might be done), as it is to dissociate them."[39] Finally, he explicitly rejects the equivalence between the Roman Church and the Mystical Body: "We shall not reduce the Mystical Body of Christ to equivalence with the forms of the Roman Church, nor will we water down the Church until it becomes a 'body' conceived in an entirely 'mystical' fashion."[40] De Lubac therefore rejects an overly materialistic application of the physical image of body to the question of Church membership, noting that "the absolute and univocal identification of the (mystical) body of Christ with the visible institution founded by him has led to extreme theories of who exactly does or does not belong to the true Church."[41]

We can conclude, therefore, that in his thought in 1967 the Mystical Body is much more extensive than the Church although all members of the Church are also members of the Mystical Body. Yet, paradoxically, the Church also extends its visibility, transcends what Christianity is, and yet the very reaching beyond is itself Christianity.[42] This extends the visible Church to an invisible realm. Does this extension, then, equate the visible Church with the Mystical Body and therefore negate those statements where de Lubac draws a distinction between them? It is difficult to say, caught as we are in what is either an ambiguity in de Lubac or the mystery of the paradox of the Church that is at once visible and invisible. Regarding

---

1944. Elsewhere in this work he refers to the union between Christ and the faithful as a "physical union" (53). For a discussion of the differences and similarities between the Incarnation and the Church see Heribert Mühlen, *Una Mystica Persona* (Munich: Verlag Ferdinand Schöningh, 1967), 173-216; also Yves Congar, "Dogme Christologique et ecclésiologie: vérité et limites d'un parallèle," *Sainte Eglise* (Paris: Cerf, 1963), 69-104.

38. De Lubac, *The Church: Paradox and Mystery*, 24.
39. Ibid., 28.
40. Ibid., 27.
41. Ibid., 20.
42. Ibid., 27.

the relation of the Church to the Mystical Body, we can conclude, despite the lack of clarity, that de Lubac's thought developed from *The Splendour of the Church* to *The Church: Paradox and Mystery,* the former strongly reflecting *Mystici Corporis* and the latter reflecting *Lumen Gentium.*

The Church as a Continuation of the Incarnation

In spite of these ambiguities, de Lubac retains the image of the Church as the body of Christ. This image, based as it is on the image of the head and members, is Pauline in origin. However, it is important to note that when the union of the body, the Church, to its head, Christ, is compared with the union of humanity and divinity in Christ, the Pauline image is being read through the Chalcedonian formula and is thus an interpretation of the Pauline image through a later doctrinal statement. The Church is then compared with the humanity of Christ, and its union with Christ is represented as structurally the same as humanity's union with divinity in the personal unity of the Christ.

Analogy with the Hypostatic Union

This analogy fails, however, because Christ as both human and divine represents more than just divinity. When the Church is joined to Christ, it is joined to Christ in his humanity and divinity. When de Lubac notes the ambiguities inherent in considering the Church as a continuation of the Incarnation, he sees the difficulties resulting from such a comparison, but does not note their source in an analogy that necessarily equates the union of Christ and the Church with that of the divinity and humanity in Christ. Once this difficulty is perceived, the Pauline image of head and members can no longer be read with reference to the Chalcedonian formula.

When the Church's union with Christ is compared analogously to the hypostatic union, there is a communication of idioms between the Church and Christ. However, the use of theological language originally designed to describe the union of humanity and divinity in Christ to describe the presence of divine and human elements in the Church or the relationship between Christ and the Church is problematic for both the

Christology and the ecclesiology which results. On the one hand, if the Church is joined to Christ as humanity is joined to divinity, this results in a hypostatic unity. In this instance the relationship between Christ and the Church could not be free, resulting in an orthodox Christology but in a heterodox ecclesiology. If, on the other hand, the Church is joined to Christ in a covenantal relationship, this results in a Nestorian Christology as the *anthropos* is joined to the *Logos*.[43] Because in this case the unity of the Logos-anthropos is intrinsically covenantal, the corresponding Christology is adoptionist. Here the ecclesiology is orthodox, but not the Christology. Consequently, when one attempts to compare the Christ/Church relationship to the God/man relationship one jeopardizes either the ecclesiology or the Christology.

This does not mean, however, that it is always inappropriate to compare the union of divine and human elements in the Church with the mystery of the incarnate Word. This comparison can be made without presuming that the ecclesial union of humanity with divinity represents the union with the Logos rather than with the incarnate Logos. For example, in *Lumen Gentium* the social structure of the Church is compared with the Logos's assumed nature while the Spirit of Christ which vivifies it represents the divine element in the Church.[44] This is different, however, from saying that the Church is joined to Christ as humanity is joined to divinity in Christ, which is the implication of the communication of idioms between the two.

Values of the Image of the Church as the Body of Christ

If de Lubac as well as other theologians emphasizes an organic image of the Church that risks absorbing the Church into Christ — with the result that in recognizing the close union of the two they do not account adequately for their discontinuity — it is because there are values that such an image preserves despite its risks and ambiguities. De Lubac tries to

---

43. From another perspective than the one described here, Yves Congar discusses the problems of Nestorianism and Monophysitism in regard to the Church in *Christ, Our Lady and the Church,* trans. Henry St. John (Westminster: The Newman Press, 1957). French original: *Le Christ, Marie et l'Eglise,* 1952.

44. *Lumen Gentium,* I, 8.

avoid a notion of the Church as a transcendent, quasi-Platonic hypostasis, an invisible Church which is wholly "interior" or "spiritual." He achieves this by identifying the visible institutional Church with the Mystical Body of Christ.[45] Second, he avoids a nominalist and merely pragmatic concept of the Church as a federation of local assemblies or as the gathering of individuals which results in an organism brought into being after the event of conversion by the community of believers.[46] A federation is the antithesis of an organic image of the Church; by contrast, the image of the Church as body, especially when identified with the prior unity of the human race, intends an ontological rather than sociological description of the Church. De Lubac's theology of the Eucharist as causative of the Church, as gathering the believers, prohibits a view of the Church as an organization created by believers. An organic image of the Church primarily tries to preserve the Church from any consideration of it as a merely human society. This is also why de Lubac stresses that there are both divine and human elements in the Church. Finally, the unity of the body or organism assures the unity of the Church. This unity is more than a moral or spiritual unity since de Lubac opposes the notion that there can be several independent Christian societies linked by a "spiritual unity."[47] This underscores de Lubac's preference for physical imagery. True "spiritual unity" is achieved only by incorporation into the body of Christ which is the Church.

One final value of the image of the Church as the body of Christ is that it distinguishes the Church from the "people of God" of the Old Testament by emphasizing the discontinuity of the new dispensation, the newness achieved in Jesus Christ. De Lubac himself does not compare or contrast the Church as the "people of God" and the Church as the "body of Christ," but he does emphasize the newness and the discontinuity of Christ in comparison with the figures of the Old Testament.[48] He also speaks of the Spirit as the soul of the body, as the vital principle of the body.[49] The newness wrought by Christ and the life achieved in the unity of the body through the vital principle of the Spirit is the life of grace. In

---

45. De Lubac, *The Splendour of the Church*, 76.
46. Ibid., 92ff.
47. Ibid., 57.
48. De Lubac, "The Christian Newness," *The Sources of Revelation* (New York: Herder and Herder, 1968), 159-229. French original: *L'Ecriture dans la Tradition* (Paris: Aubier, 1967).
49. De Lubac, *The Motherhood of the Church*, 20.

contrast to the association of the people of God of the Old Testament through blood and race, we are incorporated into Christ and become children of God, like him, through grace. This does not mean, however, that the Jews as Jews are outside the order of grace. The freedom of graced membership in the body of Christ precludes any narrow interpretation of who is and who is not graced. This means, finally, that it is only through incorporation by grace rather than by blood and race that we constitute the body of Christ. Consequently, the organic image of the Church accounts for our life in grace at the same time that it emphasizes the unity of the body.

Problems of the Image of the Church as the Body of Christ

A central question, however, is whether in considering the Church as a continuation of the Incarnation, de Lubac contributes to a Christomonistic ecclesiology. This type of ecclesiology absorbs the Church into Christ without adequate observance of the distinction between the two. There are texts where de Lubac makes this comparison:

> There, then, is the Church, human and divine at once even in her visibility, "without division and without confusion," just like Christ himself, whose body she mystically is.[50]

When de Lubac refers to the image of the body in Paul, he refers to the Church as an organism which is

> "the unity of a totality,"[6] for all the Christians who go to make it up, "being assimilated to Christ, are the same One;"[7] . . . . The Head "is of one nature with His Members,[2] to which He communicates power, movement and energy," — so much so that the two names "Church" and "Christ" would seem to be interchangeable, as we can see as early as St. Paul.[3]

---

6. Dom Jacques Dupont, O.S.B., *Gnosis: Le Connaissance Religieuse dans les Epitres de Saint Paul* (1949), p. 426. There is a particular insistence on the unity of the body and the Spirit which animates it in Ephes. iv. 4.

7. L. Cerfaux, *Théologie de l'Eglise*, p. 255. Cf. Godescalc, *De Praedestinatione:* "Non

50. De Lubac, *The Splendour of the Church*, 69.

modo caput Ecclesiae Christus, verum etiam ipsa Ecclesia tanquam sui capitis corpus et membra cum capite suo dicatur et sit Christus, ut ait apostolus . . ." (p. 219 in Lambot's edition of 1945).

2. Louis Chardon, O.P., *La Croix de Jésus,* ed. F. Florand, p. 37.

3. Cor. xii.12: "For as the body is one and hath many members; and all the members of the body, whereas they are many, are one body; so also is Christ." Cf. St. John Chrysostom, *in loc.:* "In place of Christ he puts the Church. . . . He names Christ instead of the Church, thus designating the body of Christ" (PG, 61, 249-53): Acts xxii.7-8.[51]

As we have seen, there are problems with such a close identification. Yet, de Lubac does distinguish the Church from Christ when he characterizes the relationship between head and members as one of subordination where Christ leads and governs and the Church submits.[52] He asserts that there is no confusion between head and members.[53] This difference is evident in the fact that although the Church is holy, she is sinful in her members.[54] This qualitative distinction between the head and members is another reason for supposing Christ not to be so much a member of the body as the head of the *totus Christus.* One concludes, therefore, that some of de Lubac's descriptions or citations do admit of a certain Christomonism, but these are counterbalanced by other texts which correct this tendency.

Nonbelievers and the Body of Christ

Before leaving our consideration of the organic image of the Church in de Lubac's theology, it is important to note an important difference between his theology and that expressed in *Mystici Corporis.* Where the encyclical emphasizes the Church as the Roman Catholic Church, in *Catholicism* de Lubac's view of the Church is rather that of the totality of the human race called to be members of the Body of Christ.[55] Even though we have seen that in *The Splendour of the Church* de Lubac identifies the

51. Ibid., 83-84.

52. Ibid., 84.

53. Ibid., 112.

54. De Lubac, *The Church: Paradox and Mystery,* 24.

55. This is similar to the statement in *Lumen Gentium,* I, 7: "For by communicating his Spirit, Christ mystically constitutes as his body those brothers of his who are called together from every nation."

Mystical Body with the Roman Catholic Church, in another passage he reflects the same universalism characteristic of *Catholicism:*

> Following in the footsteps of St. Thomas, we can give the name "Church" to that gigantic organism which includes the host of angels as well as men, and even extends to the whole of the cosmos as well.[5]

5. St. Thomas, *De Veritate*, no. 29, a. 4, obj. 5: *In Ephes.,* ch. i, lect. viii, etc.: so also Romano Guardini, *Vom Sinn der Kirche,* 1922, p. 11. Opinion is divided concerning St. Paul's views on this subject (in the captivity Epistles); cf. L. Cerfaux, *La Théologie de l'Eglise Suivant Saint Paul,* 2nd ed., 1948, pp. 255-7. The reservations there made seem to be justified, as do those of Frs. Huby and Benoit in the *Revue Biblique* for 1937, pp. 354-5. Cf. Ambrosiaster, *In Eph.:* "Omnem Ecclesiam dicens summatim totum comprehendit, quod in caelo est et in terra": Heb. xii.22-3 and I Tim. v.21: *Acta et Decreta SS Concilii Vaticani.* Collectio Lacensis, vol. vii, cols. 326-7 (Bartolommeo d'Avanzo's report).[56]

This universalism touches on the issue of how all of humanity is related to the Church and thus how salvation is not found apart from the Church.

Since all humanity obviously does not belong to the Roman Catholic Church, the question arises of the relationship of nonbelievers to the Church. In this regard de Lubac rejects such positions as the one which denies grace to nonbelievers, salvation by recourse to miracles, and the hypothesis of a natural salvation whereby the greater part of humanity would be cast into the twilight of Limbo.[57] De Lubac considers that the salvation of everyone is achieved through Christ who gives a more or less obscure revelation of the Father to everyone, that the grace of Christ is of universal application. He describes the role of the Church in the salvation of nonbelievers through the principle of the unity of the human race:

> The human race is one. By our fundamental nature and still more in virtue of our common destiny we are members of the same body. Now the life of the members comes from the life of the body. How, then, can there be salvation for the members if, *per impossibile,* the body itself were not saved? But salvation for this body, for humanity, consists in its receiving the form of Christ, and that is possible only through the Catholic Church. For is she not the only complete, authoritative inter-

56. De Lubac, *The Splendour of the Church,* 29.
57. De Lubac, *Catholicism,* 108.

preter of Christian revelation? Is it not through her that that the practice of the evangelical virtues is spread throughout the world? And, lastly, is she not responsible for realizing the spiritual unity of men in so far as they will lend themselves to it? Thus this Church, which as the invisible Body of Christ is identified with final salvation, as a visible and historical institution is the providential means of this salvation.[58]

In de Lubac's view, nonbelievers will be saved by virtue of the mysterious bonds which unite them to the faithful. Nonbelievers are saved because they are an integral part of that humanity which is to be saved.[59] Consequently, those who do not belong exteriorly to the Church can be saved, but their salvation is through the Church by virtue of the unity of the human race.[60] Salvation is through the unity of the body.

---

58. Ibid., 110-111. De Lubac finds the concept of the unity of the human race in patristic literature. However, this is also a concept of the Romantics. The similarity between this text and the following text, Geiselmann's description of Johann Adam Möhler's (1796-1838) thought, is striking: "As, however, the universe is represented for us men by humanity, the individual can only know God to the extent that he is and remains a member of mankind as a whole. Just as Möhler develops the knowledge of God as the creator of the universe from the metaphysics of man's immanence in God, so too does he develop the non-recognition of God by man from the metaphysics of man's separation of himself from the universe. Accordingly, all non-recognition of God is based on man's cutting himself off from the whole and so failing in his vocation to be a member of the universe. So little does this Romantic among the theologians consider the autonomous individual of the Enlightenment view of man truly to represent the nature of man that it is precisely by being separate and individual that the fall from God is accomplished. For what is the autonomous self-sufficient individual, if not man detaching himself from the whole, cutting himself off from the whole and making himself the centre? But that is precisely what constitutes the nature of sin, for such separation is equivalent to falling from God." Josef Rupert Geiselmann, *The Meaning of Tradition*, trans. W. J. O'Hara (London: Burns & Oates, 1966), 55-56.

59. De Lubac, *Catholicism*, 116.

60. This, however, raises a question concerning nature and grace. If humanity is created as a whole and redemption consists in restoring the lost unity of the whole, this amounts to a natural salvation. The alternative is that the original unity of the human race is graced and a restoration to unity is at the same time a restoration to grace. Moreover, since the unity of the body is at the same time its union with Christ, the question arises whether the *totus Christus* is not only eschatological, but also primordial. This in turn invokes the question of the preexistence of Jesus Christ. These are systematic questions beyond the scope of the present study since de Lubac does not examine the systematic implications of his concept of unity. The International Theological Commission briefly discusses the problem of the preexistence of Jesus Christ in its publication,

This represents an extension of the dogma of the communion of saints. Those people who do not find themselves within the normal condition of salvation are saved through their ties with the faithful.[61] Thus de Lubac's presupposition regarding the unity of the human race allows him to account both for the necessity of the Church for salvation and for the salvation of those people apparently outside the Church. Consequently, in de Lubac's soteriology the concept of the Mystical Body is inclusive rather than exclusive.

Conclusion

The thesis that the Church is the social embodiment of grace in the world is closely tied to an incarnational view of the Church as demonstrated here in the theology of Henri de Lubac. The union between Christ and his Church assures the graced character of the Church while the relationship between the body of Christ and the body which is the Church assures that this grace is embodied. The distinction between the historical body of Christ and the fullness of that body which is achieved in the Church at the end time qualifies this identification and avoids collapsing the Church into Christ or vice versa. Even though de Lubac's comparison of the Church to the Incarnation runs the risk of not adequately distinguishing between Christ and his Church, he compensates for this difficulty in his theology by using other images of the Church. The image which maintains the distinction between Christ and Church at the same time that it expresses the close union between them is that of the Church as the Bride of Christ.

"Theology, Christology, Anthropology," April 1983, 13-17, and suggests that in the light of Jesus' exaltation, "the origin of Jesus Christ is openly and definitively understood: sitting at the right hand of God in his post-existence (i.e., after his earthly life) implies his pre-existence with God from the beginning before he came into the world. In other words, his eschatological state can be no different from his pre-incarnation state and vice versa" (p. 14). This short statement, however, needs further development since Christ's wounds are historical and irrevocable, therefore hardly a condition of his pre-Incarnation state.

61. De Lubac, *Catholicism*, 116.

Part II: The Church as the Spouse of Christ

In de Lubac's ecclesiology, the image of the Church as the spouse of Christ ranks second in importance after the image of the body of Christ. The discussion of the Church as the spouse of Christ first situates this image of the Church in relation to the image of the Church as the people of God, showing, incidentally, that de Lubac places less emphasis on the image "people of God" than does *Lumen Gentium*. Secondly, the image of the Church as spouse will be seen to be inseparable from a consideration of Mary as a type of the Church. This typology is examined both from the perspective of Blondel's notion of the "concrete universal" and from that of spiritual exegesis. This examination results in the conclusion that the Church viewed as the spouse of Christ represents a model of the use of the principles of spiritual exegesis both in the tradition of the Church and in de Lubac's theology.

Spousal Imagery in Relation to Other Images

In de Lubac's theology the image of the Church as the bride of Christ follows naturally upon the image of the Church as the body of Christ. He comments:

> the analogy of the body, as is only to be expected, often leads them [the Fathers] (as it had St. Paul)[106] to that of the Spouse. "Christ and the Church are no longer two beings, but one flesh, for it has been said to the spouse: you are the members of Christ" (Origen).[107]

---

106. Cf. Dom Paul Andriessen, "La nouvelle Eve, corps du nouvel Adam" in *Recherches bibliques*, 9, 1965, pp. 87-109. See also André Feuillet, *La Christ Sagesse de Dieu d'après les Epitres Pauliniennes*, p. 368.

107. *In. Matt. comm.*, bk. 14 (Klostermann B., p. 326). Cf. In. Cant. Comm., I, 1, n. 7, etc.[62]

The Church considered as spouse and mother is a favorite theme in de Lubac's ecclesiology, a theme which he calls the patristic theme *par*

---

62. De Lubac, *The Church: Paradox and Mystery*, 55-56. This chapter, "Lumen Gentium and the Fathers of the Church," is also printed in *Vatican II: An Interfaith Appraisal*, ed. John H. Miller (Notre Dame: University of Notre Dame Press, 1966), 153-175.

excellence.[63] De Lubac observes that the image of the Church as the spouse of Christ, occurring in four passing references in *Lumen Gentium* (nos. 6, 7, 9, and 39), is subordinated to the image of the Church as the people of God as it had previously been subordinated to the image of the Mystical Body.[64] De Lubac regrets the subordination of the treatment of Church as spouse and mother to the treatment of the Church as the people of God since in his opinion the former is as well founded in Scripture and the Fathers as the latter.[65] In de Lubac's own writing the image of spouse follows the image of the Mystical Body while the image of the people of God is mentioned only in passing or in the context of a discussion of *Lumen Gentium.*[66]

Although de Lubac acknowledges the value of the phrase "people of God" to designate the Church, he questions the proof which argues from the origin of the word *Ekklesia,* the Greek translation of the biblical *Qahal Yahweh,* the assembly of the people of God. He acknowledges that this etymology is correct, but questions whether the patristic usage had this origin, and therefore this meaning, in mind. He further notes that the phrase does not communicate the newness of the Church in relation to the people of God of the Old Testament and the discontinuity of the new Christian creation.[67] Where *Lumen Gentium* uses the phrase to emphasize

63. Ibid., 55. Hubert Schnackers in *Kirche als Sakrament und Mutter: zur ekklesiologie von Henri de Lubac* (Frankfurt am Main: Peter Lang, 1979), 106-112, is much more optimistic about the place of the image of the Church as the "people of God" in de Lubac's theology than I am. De Lubac refers his readers to Dom Vonier, *The People of God,* especially ch. 8, for material on the importance of the idea of the people of God for ecclesiology and its inadequacies when treated alone. (*The Church: Paradox and Mystery,* 45.) Similarly, in *The Motherhood of the Church,* 12, de Lubac speaks of the gospel as a "new covenant" whose consequence is the new people of God, a people who will be characterized by its status as the "Body of Christ." Once again we see here the association de Lubac makes between the "people of God" and the "body of Christ." For additional discussions on the relationship between the images "people of God" and "body of Christ" see Herwi Rikhof, *The Concept of the Church: A Methodological Inquiry into the Use of Metaphors in Ecclesiology* (Shepherdstown, WV: Patmos Press, 1981); Cardinal Ratzinger, "The Ecclesiology of Vatican II," *Origins* 15 (#22, November 14, 1985): 370-376. Both of these writers show that the image "people of God" needs to be interpreted in conjunction with the image "body of Christ."

64. De Lubac, *The Church: Paradox and Mystery,* 45.

65. Ibid.

66. See de Lubac, *The Splendour of the Church,* 36.

67. De Lubac, *The Church: Paradox and Mystery,* 41.

the continuity between the Testaments, de Lubac claims that the phrase resonates differently than it does when used by the Fathers. De Lubac prefers to stress the radical transformation effected by Christ and criticizes *Lumen Gentium* for not underlining this newness effected by the coming of the Messiah and the infusion of the Holy Spirit.[68] De Lubac's criticism here is consistent with his analysis of the relationship between the allegorical and literal or historical sense of Scripture. Just as the allegorical sense represents a transformation of the literal sense, so the Church represents a transformation, rather than a continuation, of the people of God of the Old Testament.

Positively, de Lubac affirms that the term "people of God" "allows a better understanding of an essential character of the idea of the body of Christ in that it clearly indicates the distance to be kept between the head of the body and the other members."[69] Second, it evokes the historical dimension of the Church and the complex relationship between the Old and the New Covenant.[70] Third, in his opinion the image "people of God" completes the analogy of the body of Christ by bringing out the fact that the body is growing, that there is a salvation history.[71] He is aware, however, that neither the expression "body of Christ" nor "people of God" constitutes a definition of the Church, but are privileged paths by which we attempt to approach in faith the heart of the mystery which is the Church.[72] This shows, first, that de Lubac is careful to maintain the distinction between Christ and the Church in spite of other texts where he seems to identify them more closely. Second, the fact that he sees as a primary value of the term its clarification of his own preferred image, the body of Christ, is consistent with his heavily incarnational ecclesiology centered on the concept of the body.

---

68. Ibid., 43.

69. Ibid., 41. Here again Christ, as head, is an organic member of the body.

70. Angelo Scola, *De Lubac: A Theologian Speaks, Interview of Henri de Lubac* (*Trenti Giorni,* trans. Stephen Maddux [Los Angeles: Twin Circle Publishing Co., 1985], 15). The French version of this interview was published in the July 19, 1985, issue of *France Catholique.*

71. Ibid., 8.

72. Ibid.

Mary as Type of the Church

A consideration of spousal imagery of the Church is inseparable from a consideration of the relationship between Mary and the Church. For de Lubac the connections between Mary and the Church are not only numerous and close, but the two form "one single and unique mystery."[73] Consequently, the same biblical symbols, such as the New Eve, the Ark of the covenant, the City of God, the woman — foe of the serpent, and the woman — victor over the dragon, are applicable to both Mary and the Church. However, it is Mary as virgin and mother who images the Church most closely. Mary, as virgin and mother, is a type of the Church both from the point of view of her spiritual receptivity and her motherhood with regard to Christ.[74] As Mary gave birth to Christ, so the Church gives birth to Christians in the sacrament of Baptism and, in a sense, to Christ in the sacrament of the Eucharist.[75] The purity and spiritual receptivity of Mary are associated with the Church's fidelity in an integral faith, a firm hope, and sincere charity.[76] In the relationship of Mary to the Church, Mary as a "concrete universal" or "type" comprises in an eminent degree all the graces and the perfection of the Church.[77] De Lubac comments that in Mary "the whole Church is outlined" and at the same time already completed. Mary is both the "seed" and the "pleroma" of it, the perfect form of the Church.[78] In her personal relationship to her Lord, Mary appears by anticipation as the perfection of the Church and is therefore an eschatological figure.

Because of the similarity in their motherhood, de Lubac alludes to an "exchange of idioms" between the Church and Mary.[79] This "exchange of idioms" parallels the "exchange of idioms" between Christ and the Church, but an examination of each reveals that they differ. In the Mary-Church relationship the similarity can be properly regarded as an identity, for Mary in her response to God is a microcosm of the Church, the particular from which the universal derives its existence. On the other hand, the exchange of idioms between Christ and the Church is based on

73. Ibid., 240.
74. De Lubac, *The Church: Paradox and Mystery,* 57.
75. Ibid., 249.
76. *Lumen Gentium,* VIII, 64.
77. De Lubac, *The Splendour of the Church,* 259.
78. Ibid.
79. Ibid.

the union of humanity and divinity in both, which, as we have seen, is not a strict identity.

Mary and the Church in Spiritual Exegesis

To place this relationship in the context of spiritual exegesis, to which the categories of type and antitype belong, Christ and Mary are related to the allegorical sense as the Church is related to the anagogical sense when they are considered as types for which the Church is the antitype. However, there is a degree of fluidity or flexibility here. Insofar as Mary is viewed as the antitype of Old Testament figures, as the new Eve, for example, she is considered in the light of the allegorical sense. On the other hand, insofar as her relationship to her Lord is considered as a particular, concrete instance of the Church's relation to him, she is considered in the light of the tropological sense. Similarly, the Church is sometimes considered in the light of the allegorical sense, when viewed as antitype of Old Testament figures, and sometimes in the light of the anagogical sense, when viewed eschatologically. One concludes, therefore, that neither Mary nor the Church is associated absolutely with a particular spiritual sense, but that the spiritual senses provide different perspectives from which to view them.

Since both Mary and Christ are types of the Church, but are so differently, there is danger that the very category of "type" risks ambiguity. However, it is necessary to recall that spiritual exegesis is not a scientific method and therefore can be neither interpreted nor applied in a rigid and absolute manner. It is rather suggestive and descriptive. Nevertheless, one general difference between Marian and Christic typology is that where Christ is understood as a type of the Church, the union of head and members is figured in the union of humanity and divinity in Christ. Where Mary is a type of the Church, the image is not predominantly that of the union of head and members, but the more explicitly spousal covenantal image. In this instance the Church is the body, not as opposed to Christ as the head, but as the feminine element in correlation to the masculine. Thus the typology changes from a head-body relation to a man-woman relation.[80] The differ-

---

80. Jean Daniélou notes the relationship between the two images in *The Development of Christian Doctrine before the Council of Nicaea*, vol. I: *The Theology of Jewish Christianity*, trans. John A. Baker (London: Darton, Longman & Todd, 1964), 306-307.

ence can be considered as one of emphasis since the images of the body and of marriage are very closely associated in the text from the Epistle to the Ephesians:

> Husbands, love your wives, as Christ loved the Church. . . . Even so men should love their wives as their own bodies. . . . For no man ever hates his own flesh; but nourishes and cherishes it, as Christ does the Church; because we are members of his body. For this reason a man shall leave his father and mother, and be joined to his wife, and the two shall be one [Gen. 2:24]. This is a great mystery: and I take it to mean Christ and the Church. (Eph. 5:25-32)

Here the Church as comprising the members of the body of Christ is compared to the one flesh of marital union. The close juxtaposition of these images of the Church is perhaps one indication that too distinct a dichotomy between the imagery of head and members and covenantal, marital imagery is foreign to the biblical text. De Lubac's theology, in using both images, finds itself squarely within this tradition. Potential ambiguities as well as the fact that both Mary and Christ can be associated with various spiritual senses of Scripture indicate that spiritual exegesis does not determine de Lubac's theological conclusions any more than it constitutes a method for arriving at dogma. The faith of the Church is prior to the theological method. Spiritual exegesis represents a tool with which the interrelationship of the mysteries of faith can be expressed. There is consequently a certain fluidity and flexibility in the use of spiritual exegesis. In whatever sense Mary and the Church are considered, it remains true that they are historical figures whose ultimate meaning is only grasped in faith.

Mary and the Church as Universal Figures: The Concrete Universal

Christ and Mary, as eschatological figures, are also universal figures. The problems such a statement raises are legion since one can immediately ask how a figure can be at once historical, with all that entails in terms of beginnings and endings, of birth and death; and at the same time be universal. The difference between the historical and the universal, however, depends on the perspective from which the problem is viewed. To consider solely the historical limits of a person is to confine oneself to an immanent concept of history. One limits oneself to the empirical and the phenomenological. It is from this stance that most of the challenges posed to the Church by the contemporary "historical consciousness" derive. An alternative viewpoint is given in Teilhard de Chardin's poem "L'Eternel Féminin" for which de Lubac has written a book-length commentary.[81] In this poem Teilhard has Beatrix say:

> I am the Church, the bride of Christ.
> I am Mary the Virgin, mother of all human kind.[82]

One notes here the identification of bride, mother, virgin, Mary, and the Church, an indication that for an eschatological, integral figure there is no discontinuity between these seemingly contradictory sexual roles. Such a figure can simultaneously be bride, mother, and virgin. Unfallen femininity is integral rather than fragmented. If Mary and thus the Church can be considered the mother of all humankind, this title immediately connotes a universalism and some type of priority over the rest of humankind. The theological foundation for such a treatment of Mary is her identification with created Wisdom.[83] Once Mary is seen to be a type of the Church, it is a short step to attribute to the Church the same attributes as are accorded to Wisdom and, in a second instance, to Mary. De Lubac comments that "having issued from God and being co-extensive with the whole history of the cosmos and the whole adventure of man, she [the feminine] leads all God's creation back to him in a reversal of movement."[84] Within such a perspective Mary and the Church function as exemplars, and the doctrine of the fall and redemption has a strong flavor of a Platonic *exitus-reditus*. De Lubac notes the marked Platonic flavor, but affirms the biblical cast of the poem, whose spirit he calls "completely Christian."[85] One difference between the Platonic and the Christian character here is that for the Platonic tradition, as for later

---

81. De Lubac, *The Eternal Feminine,* trans. René Hagne (New York: Harper and Row, 1971). French original: *L'Eternel Féminin* (Paris: Aubier, 1983; original edition, 1968).

82. Ibid., 26.

83. See Proverbs 8; *The Eternal Feminine,* 95; and *The Church: Paradox and Mystery,* 86. Such an identification, of course, is only accomplished within the practice of spiritual exegesis.

84. De Lubac, *The Eternal Feminine,* 26.

85. Ibid.

Gnosticism, the historical interval separating the *exitus-reditus* is annulled, whereas in Christianity, history is all-important, being the history of salvation.

For Teilhard, the feminine is not an abstract principle since its perfection is realized in a personal being — the Virgin Mary.[86] In spite of the strong exemplarism in Teilhard, the most Christian element in his thought here may be the principle that the universal exists because of the particular. That is, the particular is not merely an instance of the universal, but that which is universal only has existence in the particular. Specifically, the ideal universalized as the feminine exists in its unitive and spiritually receptive function because a particular, concrete, historical woman embodied such perfection in her own being. This transforms Platonic exemplarism into its mirror image, in which all is reversed. The real is not dehistoricized so that the particular is only an imperfect image of an ideal and perfect reality, but the universal exists because it has been achieved in historical particularity. Thus a universal principle, here the feminine, becomes a symbol of a concrete person in whom it attains its highest realization.[87]

The concrete is not a symbol of the universal, but the universal becomes a symbol of the concrete. As de Lubac notes: "Wisdom is not a hypostasis which, in its created aspect, is realized in the Virgin."[88] Elsewhere he comments:

> It is not the universal which takes on for us the appearance of the personal in order that it may make itself apprehensible by giving itself mythical expression; the universal does not become more or less personal and so acquire an added attribute. It is the personal which becomes universal, to the degree in which (subject to certain conditions) it realizes more profoundly its own specific character. Universality is the prerogative of the strongest personality.[89]

86. Ibid., 19.

87. Ibid., 20, 103, 119. That this is a fairly accurate assessment of Teilhard's thought is evident from de Lubac's statement: "For Teilhard, 'Platonic' errors will be, not suppressed, but integrated by 'reversal' in the dialectic of agape. It is this of which 'Beatrix' is the sign" (M. Bathélemy-Madaule, *Le personne et la drame humain*, 113). Cited in Henri de Lubac, *The Eternal Feminine*, nn. 64, 229.

88. *The Eternal Feminine*, 95.

89. Ibid., 118. See also Henri de Lubac, "L'Universel concret," *Teilhard posthume: réflections et souvenirs* (Paris: Fayard, 1977), 121-132.

The concept which enables Teilhard as well as Hans Urs von Balthasar[90] to develop this perspective of the relation of the universal to the particular is Blondel's notion of the "concrete Universal."[91] This universal is always personal, never an abstraction.[92] Christ as both individual being and absolute norm is, of course, the concrete Universal, but the same principle is applicable to Mary when her universality is perceived as the feminine.

The Concrete Universal Correlated with Spiritual Exegesis

The concept of the concrete universal is easily related to the typological relationship of Christ to the Church and of Mary to the Church although de Lubac himself does not draw this connection between Teilhard's work and the intellectual framework of his own work.[93] In the Christ/Church relationship, de Lubac describes Teilhard's Christ as "truly the center and cohesive bond of the whole body of monads destined to build up glorified man — the "universal Christ."[94] De Lubac comments that Christ is the bond because he is first "God incarnate, God-man, Jesus, the being born of the Virgin."[95] The "glorified man" is none other than the *totus Christus* — the body of "monads" or members united in Jesus Christ. In other words, the particularity of the concrete universal corresponds to the typological figure, Jesus Christ, the God-man. The universal present with the concrete particularity represents his eschatological fulfillment — here the *totus Christus*. Although de Lubac's commentary on Teilhard does not compare the concrete universal with spiritual exegesis, the similarities remain and are evident.

What has been described here as the relationship of the concrete to the universal, of the type to the antitype, can in the Latin tradition be

---

90. Hans Urs von Balthasar, *A Theology of History* (New York: Sheed and Ward, 1963). The English is a severe abridgment as well as translation of the German original, *Theologie der Geschichte*, 2nd ed. (Einsiedeln, 1959).

91. Maurice Blondel, *Exigences philosophiques du Christianisme* (Paris: Presses Universitaires de France, 1950).

92. De Lubac, *The Eternal Feminine*, 121.

93. However, in another context de Lubac does refer to Mary as "the universal creature." *The Splendour of the Church*, 267.

94. De Lubac, *The Eternal Feminine*, 122.

95. Ibid.

described as the relationship of the species to the genus. De Lubac cites Ticonius's comment that Scripture conceals the species under the genus, for example, the whole body under a member.[96] The genus is the more inclusive category which includes the species as animal includes rational animal. In this view the Body is the genus and the member is the species. Thus in Mary we see *in specie* what is realized in the Church *in genere,* and the genus is anticipated in the species. In other words, Mary is the effective figure of the Church. The relationship of the species to the genus within this tradition of exegesis is clearly analogous to that of the concrete to the universal within Blondel's and Teilhard's terminology.

Regarding other members of the Church, we can apply to the individual person *specialiter* what is said of the Church *generaliter.*[97] The relationship here between the use of *generaliter* and *specialiter* mirrors the relationship between the allegorical and anagogical senses, where Scripture is interpreted with reference to the Church, and the tropological sense, where Scripture is interpreted with reference to an individual.[98] Thus according to the tropological sense, each faithful soul is the "city of God," "ark of the covenant," etc., but this is true in a special sense of Mary, and, in the most complete sense, of the Church.

A notable example of spousal typology is found in the Canticle of Canticles. De Lubac calls this use of spiritual exegesis "perfectly objective."[99] It is de Lubac's judgment that even a naturalist exegesis of the Canticles is unable to avoid all use of allegory,[100] and that this book was admitted to and retained in the Jewish canon of Scriptures because the Jews saw it as a symbolic expression of the love between Israel and God.[101] Since the Church, after the Incarnation, carried on the role of Israel, the first Christian commentaries on the Canticle were ecclesial and Christological.[102] The transition from the Jewish interpretation of the Canticle

---

96. De Lubac, *The Splendour of the Church,* 264.

97. Ibid. However, de Lubac notes that in order to give Mary her proper preeminence, the term *specialiter* was reserved for her and *singulariter* was used for other individuals.

98. Ibid., 267.

99. Ibid., 268.

100. Ibid. In this regard de Lubac cites P. Villiard, *Le Cantique des Cantiques d'après la tradition juive,* 19-29; A. Feuillet, *Le Cantique des Cantiques, Etudes de théologie biblique,* in the series Lectio Divina, 1953, 248.

101. Ibid., 269.

102. Ibid., 270.

to the Christological interpretation represents the transition from the historical sense of Scripture to the allegorical sense.[103] When the Canticle is read with reference to an individual person, as is often done in mystical literature, such an interpretation then represents a transition from an allegorical interpretation to a tropological one. The close relationship between the allegorical and the tropological meanings, reproduced in the close relationship between ecclesiology and spirituality, is expressed in de Lubac's words: "the life of the spirit reproduces in the soul the mystery of the Church herself."[104] The spiritual interpretation of the Canticle is so closely linked with the life of the Church in its relationship to God that de Lubac concurs with Claudel that a failure to interpret the poem allegorically, therefore "mystically," strikes at "the deepest theological roots of our faith."[105]

Conclusion

An analysis of de Lubac's treatment of Christ and Mary leads to the conclusion that Mary is an eschatological figure as Christ is an eschatological figure. As such they are defined in their relation to the Church. Within his thought as structured by the principles of spiritual exegesis and the concept of the "concrete universal," one may ascertain the following characteristics of such eschatological figures. First, they are concrete, historical persons. Second, in their person they realize individually what will only be complete eschatologically. Thus, although Christ and Mary are types of the antitype which is the Church, this in no way relegates the figure or type to the "unreal," "transitory," or "ideal." Third, as eschatological figures Christ and Mary have a reality independent of the Fall and ontologically prior to it. As eschatological figures they look to an eschaton, a redeemed world, and they themselves cause this redemption but are not themselves redeemed since they represent in their persons integral redeemed humanity. This is what the doctrine of the Immaculate Conception ultimately means, that Mary, as sinless, is integral. This does not, however, imply any supracreaturely status for Mary, for she is an eschato-

---

103. Ibid., 271.
104. Ibid., 272.
105. Ibid., 268, citing *Paul Claudel interroge le Cantique des Cantiques,* 13.

logical figure in a way different from Christ. It is her fiat which represents, under the grace of Christ, humanity's acceptance of God's self-offer in Jesus Christ and thus represents humanity's free participation in the New Covenant. The historical presence of eschatological figures represents the presence of the New Covenant within history since it is in these two figures, Christ and Mary, that the Covenant is offered and received.

We have seen that the principles for an interpretation of the Church as the Spouse of Christ rest in the principles of spiritual exegesis. This image not only represents an allegorical reading of the Canticle of Canticles, but is also an instance of a correlation of type/antitype when the Church is viewed from the perspective of Marian theology. First, such an interpretation is only possible within the perspective of faith and operates on the principle of the analogy of faith. Second, the interpretation presupposes a unity within Scripture. Third, the critical methodology of such an interpretation is synthetic rather than analytic. This means that details are viewed only in relation to the whole as "a partial sign and not a detachable piece.[106] What is important is not every detail of spiritual exegesis, which can sometimes be applied excessively, but the broader relationship between the Old and New Testaments, between the two covenants they represent, and between Christ and the Church. De Lubac concludes that although spiritual exegesis often seems fanciful and appears to create a mass of detail, it results in "the true sense" and a unity of the Scriptures.[107] Finally, the traditional interpretation of the Canticle rests on a profound symbolism which we may consider as "rooted in the actual being of things."[108] Thus spiritual exegesis and the spousal imagery of the Church rest on an ontology which is the new creation resulting from God's alliance with his people. However, de Lubac's theology does not develop a metaphysics based on the covenant, but limits itself to its scriptural and patristic expression. This section, then, has shown that the image of the Church as the spouse of Christ represents a clear example of the use of spiritual exegesis as a theological method which provides a vehicle for expressing the relationship between the particular and the universal, the tropological and the allegorical and anagogical senses, in short, the relationship between Mary and the Church and that between the Church and Christ.

106. Ibid., 276.
107. Ibid.
108. Ibid., 277.

Part III: The Church as the Sacrament of Christ

In addition to considering the Church as the body of Christ and as the bride of Christ, de Lubac considers the Church as a sacrament of Christ. A number of theologians, including Otto Semmelroth, Karl Rahner, Leonardo Boff, Edward Schillebeeckx, Yves Congar, and Avery Dulles, have favored this way of conceptualizing the Church.[109] This concept of the Church was used at the Second Vatican Council; the document *Lumen Gentium* refers to the Church as sacrament three times.[110] Although rooted in the theology of such traditional authors as Augustine and Aquinas,[111] the use of the term "sacrament" in reference to the Church is comparatively new in the more recent history of ecclesiology. The widespread use of the term, however, can be misleading since it is not used univocally by all authors. One of the crucial differences lies in the referent of the sacramental symbol which is sometimes taken to be Christ and sometimes human history or even the worshiping community. To see the difference it is helpful to situate de Lubac's work in relation to that of Edward Schillebeeckx, who represents a notion of ecclesial sacramentality counter to that of de Lubac. The choice of Schillebeeckx is not arbitrary, but sanctioned by de Lubac's own explicit criticism of him.

---

109. Otto Semmelroth, *Die Kirche als Ursakrament* (Frankfurt: Verlag Josef Knecht, 1955); Karl Rahner, *Church and Sacraments,* Quaestiones disputatae 9 (New York: Herder and Herder, 1963); Leonardo Boff, *Die Kirche als Sakrament im Horizont der Welterfahrung* (Paderborn: Verlag Bonifacius-Druckerei, 1972); Edward Schillebeeckx, *Christ, the Sacrament of the Encounter with God* (New York: Sheed and Ward, 1963), esp. ch. 2: "The Church, Sacrament of the Risen Christ," 47-89. Schillebeeckx's position as expressed here undergoes some modification in *Approches théologiques,* vols. 3 and 4 (Brussels and Paris: Editions du C.E.P., 1967). See also Yves Congar, *The Church That I Love* (Denville, N.J.: Dimension Books, 1969); *Un peuple messianique* (Paris: Cerf, 1975); Avery Dulles, *Models of the Church* (New York: Doubleday & Co., 1974), 58-70.

110. *Lumen Gentium,* I, 1; II, 9; VII, 48.

111. On Augustine's use of the concept see Y. Congar, "Introduction générale," *Oeuvres de St. Augustine,* vol. 28, Traités Anti-Donatists (Bruges: Desclée de Brouwer, 1963), 86-115. On Aquinas see Y. Congar, *The Mystery of the Church* (Baltimore: Helicon, 1960), ch. 3, esp. 113-116. For an overview of its use in the nineteenth and twentieth centuries see Matthaus Bernards, "Zur Lehre von der Kirche als Sakrament aus der Theologie des 19. und 20. Jahrhunderts," *Münchener theologische Zeitschrift* 20 (1969): 29-54. Leonardo Boff gives a comprehensive history of the concept in *Die Kirche als Sakrament im Horizont der Welterfahrung.*

Ecclesial Sacramentality in De Lubac's Theology

For de Lubac, the Church is a sacrament of Christ just as Christ is a sacrament of God:

> If Christ is the sacrament of God, the church is the sacrament of Christ
> for us; she represents him, in the full ancient meaning of the term: she
> really makes him present to us. She not only carries on his work, but
> she is his very continuation, in a sense incomparably more real than any
> human institution can be said to be a continuation of its founder.[112]

Three observations can be made regarding de Lubac's identification of the Church as sacrament. He presumes a communication of idioms between Christ and the Church. The notion of sacramentality is grounded in a mystical signification in the sense understood by spiritual exegesis. Finally, a sacrament is an efficacious mediatory sign between the human and the divine.

De Lubac's point of departure is the communication of idioms between Christ and the Church. As noted in the earlier discussion of the image of the Church as the body of Christ, this communication of idioms preserves the inseparability of the divine and the human elements in the Church. When these elements are held together in all their paradoxical tension, one avoids a merely secular and sociological understanding of the Church as institution. To consider the Church as sacrament is never to speak of the Church alone or to let our vision stop short at the Church, but to consider the Church always in relation to Christ.[113] Furthermore, the divine element is intrinsic to the human element in the Church, thus avoiding a dualism between the two. When de Lubac speaks of the mystery of the causality of the sacraments, he states that such a causality does not "reside so much in the paradoxical efficacy in the supernatural order of a rite or a sensible gesture as in the existence of a society which, under the appearances of a human institution, hides a divine reality.[114]

Second, de Lubac interprets the sacramentality of the Church in regard to Christ as a relation of mystical identity.[115] Head and members are one body. The Bridegroom and Bride are one flesh. He even states: "Christ is

---

112. De Lubac, *Catholicisme*, Coll. Traditions chrétiennes 13 (Paris: Cerf, 1983), 50.
113. De Lubac, *The Splendour of the Church*, 164.
114. De Lubac, *Catholicisme*, 51.
115. De Lubac, *The Splendour of the Church*, 152.

thus His Church."[116] Here "mystical" has the same significance as does the Church/Eucharist correlation prior to the middle of the twelfth century, evidence that de Lubac's sacramental theology is grounded in the sacramentality inherent in spiritual exegesis. In other words, de Lubac perceives the relationship of the sign and that which is signified in sacramentality to be analogous to that between type and antitype within spiritual exegesis.

Third, the sacramentality of the Church is related to its character as sign. Here again the human reality is the sign of divine reality. In *The Splendour of the Church,* de Lubac notes that the Church is "the sacrament of Christ as Christ Himself, in his humanity, is for us the Sacrament of God."[117] De Lubac describes sacramentality as the "sensible bond between two worlds."[118] Rather than being something intermediate between two worlds, a sacrament mediates by making present that which it evokes.[119] In other words, the human element in the Church makes the divine element present by making Christ present. De Lubac describes the Church's unique mission as that "of making Christ present to men."[120] Crucial to his notion of sacramentality is that the sign makes Christ present. The referent of the sacramental symbol is therefore not immanent, but transcendent.

De Lubac maintains the distinction between the human and the divine at the same time that he asserts their union. If Christ is indeed his Church, as de Lubac states, this does not imply that Christ is so immanent to the Church as to be absorbed or assimilated into the Church any more than grace is absorbed into nature. The structure of paradox which governs so much of de Lubac's thought demands that Christ and Church, grace and nature, be distinct at the same time that they are united. In 1953 de Lubac warned about a kind of immanentism which he calls a "sacramentalism turned inside out." The referent of the symbol or sacrament then becomes the Church, the world, or humanity once it has been identified with Christ or grace after the dialectic of paradox has collapsed:

> In its essentials this system of thought stems equally from Hegel and Comte, and it is at present widespread. According to it, God is not

---

116. Ibid., 153.

117. Ibid., 147.

118. Ibid., citing Joseph de Maistre, "Lettre à une Dame Russe," *Works* 8 (London: Allen & Unwin, 1965), 74.

119. De Lubac, *The Splendour of the Church,* 147.

120. Ibid., 161.

"dead"; He is assimilated. He becomes the symbol of man, as man has become the truth of God. Thus the Church becomes that great being whose cult prepares peoples formerly monotheistic for the cult of the one and only true Supreme being; she is the sacrament of Humanity, over an indispensable transition period. And thus is made manifest what Comte called "our growing tendency towards a real homogeneity between worshipers and the beings that are worshipped." According to this interpretation — which at the same time claims to be a philosophy of history — the growing interest of Catholicism in the dogma of the Church marks . . . a new stage in the opening perspective of faith in God. It is one step further in the long process of immanentizing which is finally to "lead to the complete elimination of the fictitious being."[2] Thus man will acquire the disposition to enter into himself and prepare for his apotheosis, and thus, perhaps, "finally the religion of God made man will end up, by an inevitable dialectic, in an anthropology." By ripening the dogma of the Incarnation to its fruition in the dogma of the Church, Catholicism will give its final stage of development and itself contribute to the liquidation of all theology; for it will lead us to an eventual realization that religion was "the fantastic realization of the human essence" and that it should be treated "as the symbolic expression of the social and human drama" which is alone real.

---

2. Auguste Comte, *Système de Politique Positive*, vol. ii, p. 108; vol. iii, p. 455; cf. p. 433 on the subject of medieval Catholicism. There are similar ideas in Proudhon.[121]

This citation demonstrates de Lubac's awareness in 1953 of a problem in regard to the sacramentality of the Church which became more pronounced after the Second Vatican Council. In 1980 de Lubac sharply criticized Edward Schillebeeckx's use of the term "sacrament of the world" for the Church because the referent of the sacrament becomes the world rather than Christ, thus reflecting an immanentism of the type described above.[122]

---

121. Ibid., 165-166. The quoted expressions are from M. Maurice Merleau-Ponty, who is himself quoting and justifying Marx, in his *Sens et Non-sens*, 151-258, cited in *Méditation sur l'Eglise*, 194-195. De Lubac gives the same warning in "Liminaire," in *L'Eglise de Vatican II*, vol. II, ed. G. Barauna (Paris: Cerf, 1966), 27.

122. De Lubac, *A Brief Catechesis on Nature and Grace*, trans. Richard Arnandez (San Francisco: Ignatius Press, 1984), 191ff. French original: *Petite catéchèse sur Nature et Grâce* (Paris: Arthème Fayard, 1980).

De Lubac's Criticism of Schillebeeckx

One of the most serious questions in sacramentality today is the question concerning the referent of the symbol. Is the Church a sacrament of Christ or a sacrament of the world? This question, however, is complicated by some of the work by de Lubac himself on the relationship between nature and grace, the problem being whether, when a dualism between nature and the supernatural is denied, the supernatural is absorbed into nature. In much of the contemporary literature the problem of nature and grace often appears as the relationship between a person's expectation for the future here on earth and the eschatological Kingdom.[123] Despite the shift in the terms of the discussion, it is only in reference to the distinction between nature and the supernatural that the Church's role in the world can be grasped. That is, a position on the relationship between nature and the supernatural necessitates certain conclusions concerning the relationship between the Church and the world. Conversely, the relationship between the Church and the world necessarily implies a corresponding theology of nature and grace. A comparison of Schillebeeckx and de Lubac on these points clarifies the differences in their respective sacramental theologies.

The following, then, is Schillebeeckx's text as cited by de Lubac:

> The Church manifests, as in a sacrament, what grace the *eheveh asher eheveh* is already accomplishing everywhere in human-existence-in-the-world.
>
> In this context it is fitting to quote one of the most felicitous passages in the Constitution *Lumen Gentium:* "In Christ, the Church is as it were the sacrament, i.e., the sign and instrument, of intimate union and of the unity of the entire human race" (Introduction, no. 1). The Church is the "sacrament of the world." Personally, I consider this declaration as one of the most charismatic that have come from Vatican II. It stands out all the more since it is found again — as though all its consequences

---

123. De Lubac, *The Mission of the Church,* trans. by N. D. Smith, *Theological Soundings,* vol. 4 (New York: The Seabury Press, 1973), 82. Originally published as *Zending van de Kerk* (Bilthoven [Holland]: Uitgeverij H. Nelissen, 1968). In this regard see also Gustavo Gutiérrez, *A Theology of Liberation,* trans. and ed. Sister Caridad Inda and John Eagleson (Maryknoll, N.Y.: Orbis Books, 1973), 69-72.

had been felt spontaneously in advance — in the Pastoral Constitution on the Church and the world (pt. I, chap. 4, no. 42). . . .[2]

The Church, the form in which the progressive sanctification of the world shows itself explicitly (as a profane reality) by the law of the living God, is at the same time an intrinsic aspect of the history of this world sanctified by God's unconditional "Yes." . . .

. . . The deepest secret of what grace is accomplishing in the profane world, in virtue of the unknown and hence unexpressed name of God, is *named* and proclaimed by the "Church of Christ" and practically heralded in the witness afforded by her works. This is why belonging to the Church should be accompanied by an active will, full of hope, to change the face of the world through love for men. . . .[3]

---

2. The Church, says the author, "is the effective sign — the sacrament — of the union or the 'community' of all humanity in and by its union with the living God; she is the community of men living in communion with God who is life, the living one. In this universal communion the Church plays a sacramental role, i.e., she is the sign that brings this about. . . ." As Paul VI said at Hong Kong on December 3, 1970, "The Church is a sacrament of unity and of love."

3. Schillebeeckx, *Approches théologiques*, vol. 3, 145-47.[124]

De Lubac criticizes this text for the ambiguity of the term "world" and for its misrepresentation of the conciliar document by the omission of the

---

124. Ibid., 191-192. This translation of Schillebeeckx's text is the English translation of the French translation in *A Brief Catechesis on Nature and Grace*. The French translation of Schillebeeckx's text does indeed leave out the "cum Deo." This is an error in the translation since the Dutch original reads: "In Christus is de Kerk als het sacrament, dat is: teken en instrument, van de innige vereniging *met God* en van de eenheid van heel het menselijk geslacht" (emphasis added). *Wereld en Kerk,* Theologische Peilingen Deel III (Bilthoven: H. Nelissen, 1966), 124. The French translation of the Dutch which de Lubac cites reads: "Dans le Christ, l'Eglise est comme le sacrement, c'est-à-dire le signe et l'instrument, de l'union intime et de l'unité de tout le genre humain." *Le monde et l'église,* Approches theologiques 3 (Bruxelles: Editions du CEP), 145. In these essays Schillebeeckx does not envision human solidarity apart from union with Christ: "Expressed in more modern terms, this means that the source of the grace of Christ is not human solidarity itself, but human solidarity with Christ who has, however, disappeared from our empirical horizon since his death, but who wishes to remain present among us post-paschally by virtue of the Spirit of God, in his body, the Church" (*World and Church,* trans. N. D. Smith, *Theological Soundings,* vol. 4 [New York: Sheed and Ward, 1971], 124). The rest of de Lubac's criticism, however, stands, including the fact that Schillebeeckx erroneously includes the expression "sacrament of the world" in quotation marks as if it were an expression in *Gaudium et Spes,* which it is not.

words *cum Deo* in the citation from *Lumen Gentium*.[125] Second, he notes that the expression *sacramentum mundi* is Schillebeeckx's expression, not that of *Lumen Gentium*. Third, de Lubac asserts that Schillebeeckx reduces the ordinary meaning of "sacrament" in his description of the role of the Church as the manifestation of "progressive sanctification of the world (as a profane reality)," a sanctification which seems to take place without her.[126] In other words, the Church "only needs to 'name' and 'herald' what grace is accomplishing in the profane world."[127] According to Schillebeeckx, this grace exists in the world by virtue of the Incarnation interpreted as the union of divinity with humanity. The whole created order, as "created in Christ," is viewed as being in union with grace when Christ is understood as a representative figure. That is, when humanity is joined to divinity in the Incarnation, grace is joined to all of humanity or even all of creation through the representation of Jesus Christ who is the prototypical figure of our history. The implication of such an interpretation is that the order of creation is equated with the order of redemption: "Creation and covenant — these form one divine structure and this is also seen in its historical consequences."[128] Furthermore, the hypostatic union of the Incarnation is seen as an analogue of the structure of creation. When the order of grace is so identified with the world, the conclusion is that the world is Christian. Schillebeeckx logically and consistently completes this line of argumentation by extending Rahner's concept of an "anonymous" or implicit Christian to an implicit Christianity.[129] The Church, then, is a sacrament of the grace in the world which makes the referent of the sacramental symbol immanent rather than transcendent. Most significantly, therefore, de Lubac doubts whether Schillebeeckx adequately distinguishes between the sanctification of the world and the technical construction of a new politico-social world.[130]

125. Ibid., 193.

126. Ibid., 194.

127. Ibid.

128. Ibid., 55.

129. De Lubac, *A Brief Catechesis on Nature and Grace*, 219, citing *Approches théologiques*, vol. 3 (Brussels: CEP, 1967), 155.

130. This doubt appears justified from Schillebeeckx's statement in *The World and Church*, 107, that ". . . the building up of temporal society has been concretely included in the absolute and gratuitous nearness of the mystery of grace and is, as such, implicit Christianity."

In addition to de Lubac's objections to this position, one can further observe that Christ becomes an archetype of a creation which has no real need of him since grace is already given "anonymously." The only alternative is to presuppose that grace is given at the moment of creation, which in turn presupposes the preexistence of Jesus Christ and a creation in him; but this begs questions not conceived of by either Schillebeeckx or de Lubac. Second, when grace is considered as a structure of creation, it loses its character as a historical event. Apart from a covenantal view where grace is freely offered and freely received, structures cannot be free. Creation is free and *ex nihilo* from the perspective of God, but necessary and therefore not free from the perspective of humanity. Without the freedom of grace, there is no possibility of sin or conversion.

It is now necessary to look more closely at the development of Schillebeeckx's argument and at additional elements in de Lubac's theology regarding the sacramentality of the Church, particularly as it relates to the world.

Schillebeeckx's Argument

Schillebeeckx arrives at the expression *sacramentum mundi* by working a series of verbal substitutions.[131] Beginning with the word "sacrament," Schillebeeckx notes that the Greek word *mystērion*, translated into Latin as *sacramentum* and *mysterium*, denoted the divine decree, or God's plan of salvation, insofar as this has been manifest in a veiled manner and is accessible only to faith. It includes the whole of the Christian plan of salvation as prepared in the Old Testament and completed in Jesus Christ, of whom the Church is the visible presence in the world. Schillebeeckx thus concludes that the history of salvation is itself a sacrament. Schillebeeckx then works a series of substitutions on the following sentence from the decree on missionary activity in the Church:

> Missionary activity is nothing other than and nothing less than the revelation of and epiphany of the completion of God's plan of salvation in the world and in the history of the world, in which God, through the mission, visibly completes the history of salvation.[132]

131. This is a synopsis of the material in Schillebeeckx's "The Church, the 'Sacrament of the World,'" in *The Mission of the Church*, 43-50.

132. *Ad Gentes*, I, 9.

Because the Church is oriented toward mission, Schillebeeckx replaces the words "mission" and "missionary activity" with the word "Church":

> The church is nothing other and nothing less than the revelation of, epiphany of and the completion of God's plan of salvation in the world and in the history of the world in which God, through the church, visibly completes the history of salvation.[133]

This is similar to the statement from *Gaudium et Spes* which states that "In Christ, the church is the universal sacrament of salvation which manifests and realizes the mystery of God's love for man. . . ."[134] Schillebeeckx has defined sacrament as the manifestation of God's plan of salvation, and he has indicated that this plan of salvation is evident in human history. What is not clear is whether sacrament is also the effectuation of this same plan of salvation. Since this plan of salvation is for the whole of the human race, which means that God's will for salvation is universal, and since grace is seen to be present in the world insofar as God's plan of salvation is active there, Schillebeeckx concludes that

> salvation, which is in fact actively present in the whole of mankind, is given in the church, the completed form in which it appears in the world. What God has already effectively begun to bring about in the whole of mankind in an activity of grace that is not clearly expressed and recognized as such, is expressed and accomplished more clearly and recognizably as the work of grace in the world in the church.[135]

This statement does not make it clear that the grace in the world is the grace of Christ unless it is present through him as a representative figure. Then, unless Schillebeeckx grants a doctrine of creation in Christ, it does not account for the newness wrought in creation by Christ. Nor does it indicate by what role the Church is effective in being an efficacious sign of this grace. Furthermore, "activity" is of another order than "church," the latter having an ontological identity as the body of Christ (even for Schillebeeckx in these essays), while the former is an activity proceeding from the latter, but not having the ontological identity. Thus

---

133. Schillebeeckx, *The Mission of the Church*, 45.
134. *Ad Gentes*, I, 4, 45.
135. Schillebeeckx, *The Mission of the Church*, 48.

"church" cannot be substituted for "missionary activity" in the Council's statement.

Schillebeeckx does note that the Council did not state explicitly that the church is the visible sacrament of that salvation which is already active wherever people are to be found, but thinks that he has found a dialectical tension within the conciliar texts which calls for further theological clarification. In addition to the interplay of the concepts "sacrament," "plan of salvation," and "salvation history" which we have seen, he notes the tension between such concepts as the necessity of the Church for salvation and the fact that those outside the Church are able to share in salvation. He poses two distinct alternatives — whether God's salvation cannot in any sense reach the world except in and through this world's gradual and historical confrontation with the Church or whether universal salvation, already offered to the world on the basis of God's universal will to save all people, and which is already active in the world, only reaches its completed appearance in the Church. He chooses the second and concludes:

> The church is therefore both the sacrament of herself, in other words, the visible appearance of the salvation that is present in her, and, at the same time, the *sacramentum mundi;* in other words, what is present "outside the church" everywhere, wherever men of good will in fact give their consent personally to God's offer of grace and make this gift their own, even though they do not do this reflectively or thematically.[136]

A number of corollaries, not mentioned by de Lubac, can be found in Schillebeeckx's work. First, for Schillebeeckx, once human existence is seen as an expression of grace, the acceptance of actual human existence with all its responsibilities is considered an act of "theological" faith.[137] Second, the world, in the contemporary saving situation of the Incarnation, is implicit Christianity, which Schillebeeckx defines as "a distinctive, non-sacral, but sanctified expression of man's living community with the living God."[138] The Church, on the other hand, is a "set aside" sacral expression of this implicit Christianity.[139] The world and the Church, then, constitute two complementary forms of Christianity. Third, according to this view

136. Ibid., 48.
137. Schillebeeckx, *World and Church,* 99.
138. Ibid., 101.
139. Ibid.

the world is considered "holy" by virtue of the identity of the orders of creation and redemption, and any activity which builds a better world becomes an activity which inherently contributes to the eschatological kingdom and is included in the life of grace.[140] Conversely, if this were not seen to be the case, this would imply that one's activity within this world would lie outside Christianity, and there would be a dualism between the world of grace and the secular world, a dualism reflected in the two-story universe of nature and grace as articulated in some scholastic commentaries on Thomas which de Lubac criticizes in his *Surnaturel*. Fourth, the starting point is not that of theological and theoretical formulations of the traditional problem concerning the relationship between nature and the supernatural, but the existential experience of Christians who question the place of religion and the Church in their lives. This approach stresses the inherent significance of human history, which is seen as sanctified, but not sacral. The Church, on the other hand, is seen as sacral, but in a process of secularization. This means that the world, insofar as grace becomes historically visible in its distinctive form, strives to become Church. Conversely, the Church, in making the salvation of which it is the sign incarnate in the secular reality of the world itself, experiences a tendency toward what Schillebeeckx designates "sanctifying secularization." Thus there is a sort of reciprocity between Church and world in which the distance and tension between the two is minimalized. Ultimately the secular predominates in its new state of having been sanctified.

Comparison of de Lubac and Schillebeeckx

The terms of the discussion have changed, with Schillebeeckx speaking in terms of the relationship between the world and the eschatological kingdom while de Lubac speaks of the relationship between nature and the supernatural. Both perspectives are concerned with unity. There is, however, some ambiguity present in Schillebeeckx's position. On the one hand, he speaks of a unity or community of humankind based on God's universal salvific will.[141] He likewise affirms that the source of the grace of Christ is not human solidarity in itself, but human solidarity with Christ through

140. Ibid., 102.
141. Ibid., 118.

his body the Church since Christ himself has disappeared from our empirical horizon since his death.[142] Yet, on the other hand, he will state that the Church is the "momentous visible form or meaningful presence in the world of an already accomplished communion of men."[143] This raises the question whether it is union with Christ that constitutes the unity of the human race or whether the Church is merely the visible form of a unity that exists prior to it. In both instances, unity with Christ occurs apart from the Church. In either case, the relationship between Christ and the Church is not addressed, although Schillebeeckx does refer to the Church as the body of Christ. It would appear that the same unresolved tension which Schillebeeckx sees in the language of *Gaudium et Spes* occurs in his own exposition, resulting in a certain ambiguity.

In other words, he affirms the identity of the Church as the body of Christ and the necessity of the institutional Church for salvation, but he does not, in these essays, show how these themes are systematically integrated with his position on the relationship between the Church and the world. It is the lack of systematic coherence which leads to ambiguity. For de Lubac, as we have seen, the unity of the human race has been an important theme since *Catholicism*. Humanity is "organically one by its divine structure," and the Church's mission is both to reveal the unity that has been lost and to restore and complete it.[144] The efficacious sign of that unity is the Eucharist. Ultimately, the unity of the human race is a union only possible in God so that the Church, in addition to being a means of unity, is itself that "union in its consummation" because of its union with Christ. Therefore, for de Lubac, unity is not prior to the Church, but always exists through the Church. This unity exceeds the unity of faith and love described by Schillebeeckx since it is an incorporation into the body of Christ, to use the physical image so common in de Lubac's work. This is another reason for asserting the identity of the Church as the social embodiment of grace in his theology.

A second common category in the thought of both theologians is that of history. History, for Schillebeeckx, is the existential temporal order. Furthermore, he identifies salvation history with this order, which is why he can identify the construction of the temporal order with implicit

---

142. Ibid., 124.
143. Ibid., 92.
144. De Lubac, *Catholicism*, 33.

Christianity. What is missing, however, is an explicit principle of interpretation for this history. In Chapter Two, above, we saw that even an empirical, positivistic account of history requires a principle of interpretation beyond the empirical data. De Lubac, on the other hand, finds his principle of interpretation in the Christ event and envisions a theology of history based on the Christic and eucharistic unity of the two Testaments. His Christocentric concept of history presumes a realized eschatology mediated through the Church sacramentally. Schillebeeckx also acknowledges that Christ is present to his Church sacramentally since his death, but the temporal order assumes a more mediatory role than it does for de Lubac because of the presence of grace operative there. Thus, one can conclude that in effect the temporal order becomes the primary sacrament and the Church as the sacrament of the temporal order, the *sacramentum mundi,* is a sacrament derivatively. Admittedly this contradicts Schillebeeckx's earlier presentation of the sacramentality of the Church in *Christ, the Sacrament of the Encounter with God,*[145] but it is nevertheless the conclusion one reaches when following the logic of the essays in *Theological Soundings.* In other words, for de Lubac, the Church is causative of unity and grace while for Schillebeeckx, even when accounting for the ambiguities present in his exposition, the Church is a sign of a unity and grace already operative on another basis.

De Lubac's Hermeneutic of Paradox

The hermeneutical principle of paradox which forms the basis of de Lubac's thought challenges Schillebeeckx's conclusions. Ultimately de Lubac responds to the dialectical tension between Church and world within the framework of an analogous tension between the dialectical pairs of nature and the supernatural, the order of creation and the order of redemption, immanence and transcendence. Such a dialectic is fundamentally phenomenological, founded on the existential experience of being fallen, and inspired by the Augustinian tradition, although de Lubac also attempts to draw upon the Thomistic and Aristotelian categories of accident and substance which are not phenomenological or

145. Edward Schillebeeckx, *Christ, the Sacrament of the Encounter with God* (Kansas City: Sheed, Andrews and McMeel, 1963).

experiential, but which deal with nature and structure. This mixture of two levels of discourse leads to some ambiguities within de Lubac's thought, leaving him vulnerable to an interpretation which he himself would not acknowledge. The fundamental problem will be whether grace can be considered a structure of creation or whether transcendence, grace, and redemption are present within creation only in the event of Christ, who represents divine immanence within history. As a free historical event, Christ, and thus grace, can never be considered a necessary structure of creation.

Nature — Supernatural

The first question is whether nature and grace, the world and the eschatological kingdom, are the same order or different orders. De Lubac himself is ambiguous here, for he both affirms the distinction between the two orders and denies it. For example, in *Athéisme et sens l'homme* (1968) as well as in *A Brief Catechesis on Nature and Grace* (1977), he cites Jean Mouroux, who says:

> There are not two different orders, but only one, that of the Covenant for which Creation is the first moment and for which Christ is the Alpha and the Omega, the center [sic] and the end; and this order is supernatural.[146]

On the other hand, also in *A Brief Catechesis on Nature and Grace*, de Lubac cites Pascal's description of the supernatural:

> "It belongs to a different order." That is the decisive word, which demolishes the pretension of eliminating the supernatural in the name of scientific progress.[147]

146. "S'il y a, dans l'univers, des niveaux d'analyse différents (création, péché, rédemption), il n'y a pas deux ordres différents, mais un seul, celui de l'Alliance dont la création est le premier temps, dont le Christ est l'Alpha et l'Oméga, le centre et la fin; et cet ordre est surnaturel." *Athéisme et sens de l'homme: Une double requête de "Gaudium et spes"* (Paris: Cerf, 1968), 101, citing Mouroux's "Sur la dignité de la personne humaine," in *L'Eglise dans le monde de ce temps,* "Vatican II," n. 65b (Paris: Cerf, 1967), 232. De Lubac cites the identical text in *A Brief Catechesis on Nature and Grace,* 190.

147. De Lubac, *A Brief Catechesis on Nature and Grace,* 29.

De Lubac's apparent or actual contradiction results from his desire to maintain the distinctiveness of nature and the supernatural at the same time as he attempts to avoid a dualism between the two. For if there are different orders, the question is whether this represents a return to the dualism between nature and grace which Blondel and de Lubac himself have refuted.

In *A Brief Catechesis on Nature and Grace* de Lubac, rather than describing the relationship as an identification or a superimposition of one on the other, maintains the distinctiveness of the two orders of nature and grace, but describes their relationship as a circumincession.[148] The very fact that he insists on the use of the adjective "supernatural" rather than the substantive "supernature" is indicative of his efforts to avoid a dualism even as he maintains a distinction. The supernatural is not a "supernature" with its own consistency and its own subsistence, something that would be "added" to human nature.[149] Yet the tension is continually between union and distinction, and one must not equate union with identification, there always being a distance between nature and the supernatural because of their incommensurability. In de Lubac's words, the pair "nature-supernatural" must be thought of at the outset as a relationship of opposition, of spiritual otherness, and of infinite distance; but if a person so wills, it resolves itself finally into an association of intimate union.[150] However, even in the closest union, there is distinction. This maintains both the absolute transcendence of God and grace and the deep realism of the quality of "children of God." Therefore the alternative to extrinsicism is not immanentism but transformation, incorporation, adoption, where the supernatural remains totally other, not identified with nature, but where nature becomes a "new creation," qualitatively different. De Lubac clearly states that "we must take care not to confuse the 'progress of this world' (itself a very ambivalent term) with the 'new creation'."[151]

---

148. Ibid., 43. This appears to describe the Old Testament–New Testament relation that dominates his similar analysis of the relationship between the allegorical and the literal senses.

149. Ibid., 49.

150. Ibid., 101. Once again, supposing nature and the supernatural to be historical, this is analogous to the dialectic of conversion within the Old Testament–New Testament dialectic. The Old Testament is not annulled, but transformed.

151. Schillebeeckx, *World and Church*, 129-130.

The Order of Creation and the Order of Redemption

The question of the relationship between nature and grace, Church and world, is also the question of the relationship between the order of creation and the order of redemption. It is important that they be seen as united, but not identical.[152] If this distinction is not retained, redemption is equated with the perfection of creation and world progress becomes world salvation. Simply to identify creation and redemption, however, fails to recognize yet another difference between nature and grace. "Grace" can also mean forgiveness, mercy, and pardon.[153] De Lubac notes that when grace is considered in this sense, the distinction between nature and grace is much more radical than in the general differentiation between nature and the supernatural:

> between sinful human nature and divine grace we have not only a dissimilarity, a heterogeneity between two orders of being, an infinite distance that man alone cannot bridge. There is antagonism, violent conflict.[154]

At this point the language changes from that of "elevation" or even "transformation" to "conversion." De Lubac switches from nature-supernatural, a correlation of humanity with the divine, to fallen-redeemed, a correlation of two states of humanity. He apparently does not notice that the change represents not only a change from the abstract and the theoretical to the existential, but a different correlation. Nevertheless, in this context "nature" is no longer part of the remainder concept of "pure nature" when considered in contrast to the supernatural quality, grace, but becomes the existential experience of a sinful human being. Within this more existential framework the difference between the order of redemption and the order of creation is more distinct. As de Lubac says: "If the union of nature and the supernatural was brought about in principle by the mystery of the Incarnation, the union of nature and grace can be fully accomplished only through the mystery of the redemption."[155] In effect, this responds to a structural problem of the relation between nature and grace in terms of

---

152. De Lubac, *A Brief Catechesis on Nature and Grace*, 118.
153. Ibid., 119.
154. Ibid., 121-122.
155. Henri de Lubac, *Athéisme et sens de l'homme* (Paris: Cerf, 1968), 132.

the historical event of the redemption. An analysis of nature and grace, creation and redemption, and, therefore, Church and world, is incomplete without a consideration of the role of the Cross. It is the Cross which effects the "new creation" and represents the difference between the two orders. De Lubac borrows the words of Teilhard de Chardin to express the difference:

> The Cross of Jesus signifies to our thirst for happiness that the term of creation is not to be sought within the temporal zones of our visible world, but that the effort expected from our fidelity must be consummated beyond a total metamorphosis of ourselves and beyond everything which surrounds us.[156]

Consequently, creation, even as graced, is not the term of our supernatural desires, and the "new creation" is something qualitatively, not merely quantitatively, different from creation. If the Cross is the resolution of the polarities mentioned, this resolution is none other than the New Covenant since the Cross is the "blood of the Covenant." This represents a historical resolution of the polarities, not only in the Incarnation-Redemption, but in the Eucharist where the Covenant is actualized sacramentally.

Immanence–Transcendence

In addition to the pairs nature-supernatural, world-Church, and creation-redemption, we have immanence-transcendence. The question is whether in the Incarnation, when the Logos became human, divinity became immanent to humanity in such a way that the supernatural, in becoming immanent, is no longer transcendent to human history. However, here as elsewhere, absolute dichotomies are misleading. The categories of transcendence and immanence, seemingly opposed or contradictory, are not as distinct as they might first appear. De Lubac remarks that the two notions are intimately interwoven insofar as the very idea of transcendence, far from being reduced to a type of exteriority, necessarily implies immanence. In other words, nothing can limit or oppose that which is

---

156. Ibid., 41. See Schillebeeckx, *World and Church*, 130; and Karl Rahner, "Membership of the Church according to the Teaching of Pius XII's Encyclical *Mystici Corporis*," *Theological Investigations*, vol. II (London and Baltimore: Helicon Press, 1963), 1-88.

transcendent, but the transcendent penetrates everything absolutely.[157] Nevertheless the distinction between transcendence and immanence remains. Just as de Lubac holds the supernatural to be distinct from nature, so transcendence is never lost even when that which is immanent is described as a penetration of transcendence.

The Correspondence between Paradoxical Pairs

That there is a correspondence between transcendence, the Church, and the supernatural, on the one hand, and immanence, the world, and nature, on the other hand, is evident in de Lubac's statement that "every notion which tends to bring down the supernatural order to the level of nature tends, by that very fact, to mistake the Church for the world, to conceive of her after the model of human societies."[158] If this should happen, the Church would simply end up duplicating services and institutions better and more properly available elsewhere.[159] Even though there is a correspondence between them, the pairs of distinctions are not equivalent to each other. For example, to equate the Church with grace or the supernatural begs a lot of questions. The Church is not the same as redemption although it is an instrument of redemption. Grace is not limited to the visible Church. One cannot speak of the Church, human as well as divine, as transcendent. Yet, on the other hand, the penetration of transcendence is immanence; nature is graced; God's salvific will is universal; and redemption occurs within creation. The similarity of the terms is found in the fact that grace has a transcendent quality not totally reducible to immanence, and that the Church's mission is a salvific one. The term of each pair is in union with the other term, yet distinct from it. By maintaining the distinction as well as the tension between Church and world, nature and grace, transcendence and immanence, the Church's mission of reminding people of their supernatural vocation and communicating the gift of divine life through her sacred ministry is preserved. If the distinctions are lost, the Church would simply disappear. Arguments that implicit

157. De Lubac, *Athéisme et sens de l'homme*, 41.
158. Ibid., 109-110.
159. Ibid., 112.

grace has an inner dynamism that seeks explicit expression are less than convincing.[160]

The Incarnation: Basis for the Hermeneutic of Paradox

The model for the tension between identification and distinction, as fundamental as it is pervasive in de Lubac's theology, is the hypostatic union of the divine and human natures in Christ. It is only as analogous to the ultimate paradox of Jesus Christ, the God-man, that the relationship between the two orders can be understood. We have seen the problem of identification and distinction when this is extended to the relationship between Christ and the Church. The same problem exists in regard to the relationship between the order of creation and the order of redemption, between the Church and world, between nature and grace, but in these instances de Lubac's sense of the transcendent quality of grace and of the radical rupture and newness achieved in Christ enables him to maintain the distinction. Ironically, some theologians who tend to conflate the two orders appeal to his work on nature and grace as a foundation for their secularity. However, to say that "pure nature" has no existential reality or to deny that there are two finalities for a human being, one natural and the other supernatural, is not thereby to deny a distinction between nature and the supernatural.[161] Consequently, the supernatural is not eliminated in the name of scientific progress,[162] and an "infinite disproportion" is seen to lie between our concrete human nature and our graced destiny even though there is but one destiny and that is supernatural.[163] The divine order is paradoxically in opposition to, but in union with, the human order.

---

160. Schillebeeckx, *World and Church,* 126. See also Karl Rahner, "Membership of the Church according to the Teaching of Pius XII's Encyclical *Mystici Corporis,*" 1-88.

161. De Lubac, *A Brief Catechesis on Nature and Grace,* 29.

162. Ibid., 32.

163. See de Lubac, *Surnaturel: Etudes historique,* Coll. Théologie 8 (Paris: Aubier, 1946); *Augustinisme et théologie moderne,* Coll. Théologie 63 (Paris: Aubier, 1965); English translation: *Augustinianism and Modern Theology,* trans. Lancelot Sheppard (Montreal: Palm, 1969); *Le mystère du Surnaturel,* Coll. Théologie 64 (Paris: Aubier, 1965); English translation: *The Mystery of the Supernatural,* trans. Rosemary Sheed (New York: Herder and Herder, 1967).

Implications of Paradox for the Relationship between Church and World

This distinction carries implications for the relationship between the Church and the world, a relationship ultimately founded on the type of anthropology presented by de Lubac in *Surnaturel.* A human being's vocation and ordination to a supernatural destiny prohibits a view of the Church and the world as two powers existing side by side or one superimposed on the other.[164] Consequently, there is a sense in which the world, humankind, is called to become Church as Schillebeeckx has indicated. That de Lubac would not oppose this seems apparent from his notion of the unity of the human race and his view that the restored unity is incorporation, in varying degrees, into the body of Christ which is the Church. The problem is whether the converse is true, that is, whether the Church is also becoming world. It is at this point that the question of the assimilation of grace into nature, the Church into world, is at issue. This, I believe, is where de Lubac parts company with Schillebeeckx. If, as is the case, a dualism between Church and world is rejected on the basis of the supernatural destiny of the human person, a destiny which negates a dualism between nature and grace as if there were natural destiny, the dualism is resolved in favor of the Church, in the one instance, and grace, in the other instance. If the world, even given the ambiguity of the term, is defined as that which is not Church, it is impossible that the Church should become world, or secularized, which is the equivalent, for this would mean that the dualism would be resolved in favor of nature. This is not to argue, however, for a material separation of the sacred and the profane resulting in either a political and social life separate from and ultimately uninformed by religious values, or a religious life restricted to cultic worship. Nor is it an argument for a theocracy. The final distinction between identification and union implies that the Church does not assume tasks proper to the secular order any more than the secular order can subject the whole of a person's life to it. Yet it does mean that the secular

---

164. Yves Congar, "The Role of the Church in the Modern World," in *Commentary on the Documents of Vatican II,* ed. Herbert Vorgrimler (New York: Herder and Herder, 1969), 212, draws a connection between de Lubac's work on nature and grace and the relationship between the Church and the world, as does Gustavo Gutiérrez in *A Theology of Liberation,* rev. ed. (Maryknoll: Orbis Books, 1988), 44-46.

life is lived with a view to its supernatural destiny and that secular activity can have religious significance.

The Opposite Alternative: Assimilation of Nature into Grace

Another question remains. In de Lubac's theology, if the world is to become Church, does this mean that nature is assimilated to grace or the supernatural so that there is only grace? The distinction between nature and grace, so strongly emphasized by de Lubac, prohibits this interpretation of his work. In addition, he specifically describes grace as an accident:

> The supernatural . . . is that divine element which man's effort cannot reach (no self-divinization!) but which unites itself to man, "elevating" him as our classical theology used to put it, and as Vatican II still says (*Lumen Gentium,* 2), penetrating him in order to divinize him, and thus becoming as it were an attribute of the "new man" described by St. Paul. While it remains forever "un-naturalizable," it profoundly penetrates the depths of man's being. In short, it is what the old Scholastics and especially St. Thomas Aquinas called (using a word borrowed from Aristotle which has been completely misunderstood) "accidental form" or an "accident."[60] Call it an accident, or call it a habitus, or "created grace": these are all different ways of saying (even if one thinks they need various correctives or precisions) that man becomes in truth a sharer in the divine nature."

---

60. St. Thomas Aquinas, *Summa Theologica* I-II, q. 110, a. 2: "Utrum gratia sit qualitas animae," and ad 2: "Quia gratia est supra naturam humanam, non potest esse quod sit substantia aut forma substantialis, sed est forma accidentalis ipsius animae. . . ."[165]

We are dealing with very fine distinctions here. Grace is not a separate order having its own subsistence which is imposed on nature, yet it is not nature. It is rather a principle of transformation permitting a participation in the divine nature. The models de Lubac uses to describe the relationship between nature and grace are the Trinity, in the circumincession of the persons of the Trinity who, although distinct, possess the same Godhead, and Jesus Christ, in the hypostatic union of his divine and human nature:

165. De Lubac, *A Brief Catechesis on Nature and Grace,* 41-42.

. . . in Jesus Christ the Transcendent made itself (partially) immanent, since God's gift has been implanted in the depths of man's nature — for the two elements which we deal with here, nature and the super-natural, have not become an intermixture or confusion but have been joined in intimate union in dependence on and in the image of the two natures in Christ.[60]

---

60. The "boundary line" established at Chalcedon, which keeps the two natures distinct and not compounded, "is not really a boundary line; in fact it is there to make possible the immediate union, the holy espousals between God and the creature": Von Balthasar, *La Foi du Christ,* 79.[166]

A question not even raised in this context is whether nature exists in a "pure" state, that is, not enlivened by the principle of supernatural life. That is a question outside the present discussion. At issue here is whether there is a distinction between the two. The evidence here is that they are distinct, yet united.

Conclusion

The comparison between Schillebeeckx and de Lubac on the sacramen-tality of the Church leaves many questions unanswered. The great themes which challenge ecclesiologists are: What does it mean for the Church to be an efficacious sign of grace? How can we account for this at the same time we affirm that grace is operative outside of, but not independent of the visible Church? How can the Church be necessary for salvation if grace is already in the world? Neither de Lubac nor Schillebeeckx gives complete and satisfactory answers. Even though de Lubac has written much about the Church, he acknowledges that he has never written an ecclesiology.[167] What is certain is that he attempts to avoid both a theocratic and a secularist distortion of the Church. Equally certain is that for de Lubac the sacramentality of the Church lies in its relationship to Christ. In the final analysis, one concludes that de Lubac perceives the Church as struc-tured in the same way as the tradition has thought of Jesus Christ, as an unmixed union of the human and the divine. Consequently, an analysis

166. Ibid., 85.
167. Statement in a conversation with the author in May 1984.

of his thought ends in a series of paradoxes: nature and the supernatural, transcendence and immanence, creation that is graced and redemption which saves, a Church which is both human and divine, for it is only paradox which is capable of expressing the mystery of such a union that retains the distinction of the two terms. However, there is only one paradox, the God-man Jesus Christ, and if the Church is paradoxical, it is only in imitation of the one she makes present. This paradox is held together by the historical event of Jesus Christ. Thus Jesus Christ is not only the model, but the incarnate presence and resolution of paradox.

In de Lubac's thought the sacramentality of the Church lies within this paradoxical structure. The visible Church is not the sacrament of history (Gutiérrez) or the sacrament of the world (Schillebeeckx), but the sacrament of the Lord whose body she is. Thus the image of the Church as sacrament is, in his thought, another manner of speaking of the Church as the body of Christ. The category of sacramentality functions as a healthy corrective to the bodily imagery because it limits too close an identification between Christ and the Church. The difference is more clearly seen if sacramentality is perceived as a category proper to the temporal order and the referent of the sacrament is perceived as lying beyond that order. Thus the Eucharist and the Church are sacraments within time and signify the *totus Christus,* which is complete only eschatologically. Once again, the divisions within spiritual exegesis make this clear. The body of Christ born of the Virgin, the eucharistic body, and the *totus Christus* are the same body, yet different modes of being the same body. In a similar manner, the Church as sacrament of Christ is Christ, yet is different, and the difference can, at least in part, be expressed as the difference between a sacramental mediation of that which is complete eschatologically and its full eschatological manifestation. Even though de Lubac's theology has a strong eschatological orientation, most strongly evident in the structure of spiritual exegesis, and most particularly in reference to the anagogical sense, he does not explicitly develop this aspect of sacramentality. However, one can conclude to it from his work on spiritual exegesis and the relationship between the Church and the Eucharist as shown in *Corpus Mysticum.*

This chapter has presented three ways of viewing the Church in relationship to Christ: as the body of Christ, as spouse of Christ, and as sacrament of Christ. Each approach has facilitated a particular insight into the nature of the Church. For example, the image of the Church as the

127

body of Christ expresses the union of the human and divine elements in the Church and emphasizes that the Church does not exist apart from Christ. The spousal imagery maintains the distinction between Christ and the Church at the same time as it emphasizes their union. It also is the image which exemplifies how typology functions in the relationship between Mary and the Church. A consideration of the Church as sacrament highlights the difference between a realized eschatology and an eschatology yet awaited.

A final question is whether these images of the Church ultimately remain disparate or whether a systematic correlation is possible. In other words, are the images finally coherent? De Lubac does not attempt such a correlation. In *The Church: Paradox and Mystery,* he comments that no simple image or concept of the Church wholly succeeds in defining her.[168] The Church, as mystery, can only be grasped tangentially. De Lubac approaches the issue in terms of paradox, in a series of antithetical or dialectical pairs, and in a number of images. This chapter has noted the inconsistency between a view of the Church as the body of Christ, when this is interpreted as a continuation of the Incarnation, and the covenantal, marital imagery, which prohibits such an interpretation. Does this mean that an image of the Church as body is incoherent with the covenantal image? I do not believe this is necessarily the case if one distinction is made. That is, if the Head of the body is in a covenantal relationship with the members of the body, this prevents a view of the Head as a member of the body in the same sense that we are members. Yet the image of the body remains and is coherent with the covenantal image. We have already seen that the sacramental image is coherent with, but corrects, the bodily image in the theology of de Lubac. This may not be true where the referent of the sacrament is other than the body of Christ. We can conclude, then, that although de Lubac does not attempt a correlation of these three ways of looking at the Church, they are not incoherent within the terms of his theology.

168. De Lubac, *The Church: Paradox and Mystery,* 23.

CHAPTER FIVE

An Organic Unity

THE ORGANIC UNITY OF DE LUBAC'S WORK is now manifest in the inter-connection of the major themes of history, exegesis, the Eucharist, and the Mystical Body. His spiritual exegesis is grounded in the belief that Jesus Christ is the center of history and the interpretive key to the Scriptures, their unity being found only in him. The connection between the Eucharist and the Mystical Body, both forms of Christ's presence, is perhaps most clearly grasped when both are studied within the relationship of spiritual exegesis, the Eucharist being a figure or type of the Mystical Body. The organic unity of these theological themes constitutes a vision of the Church as a social unity which perpetuates the sacramental presence of Jesus Christ in history. This statement presumes the material contained in the previous chapters, which develop at length the relationship between the Mystical Body and the Eucharist, their interpretation through the principles of spiritual exegesis, and the relationship between the Church and the body of Christ. Even though these themes have been shown to be interrelated, it is now helpful to conclude the study of de Lubac's ecclesiology by showing more precisely how the Church is the social embodiment of grace in his theology. The second part of this chapter will evaluate a few of de Lubac's major categories.

The Church: Social Embodiment of Grace

An identification in de Lubac's theology of the Church as the social embodiment of grace begins with the presupposition of the primordial unity of the human race. Salvation is envisioned as the restored unity of

129

humanity in Christ, the Church being both the means and the end of this restored unity and therefore eschatologically coterminous with redeemed humanity as the body of the whole Christ. The Church as the historical, real, and sacramental body of Christ is therefore the embodiment of grace in the world. Such a concept of the Church is fundamentally sacramental, "body" being used equivocally when it refers both to the Church and to Christ. In other words, the Church really makes Christ present in the world, but as an efficacious sign of a reality to be present in its fullness only in the eschaton. As we have seen, the Church as "body" cannot be said to be an organic continuation of Christ. The image of "bride" corrects this interpretation.[1] Only when the images of body, bride, and sacrament are used simultaneously are we able with de Lubac to approach the meaning of the Church in an undistorted manner.

The key to an understanding of the social unity of the human race within de Lubac's theology is the realization that for him anthropology is inseparable from Christology. In other words, what it means to be human is inseparable from union with Christ in the whole Christ. Supposing that de Lubac's theology is at least in part motivated by its historical context, his emphasis on the social character of Catholicism and on the human person's supernatural destiny may find its proximate historical impetus in his response to the nineteenth-century atheist hermeneutic represented by Comte, Feuerbach, and Nietzsche. De Lubac's emphasis on the social character of Catholicism not only represents a retrieval of a patristic theme consistent with the interests of the "new theology,"[2] but also responds to the neo-scholastic interpretation of human finality as well as to the nineteenth-century atheist humanism which converted theology to anthropology.[3] Auguste Comte, in particular, criticized Christianity for being

1. Henri de Lubac, *The Church: Paradox and Mystery,* trans. James R. Dunne (New York: Ecclesia Press, 1969), 21: "But this mother keeps us always in her womb and her union with her spouse is so intimate that she is his body and we, consequently, become his members."

2. This is evident from de Lubac's extensive appendix to *Catholicism,* where he excerpts material from many patristic and medieval writers in support of this theme (208-283).

3. It is beyond our task here to develop de Lubac's response to these thinkers. The reader is referred to *The Drama of Atheist Humanism* (New York: Sheed and Ward, 1950); *Affrontements mystiques* (Paris: Editions du Témoignage chrétien, 1949); *Atheisme et le sens de l'homme,* Coll. Foi Vivante 67 (Paris: Cerf, 1968). See also James Pambrum's "The Presence of God: A Study into the Apologetic of Henri de Lubac" (Ph.D. dissertation, The Institute of ChristianThought of St. Michael's College, Toronto, 1978).

individualistic and therefore inherently selfish. By stressing the unity of the human race and then interpreting this unity by its reference to Christ, de Lubac in effect converts anthropology back into theology and responds to Comte's charge of individualism.

Anthropology as Christology

One can speak of an anthropology in both an individual and a communitarian sense. In either sense one can proceed in de Lubac's thought from an anthropology to a Christology, although even when one begins with the individual one always ends with a community. In the first instance, one begins with the "natural" desire to see God and the supernatural destiny of an individual as union with Christ in the "whole Christ." In the second, one begins with the presupposition of the primordial unitary nature of the human race and a concept of salvation as restored unity in Christ. Here the Church is identified with the whole of the eschatologically redeemed human race. Once this identification is made, the next step is to examine the Church's relationship to Christ, thus arriving at a Christology of the "whole Christ." From this one can determine the kind of relationship that persons have to one another in Christ.

In the second instance, the relationship between individuals follows upon the nature of community rather than the reverse, as would be the case were the community seen to be an aggregate of individuals. Although de Lubac has studied the individual's desire for God, the second approach, which begins with the presupposition of the unity of human race, is the approach which leads to his ecclesiology and, therefore, is the one developed here to demonstrate how the Church is understood to be the social embodiment of grace. Since this unity does not exist prior to or apart from Christ, the implication is not that Christ is a particular instance of humanity but that to be fully human is somehow to be related to Christ, as at once the cause of humanity and the restorer of human unity.

We have already seen that one of de Lubac's fundamental presuppositions is the original unity of the human race and salvation envisioned as the restoration of this unity in Christ. The type of social unity experienced by humanity is not the unity of an aggregate, but that of a concrete universal. There is but one human nature possessed by all people. Furthermore, the unity of the human race is found not only in a common nature,

131

but in its common incorporation in Christ, who, as we have seen, is, in the subtle sense de Lubac attaches to this term, a concrete universal. De Lubac comments: "Christ, by completing humanity in himself, at the same time made us all complete — but in God."[4] The unity of humanity cannot be the unity of an aggregate because fundamentally it is the unity of one person, Jesus Christ, who, as the New Adam, is recapitulative of the human race.

The relationship between the universal character of the human race and the particularity of persons within it is analogous to the relationship between unity and distinction. We can set up the analogy: distinction is to unity as the personal is to the universal.[5] According to de Lubac, "the distinction between the different parts of a being stands out the more clearly as the union of these parts is closer."[6] The parts are not seen to be "fragments" but "members" of a whole. Conversely, the individuality of the parts is not lost in unity: "Unity is in no way confusion, any more than distinction is separation."[7] De Lubac uses three analogies to explain this paradoxical relationship. In the first, the science of biology demonstrates that more complex organisms require a greater internal unity than homogeneous beings whose unity is so weak that a piece of the organism produces a new organism. Second, his moral analogy points out that the psychology of a mob differs from that of an organized group.

The best paradigm of this unity, however, is the unity of the Trinity.[8] De Lubac notes that it is impossible to imagine a greater distinction within unity than that of the three Persons in the one Divine Nature.[9] In this unity individual persons are not annihilated, but are united by a bond of charity whose source is God himself. This love is not only the bond forming the unity of individual persons, but is a participation in the very life of God. De Lubac cites the following text of Origen to this effect:

> Paul calls the Holy Spirit the Spirit of Love; it is said of God himself that he is Love, and the Son is called the Son of Love. Now, . . . if this

---

4. De Lubac, *Catholicism: A Study of Dogma in Relation to the Corporate Destiny of Mankind,* trans. Lancelot C. Sheppard (New York: Mentor and Omega Books, 1964), 187.

5. Ibid., 178.

6. Ibid.

7. Ibid., 184.

8. Ibid., 53.

9. Ibid., 179.

is so we should be certain that both the Son and the Holy Spirit come from that one foundation of Godhead which is the Fatherhood of God, and that of his abundance bounteous love is infused into the very heart of the saints so as to make them partakers of the divine nature, as St. Peter the Apostle taught. And this is so, so that by this gift of the Holy Spirit there may be fulfilled the words of our Lord. "That they all may be one, as thou, Father, in me, and I in thee." That is to say: Let them be made partakers of the divine nature in the abundance of love diffused by the Holy Spirit.[10]

10. In Rom., lib. 4, n. 9 (P.G. xiv, 997)[10]

Although this text shows the human person to be in the image of God in his or her unity with other persons, in being fundamentally constituted as interpersonal by nature, the Trinitarian source of this unity is not always as apparent in de Lubac's writing as one would wish. The reason for this seems to be that the unity of the human race is more often compared to the unity of the body within a Christocentric rather than a Trinitarian model of unity between persons. The two images, however, are synthesized where he states:

> Christ, by completing humanity in himself, at the same time made us all complete — but in God. Thus we can say, in the end, taking up again St. Paul's *heis,* and St. Augustine's *una persona,* that we are fully persons only within the Person of the Son, by whom and with whom we share in the circumincession of the Trinity.[11]

Even here, however, the image of circumincession seems to imply that it is humanity as a whole united with Christ that is in a relationship of circumincession with the other persons of the Trinity rather than that the Trinity is a model of the relationship between persons. If the Trinity were simply a model, our relationship with each other would be analogous, but also extrinsic, to the relationship existing between the persons of the Trinity. Participation in the life of the Trinity would be a share in the same love which animates the Trinitarian relationship. However, in de Lubac's thought our incorporation into the Trinitarian life is more intrinsic than that. De Lubac states that through the mediation of Christ we are enfolded

10. Ibid., 53.
11. Ibid., 187-188.

within the Trinity itself.[12] This is possible through union with him as members of his Mystical Body. Thus the emphasis remains Christocentric and the image of body takes precedence over that of circumincession.

Since de Lubac envisions the Church as destined to encompass the entire human race as the restoration of that race in unity with Christ at the end time, the unity of the human race is analogous to the unity of the Church. The Church as well as the race can be seen as the unity of a single person:

> The whole Church forms, in some sort, but one single person. As she is the same in all, so in each one is she whole and entire; and just as man is called a microcosm, so each one of the faithful is, so to say, the Church in miniature.[13]

In this citation we see the same relationship between the one and the many that we saw between the Eucharist in its unitary character and its manifold manifestations. The Church, as the Eucharist, is indivisible in each manifestation, whether that be in a particular church, or, when considered in personalistic terms, in an individual person. Thus there is at least one sense in which the Church cannot be quantified. That is, the unity of the Church transcends the sum total of all the individuals in it. The Church cannot be reduced to the sum total of these individuals any more than Christ can be reduced to those who form his body. Consequently, no one person or group can misuse the concept that each faithful person is a microcosm of the Church by proclaiming "I am the Church" and then proceeding to speak unilaterally in the name of the Church. This is prohibited by the fact that the universal Church transcends its manifestation in each particular person.

Therefore, to seek an individual's relationship to the Church or to the whole Christ of whom he or she is a member is to seek a relationship to something or someone transcendent to the individual but in which the

---

12. Ibid., 182. The syntax is obscure, but this interpretation seems warranted by the French: "Entre les diverses personnes, si variés que soient leurs dons, si inégaux leurs "mérites," ne règne pas un ordre de degrés d'être, mais, à l'image de la Trinite même — et, par la médiation du Christ en qui toutes sont enveloppeés, à l'interieur de la Trinite même — une unité de circumincession" (*Catholicisme,* p. 291).

13. De Lubac, citing St. Peter Damian, *Liber qui appellatur Dominus vobiscum,* cc. 5 and 10 (PL 145.235 and 239). See Extract 48, 273. Cited in De Lubac, *Catholicism,* 167.

individual participates. In the interests of theological analysis we have not begun with the category of mystery, but we must end there. In de Lubac's words, the Church as a mystery "is somehow linked to God's design for man, whether as marking the limit of or the means of realizing this destiny."[14] As we have seen, the Church is both the limit and the means of this destiny.

The mystery of the Church is inseparable from the mystery of Christ, who is at once the supreme instance of mystery and the visible, tangible sign of salvation. The Church, then, is a mystery only derivatively, by and in its relation to Christ:

> The Church is a mystery because coming from God and entirely at the service of his plan, she is an organism of salvation, precisely because she relates wholly to Christ and apart from him has no existence, value or efficacity [*sic*]."[15]

Thus, after all the theological qualifications are made, we find ourselves faced with the assertion that the Church is one, that the Church is a person present whole and entire in each individual member, that the Church is the body and bride of Christ, and that our destiny is to be a member of that body and that bride. In short, we are faced with mystery. In that mystery we approach the truest understanding of the Church. De Lubac cites J. J. von Allmen:

> The Church affirms that her understanding of herself will come not so much from her structures or her history as from her predestination in Jesus Christ and her orientation towards the parousia.[11]

---

11. J. J. von Allmen, "Remarques sur la Constitution *Lumen Gentium*" in *Irenikon*, 39, 1966, pp. 14-15. Cf. Henri de Lubac, *Méditation sur l'Eglise*, 2nd ed., 1953, ch. 1, "L'Eglise est un mystère," and ch. 6, "Le Sacrement de Jesus-Christ." Juan Alfaro S.J., "Cristo, Sacramento de Dios Padre; la Iglesia, Sacramento de Cristo Glorificado" in *Gregorianum*, 48, 1967, pp. 2-27.[16]

De Lubac adds: "To forget this fundamental truth, to allow its slightest neglect, is to court disaster.[17] We can conclude that de Lubac's eschatological emphasis has remained true to this insight.

14. De Lubac, *The Church: Paradox and Mystery*, 13.
15. Ibid., 15.
16. Ibid., 16.
17. Ibid.

From the close association between anthropology and Christology in de Lubac's thought, we can conclude that whatever it means to be "person" cannot be divorced from the notion of the supernatural destiny of persons. This not only presupposes de Lubac's work on the natural desire to see God, the unity of this human finality as opposed to the possibility of a distinction between a natural and a supernatural finality, but also supernatural destiny conceived as communitarian union with Christ and with others in the completion of the whole Christ.

De Lubac's Response to the Atheist Hermeneutic

It can be argued that de Lubac found a response to nineteenth-century atheism in traditional sources. According to de Lubac's analysis, contemporary atheism, in combining a mystical immanentism with humanism, has three principal aspects symbolized by three names: Auguste Comte, Ludwig Feuerbach, and Friedrich Nietzsche.[18] While a complete exposition of the thought of these men exceeds the present study of de Lubac's ecclesiology, a brief indication of how this ecclesiology offers a response to the atheism of such writers as these is in order.

For Feuerbach, the human essence is not inherent in the individual considered in isolation, but only in the community in its generic being *(Gattungswesen)*.[19] To the extent that a person participates in this human essence, to that extent he assumes divinity.[20] For Feuerbach the principle of real religion is love, and "the distinction between human and divine is neither more or less than the distinction between the individual and mankind."[21] In denying God, the subject, Feuerbach did not deny the attributes of God — love, wisdom, and justice — but attributed them to the essence of humanity. The divine, then, is equated with humankind as a whole.

Nietzsche, more individualistic than Feuerbach, also sees divinity as a projection of the human. For Nietzsche, God is nothing more than the mirror of man. Since man does not dare to ascribe such power or love to

18. Henri de Lubac, *The Drama of Atheist Humanism* (New York: Sheed and Ward, 1950), vii.

19. Ibid., 10.

20. Ibid.

21. Feuerbach, *Das Wesen des Christentums,* cited in de Lubac, *The Drama of Atheist Humanism,* 10.

himself, he makes them the attributes of a superhuman being.[22] By choosing to affirm "the death of God" a person assumes his or her own fully human or "superhuman" life. Thus atheism is the foundation of a true humanism.

Auguste Comte, in his rejection of metaphysics, proposed to leave atheism, what he called a "mere temporary negativism," behind. He preferred to eliminate the concept of God by explaining "what illusion accounts for that belief and what role that belief has temporarily played" within the succession of his three theoretical states: the theological or fictitious state, the metaphysical or abstract state, and the scientific or positive state. In his words,

> The true positive spirit consists above all in perpetually substituting the study of the invariable laws of phenomena for the study of their causes properly so called, whether first or final, or, to put it briefly, it seeks to ascertain *how* rather than *why.*[23]

Positivism, in confining itself to the study of immanent phenomena, substitutes humanity for God and becomes essentially a religion of humanity.[24] Comte's view of this humanity, however, differs from Feuerbach's in that it is does not consist of humankind as a whole, but includes only those individuals who have "co-operated in the great human task," thus excluding criminals and parasites of society.[25] However, for Comte as well as for Feuerbach, humanity replaces God as an object of worship.

In contrast to this religion of humanity, Comte considered Christianity to be immoral. In his opinion, the believer regards human society merely as an agglomeration of individuals whose coming together is almost as fortuitous as it is transitory and who, each exclusively occupied with his or her own salvation, regard cooperation in the salvation of others merely as a good means of working out their own.[26] De Lubac summarizes Comte's criticism of Christianity when he says:

> Christianity is antisocial in two ways: in its conception of man and in its conception of salvation; or, to put it differently, in its doctrine and in its ethics, in its ontology and in its practical standpoint. The one is

22. De Lubac, *The Drama of Atheist Humanism,* 18.
23. From *Discours sur l'ensemble du positivisme,* cited in de Lubac, *The Drama of Atheist Humanism,* 95.
24. De Lubac, *The Drama of Atheist Humanism,* 100.
25. Ibid., 101.
26. Ibid., 107, referring to Comte's *Polit.* 3, xxxv (Letter to the Czar), 446. *Dis.,* 87.

"anarchic," the other "selfish." There is, moreover, a close connection between the two; the anarchism of Christian doctrine inevitably entails the egoism of Christian practice, so that there is no need to deal with them separately.[27]

Thus an emphasis on individual salvation is seen to destroy concern for the race, and a human person viewed in terms of his or her transcendent destiny is seen to negate the value of the temporal order in a metaphysical flight from the historical.

In de Lubac's opinion, what Comte's positivist humanism, Marxist humanism, and Nietzschean humanism have in common is antitheism in the form of antichristianism with a resulting annihilation of the human person. As we have seen, de Lubac in his Christocentrism offers an anthropology that is fundamentally communitarian rather than individualistic while at the same time enhancing the dignity of the individual. By converting anthropology to Christology, de Lubac responds to atheist humanism with a Christian humanism wherein a person realizes his greatness, not by getting rid of God, but by participating in the divine life.

De Lubac is able both to retain the value of Christianity and respond to the nineteenth-century atheist humanists by invoking the paradoxical condition of human life. He reaffirms the value of the individual at the same time as he emphasizes the communitarian character of salvation. On the one hand, the person does not constitute a final end, a "positive independent world," yet on the other hand, neither is the person subordinate to some other, supposedly higher, end such as the human species. De Lubac notes that

> to speak of the sacrifice of even one single being for the perfection of the universe is to imagine a fictitious opposition between two sorts of "good" which can only coincide. A universe whose beauty was bought at such a cost would be valueless.[28]

Consequently, even though a human person is a social being, de Lubac rejects forms of socialism which sacrifice the individual to the community.[29]

27. De Lubac, *The Drama of Atheist Humanism,* 106.
28. Ibid., 182-183.
29. See de Lubac, "The New Man: The Marxist and the Christian View," *Dublin Review* 442 (1948): 5-35. This article is expanded in "La recherche d'un homme nouveau," *Affrontements mystiques* (Paris: Editions du Témoignage chrétien, 1949), 2-92.

In response to the immanentism of atheist humanism, de Lubac stresses the transcendent with its correlative, mystery. In a passage contrasting the categories of myth and mystery, de Lubac notes the different use of symbols in each. The symbols of myth link us with Nature, attuning us to her rhythm but also enslaving us to her fatal powers. People mold these symbols as they please with the result that natural symbols can be the projection of human terror and desire. The symbols of mystery, on the other hand, are received from on high and reveal to a person the secret of his or her own nobility.[30] The first are immanent; the second are transcendent and revealed. The atheist humanists saw divinity as a projection of the human and consequently interpreted religious symbols in terms of myth. Where the dignity of the human is found in the divine, the symbols are received as having an existence independent of immanent human existence. From this it is evident that sacraments are efficacious symbols of mystery rather than mythical symbols of natural fatality.

De Lubac, in responding to atheist humanism, does not deny its vivid awareness of human unity nor does he seek to quench its powerful social aspirations. Instead, by emphasizing the image of God within each person, he reminds his readers that humanity is not only historical but interior, and that one aspect cannot be divorced from the other.[31] At the same time, however, he emphasizes that one person is responsible for all: "No individual has the right to escape from humanity to forge a solitary destiny; the whole of humanity has to die to itself in each one of its members in order to live, transfigured, in God."[32] In the final analysis, the impetus behind his vision of the individual in the image of God, as well as the supernatural destiny of humanity as a whole, is his concept of the supernatural. Not a "higher, richer, more beautiful Nature," it is rather "the invasion of another *principle,* the sudden opening up of a kind of fourth dimension incommensurable with all the framework provided by the natural dimensions."[33] For de Lubac, "the links between the two are close, for one, as it were, weaves the body of the other."[34] Thus the "new

---

30. De Lubac, *The Drama of Atheist Humanism,* 47.
31. De Lubac, "The New Man: The Marxist and the Christian View," 18.
32. Ibid., 34.
33. Ibid., 35.
34. Ibid., 305.

man," inseparable from the "whole Christ," is indefinable apart from the mystery of his transcendent destiny proleptically embodied in each faithful person and in the Church.

De Lubac's Categories: An Evaluation

The two main axes of this study of de Lubac's ecclesiology have been spiritual exegesis and the predominant image of the Church as the body of Christ. It will now be helpful to evaluate how they function in the light of this systematic reading of de Lubac.

Spiritual Exegesis

The categories and principles of the spiritual interpretation of Scripture provide a key to the interpretation of de Lubac's theology, the internal coherence of which is largely due to the structure these categories provide. For example, de Lubac's theological starting point, revelation in the person of Jesus Christ, is consonant with this type of exegesis. The relationship between the Church, Christ, and the Eucharist is best articulated in terms of these principles. An examination of the relationship between Christ and the Church has revealed that Christ and the Eucharist are figures of the Church when the Church is viewed as the "whole Christ," the members of Christ in union with their head. Since the "whole Christ" will be complete only in the eschaton, this relationship between type and antitype can be articulated in terms of the allegorical and the anagogical senses of Scripture. Chapter Four also showed the image of the Church as the spouse of Christ to be inseparable from a theology of Mary as type of the Church and pointed out that the very category of typology is borrowed from spiritual exegesis.

Since this type of exegesis belongs to a period of history long past, having been replaced by the historical-critical method as well as by variants of literary criticism, we might well ask, first, whether a theology based on a type of exegesis generally thought to be obsolete can be considered viable today; and, second, whether the spiritual interpretation of Scripture does not, in fact, constitute a theological method, given the fact that de Lubac's theology depends so heavily on this exegesis.

As to the first question: even though spiritual exegesis is not a contemporary method of biblical exegesis, this study of de Lubac's ecclesiology reveals that the contemporary Church has inherited and still holds as part of its culture and belief the relationship between various mysteries of faith which are the subject of this exegesis. For example, much of the liturgy is constructed within the framework of promise and fulfillment, thus incorporating the same relationship between the Old and New Testaments found in spiritual exegesis. The whole concept of *imitatio Christi,* based on the fact that the Christian participates in the life of Christ, particularly in the paschal mystery, represents an instance of the tropological sense of Scripture. The Church's Mariology, especially as articulated in the last chapter of *Lumen Gentium,* is strongly typological. The twentieth century has witnessed a proliferation of books and lectures on spirituality with a corresponding retrieval of the classical spiritual writers who themselves either practiced spiritual exegesis or were products of a time imbued with its spirit. Much of this contemporary spirituality, with the exception of that incorporating Jungian overtones or influenced by Eastern non-Christian religions, differs little from the mystical interpretation of the anagogical sense. Finally, contemporary theology evinces a strong interest in eschatology. Interpretations of this vary, depending upon whether the eschaton is taken to be the product of a progressive evolution of the historical order or an in-breaking of the transcendent into the temporal order. This latter position corresponds most closely with the view fundamental to spiritual exegesis.

One can conclude, therefore, that even though spiritual exegesis is now foreign to scientific biblical study, its categories continue to shape the Christian worldview. De Lubac does not call for a return to this method of exegesis: its time is truly past as a method of biblical study, the emphasis now being on a scientific and historical study of the literal sense of Scripture, a literary analysis of the biblical narrative, or various other exegetical methodologies. However, the fruits of this exegesis endure and serve as the foundation of a Christian vision of reality. Furthermore, considered theoretically as well as concretely, spiritual exegesis views Scripture as an interpretation of history as a soteriological event. This function of spiritual exegesis has not been exercised by the historical-critical method, which is concerned to establish what the author of a biblical text meant to say rather than to relate that message to the whole of salvation history and to Christ's saving work.

The answer to the second question, whether or not spiritual exegesis can be considered a theological method, depends on an understanding of what constitutes a theological method. Donald J. Keefe gives this description of ontological method, which, when correlated with Christian revelation, can also be said of theological method:

> A discussion of ontological method is therefore a discussion of general hermeneutics, in which all solutions to the ontological and hermeneutical problem are a priori; the ontological system must be known in some way before it is built. It is then evident that all reasoning within an ontological system must be circular, and that the entirety of the system is simultaneous with its a priori structure. The conclusions which the ontological a priori, or method, imposes, although ontological, will include an epistemology, for the structure of being and the understanding of being cannot be distinguished.[35]

The major difference between this description and spiritual exegesis is that exegesis is not concerned with ontology or being as such. It is, however, a hermeneutic which explains the meaning not only of the Scriptures but also of history. The solution to the hermeneutical problem is a priori, namely, revelation in the person of Jesus Christ. Initiated historically in the Incarnation and therefore an event rather than an abstract idea, this revelation continues to be historically present as event in the eucharistic worship of the Church. The reasoning within spiritual exegesis is circular since it both begins and ends with Christ. For example, it is possible to see the Old Testament as a prefiguration of Christ only when Christ is an a priori object of belief. This exegesis also ends with faith in Jesus Christ through an illumination of the relationship between Christ and the Old Testament (the allegorical sense), Christ and the Christian (the tropological sense), and Christ and the "whole Christ" in the eschaton (the anagogical sense). Finally, there is an epistemology governing the interpretation, namely, the tradition of the Church as the interpreter of the Scriptures in its life, belief, and worship rather than in an epistemological process immanent either to the text itself or its sociological origin.

Bernard Lonergan defines method as "a normative pattern of re-

35. Donald J. Keefe, *Thomism and the Ontological Theology of Paul Tillich* (Leiden: E. J. Brill, 1971), 7.

current and related operations yielding cumulative and progressive results."[36] For Lonergan, operations are not limited to logical operations, but may include inquiry, observation, discovery, experiment, synthesis, and verification.[37] It is more difficult to discern a relationship between this definition of method, based as it is on a scientific model of the natural sciences, and spiritual exegesis. Not all the operations are equally applicable to the biblical text. One can "inquire" into the relationship between the Old and New Testaments, "observe" similarities between types and antitypes, "discover" relationships between types, e.g., between Mary and Christ as types of the Church. However, "experiment" and "verification," especially in their scientific connotations, do not appear to be as applicable to this type of study. "Synthesis" is probably the most important operation since spiritual exegesis is primarily a synthesis of Christian doctrine through its correlation of the two Testaments and its view of the unity of the temporal order — past, present, and future — from a perspective of salvation history.

Does spiritual exegesis, however, yield "cumulative and progressive" results? Here it is important not to consider the literal, allegorical, tropological, and anagogical meanings of Scripture as progressive stages of an understanding of the biblical text since they can be applied simultaneously to the same text. Nor is the New Testament in a relationship of progression with the Old Testament since it represents a transformation of the literal meaning. The literal meaning is never discarded, nor are the other meanings deduced from the literal meaning since as mysteries of the faith they are a priori to the hermeneutical method itself. Thus it would be even more erroneous to suppose that one could "discover" doctrine by using such a method. What spiritual exegesis does is to illumine the relationships between mysteries of the faith at the same time as it grounds them in the historical order. The "discovery," consequently, is in the order of a more penetrating understanding of the text in the light of these relationships. We can conclude, then, that spiritual exegesis does not yield cumulative and progressive results in the same way that the scientific method does in the natural sciences.

From this examination of spiritual exegesis in the light of Keefe's and Lonergan's descriptions of theological method we can conclude that spir-

36. Bernard Lonergan, *Method in Theology* (New York: The Seabury Press, 1972), 5.
37. Ibid., 6.

itual exegesis does qualify as a hermeneutical method. De Lubac, however, is not engaged in a confessionally disinterested study of the Scriptures, but rather he uses the principles and relationships of spiritual exegesis for theological purposes, specifically, the correlation of such mysteries of the faith as Mariology and Christology, ecclesiology and the Eucharist. Hence spiritual exegesis functions as a hermeneutical method of theological reflection on the relationship between these mysteries rather than as an "objective" method of biblical study. Moreover, de Lubac's use of this hermeneutical method is not a self-conscious one but the result of his immersion in and assimilation of the patristic and medieval tradition formed by this exegesis. This study of de Lubac's ecclesiology points out the influence of spiritual exegesis on his theology, but this influence would not be as apparent to someone reading any one of his works in isolation from the others.

The Church as the Body of Christ

The tension intrinsic to the image of the Church as the body of Christ has been apparent throughout this study. Although the strength of the image lies in the fact that the Church really has no identity apart from Christ, we have seen that the weakness of the image is found in too close an identification between Christ and the Church, particularly when the Church is seen as an organic continuation of Christ. This danger notwithstanding, this image is necessary for de Lubac's theology, given its eucharistic and social emphasis.

The image of the Church as the body of Christ is inseparable from the eucharistic character of the Church. However, two assertions by de Lubac are difficult to reconcile. First, following medieval theology on the subject, he asserts an identity between the historical Christ, the sacramental Christ, and the ecclesial Christ. Church, sacrament, and historical person are different modes of existence of the same person, the Eucharist being the sacramental real presence of Christ, and the Church, in sacramental union with its head, constituting the "whole Christ." Second, he declares the Eucharist to be the cause of the Church. The difficulty is how at one point de Lubac can posit an identity between Church and Eucharist and at another point describe their relationship in terms of cause and effect. This difficulty is precisely the same one experienced when the Church is called the body of Christ when at the same time it cannot be identified with Christ. In other words, Christ transcends, is more than, his body and, as head of that body, cannot be considered a "member" of the body in the same sense that the Christian is a member of the body. This problem is avoided, however, given the relationship between the Eucharist and the Church. By partaking of one bread we become one body, and at that moment the Church is formed. We become what we eat, and that body is the body of Christ. We are assimilated to him, not he to us. In the Eucharist we are assimilated to the Church and to Christ in that the Church is "one flesh" with him.

The following schema may be helpful in clarifying the problem posed by the identification of the Church, Eucharist, and Christ with the correlative problem stated above, namely, the Eucharist seen as both causal of and identified with the Church:

Christ (Bridegroom)   Church (Bride)
Christ (Head)   Church (Body)
Christ (Eucharist)   Church (Sacrament of the "whole Christ")

The head/body, bridegroom/bride, and eucharistic body/Church-as-body symbols cannot be contradictory or read in isolation from one another or be understood as merely tautologous. These images, do, however illumine each other. De Lubac's discussion ultimately presupposes the identity of these pairs of covenantal interrelations. This identity occurs in two directions.

On the one hand, there is only one Christ viewed here from three perspectives as bridegroom, head, and Eucharist. Likewise there is but one Church viewed from three perspectives as bride, body, and sacrament. On the other hand, there is also an identity expressed horizontally: Christ and the Church are one flesh, one body, and one sacrament. De Lubac's difficulties and apparent inconsistencies lie in this horizontal identification which confuses the Church considered as one flesh with the Church considered as one body. He is so concerned with unity that, although he realizes and qualifies an improper identification between Christ and the Church, he does not develop a systematic resolution of the problem. Such a resolution, however, is possible on two levels: through a covenantal reading of the relationship between Christ and the Church in all three pairs and through a typological or sacramental reading of the identity of the three pairs.

In the covenantal resolution of the problem each pair represents a statement of the "cause" of the union between Christ and his Church and corresponds to one of the images of the Church examined in this study. In each case this union can be viewed as covenantal. The first pair, for example, represents the spousal imagery of the Church as the Bride of Christ. In the second the Church is viewed as the body of Christ. Since we have seen that Christ cannot be a member of the body in the same way a Christian is a member of the body, the image must be covenantal rather than organic, thus precluding a view of the Church as a continuation of the body of Christ. In the third pair, representing a sacramental iden-tification, the Eucharist, as the New Covenant, is the cause of the Church. The Church is constituted by its sacramental union with Christ, becoming at that moment body, spouse, and sacrament of Christ. By partaking of the same bread it becomes one body with Christ. Through the New Covenant effected by the Eucharist it becomes one spouse with Christ. In its sacramental union with Christ the Church becomes a sacrament of the eschatological "whole Christ."

Such a covenantal reading solves several problems occasioned by a Christ-Church identification within an organism. First, it maintains the freedom necessary to the Church's union with Christ. Second, it preserves an adequate distinction between the Church and Christ. Third, it avoids assimilating the Christian within the hypostatic union. Finally, this reading prevents the submergence of the individual in the collectivity by under-writing the covenantal character of the worship by which Christians are "one body" through their eating of "one bread." At the same time, it upholds the primacy of Christ and the sign-efficacy of the Eucharist as the event of God's covenantal immanence in his creation, in his people.

A second resolution of the problem of the identity of Christ, the Church, and the Eucharist posed by the threefold body is found within typology which represents a theology of a real symbol or efficacious sacramentality. The Eucharist is not exactly the same thing as the Church although it is a type of it; the Church is not Christ although it is a sacrament of the "whole Christ." Furthermore, while safeguarding a doc-trine of the real presence, the Eucharist is not identical with the historical Christ; it is more properly termed a sacrament of Christ. Since the time of Berengarius, however, the effort to refute his error and maintain a doctrine of the real presence has made theologians very wary of using any kind of symbolic language at all when speaking of the Eucharist. Since his problem, however, was to separate the *res* from the *sacramentum,* it remains possible to discuss the eucharistic real presence in sacramental or typological language when the sign of the sacrament is held to be efficacious and the typological language is grounded in literal truth. The realism of the Church is ultimately grounded in eucharistic realism so that the typological identification of the two in no way jeopardizes the real presence.

Within the sacramental resolution of the problem of the threefold Christic body, Christ, the Eucharist, and the Church are identified from the perspective of the sacrament rather than from the perspective of the historical person, Jesus Christ, or the Church viewed as a social institution. That is, the Eucharist is a sacrament of Christ as it is a sacrament of the Church. De Lubac's citation of *De Sacramentis* of Master Simon, who wrote in the middle of the twelfth century, is revealing in this regard:

> Why is Christ received under the form of bread and wine? It may be said that in the sacrament of the altar there are two things: the true body of Christ and what it signifies, namely his mystical body which is the Church.[38]

Thus the identification of the three bodies is made only through the medium of a sign which both reveals and hides what it signifies. In other words, it is the Eucharist as sign, most importantly an efficacious sign, which signifies the other two bodies. However, the relationship is so close that since the Eucharist *is* the real presence of Christ, Christ himself is a sign of his mystical body, the Church, just as the Eucharist is a sign of the Church. The Church is a sign of Christ, not as the person who lived two thousand years ago, but as he will be completed at the end of time. If one distinguishes the identification of the threefold body on the level of sign within a sacramental order from the relationship between cause and effect on a more literal level, an apparent contradiction between a relationship of identification and a relationship of cause and effect no longer exists.

Once the inconsistencies are resolved, the image of body serves the social emphasis in de Lubac's theology. In addition to its close association with the Eucharist, the image "body of Christ" also provides a focus for the integration of the other sacraments, emphasizing their social dimen-

---

38. De Lubac, *Catholicism,* 41.

sion. The effect of the sacraments is to establish or strengthen the bonds to the ecclesial body and, through that body, to Christ. In de Lubac's words, the sacraments are "instruments of unity":

> As they make real, renew or strengthen man's union with Christ, by that very fact they make real, renew or strengthen his union with the Christian community. And this second aspect of the sacraments, the social aspect, is so intimately bound up with the first that it can often be said, indeed in certain cases it must be said, that it is through his union with the community that the Christian is united to Christ.[39]

De Lubac comments that just as redemption and revelation, even though directed to each individual person, are fundamentally social rather than individual in nature, so "grace which is produced and maintained by the sacraments does not set up a purely individual relationship between the soul and God or Christ."[40] Each person receives such grace in proportion as he or she "is joined, socially, to that one body whence flows this saving life-stream."[41] He concludes that the causality of the sacraments is found "in the existence of a society, which under the appearances of a human institution hides a divine reality" rather than in "a paradoxical efficacy, in the supernatural order, of a rite or perceptible action."[42] This sacramental theology is entirely social and ecclesial in nature.

The central sacrament within this social and ecclesial perspective is, of course, the Eucharist. Although de Lubac does not develop the ecclesial emphasis of each of the other sacraments, he does do so for baptism and penance. Baptism is an act of incorporation in the visible Church. Since the Church is not a purely human society, this incorporation includes not only juridical, but also spiritual and mystical consequences such as the sacramental character. De Lubac even goes so far as to call incorporation into the Church at baptism a "concorporation" to emphasize that a series of baptisms does not effect a series of incorporations, but "a 'concorporation' of the whole Church in one mysterious unity" since in the one Spirit we are baptized into one body.[43]

39. Ibid., 35.
40. Ibid.
41. Ibid.
42. Ibid.
43. Ibid., 36.

The efficacy of penance is the social reintegration of the sinner.[44] In the history of the sacrament the public character of penance and pardon made it clear that "the reconciliation of the sinner is in the first place a reconciliation with the Church, this latter constituting an efficacious sign of reconciliation with God."[45] This ecclesial character of penance is precisely the reason why the sacrament requires a minister of the Church for the sacrament, for if reconciliation were solely a matter between the sinner and Christ, the presence of such a person would not be required.

A major criticism of the image of the Church as the body of Christ is that it contributes to an excessively Christocentric view of the Church at the expense of a more Trinitarian or pneumatological view.[46] In de Lubac's work, the Trinitarian and pneumatological elements of the Church are most evident in his study of the creed in *La foi chrétienne*. The creed has a threefold structure, each part expressing belief in one of the members of the Trinity. The Church is mentioned in the third part as the first of the works of the Spirit.[47] The Spirit is present in the Church as its source of sanctification[48] and its principle of life.[49] Even as the Eucharist is the cause of the Church, the Spirit, intrinsically associated with the Eucharist, is also the cause of the Church: "This Holy Spirit, by whom Christ's carnal body was prepared, intervenes too in the confection of the Eucharist for the making of his Mystical Body."[50]

The presence and activity of the Spirit in the Church is possible, however, because of the relationship between the Spirit and Christ. In de Lubac's theology the Spirit is the Spirit of Christ.[51] Thus where Christ is,

44. Ibid., 37.

45. Ibid.

46. Yves Congar in "Pneumatologie ou Christomonisme," in *Ecclesia a Spiritu Santo edocta,* Bibliotheca ephemeridum theologicorum, vol. 27 (Gembloux, Belgium: Editions J. Duculot, 1970), 41-63, points out that the charge of Christomonism is inexact. The history of the question is very complex since some theologies emphasize the economy of salvation (the Eastern tradition), while others emphasize an ontology (the Latin tradition). Congar notes, however, a contemporary concession that the Holy Spirit is the Spirit of Christ. The work and presence of Christ cannot be divorced from the Spirit and consequently cannot be considered "Christomonistic."

47. De Lubac, *Catholicism,* 22.

48. Henri de Lubac, *La foi chrétienne,* 2d ed. (Paris: Aubier, 1970), 245.

49. Ibid., 249.

50. De Lubac, *Catholicism,* 49.

51. De Lubac, *La foi chrétienne,* 287.

his Spirit is there also. De Lubac expresses the Spirit-Christ-Church relationship thus:

> Moreover, there is no other Spirit than this Spirit of Jesus, and the Spirit of Jesus is the soul which animates his body.[19] As the letter of the Law assembled the ancient people, it is the Spirit who fashions the new people.[20] Today we are in the Spirit as we are in Christ, and one can well say with Saint Paul, that we have been baptized in a single Spirit in order to form a single body or, as Saint Basil comments, in a single body to form a single Spirit.[21] The Church is "the society of the Spirit,"[22] and it is within the Church that the Spirit glorifies Jesus, as it is in the Church, in this "house of Christ" that he, Jesus, is given to us,[23] "the eternal and final covenant."[a]

19. Saint Augustine, *sermo* 268, n. 2: "Quod est spiritus noster, id est anima nostra, ad membra nostra, hoc est Spiritus sanctus ad membra Christi, ad corpus Christi, quod est Ecclesia (P.L., 38, 1232); *Sermo* 267, n. 4 (col. 1231). Cf. *Rom* VIII,9; *II Cor* III,17; *Gal* IV,6.

20. *II Cor* III,6-11; *Phil* III,3. Cf. *I Cor* XII,13; *Eph* IV,4, etc.

21. Saint Basil, *On the Holy Spirit*, c. 26, n. 61, commenting *I Cor* XII,18 (P.G., 32, 181 B). Cf. the remark of S. Tromp, *de Spiritu sancto anima corporis mystici*, I, p. 34.

22. "Societas Spiritus": Saint Augustine, *Sermo* 71, c. 19, n. 32 (FL., 38, 4620; c. 23, n. 37: "congregatur in Spiritu sancto" (col. 466).

23. Pseudo-Bede, *in Joannem* (P.L. m 92, 862 A-B). S. Augustine, *De Trinitate*, 1 XV, C. 19, n. 34.

a. Saint Justin, *Dialogue*, c XI, n. 2.[52]

The association between Church, Christ, and Spirit is so close that de Lubac cites Tertullian's statement that "where the Three are, Father, Son, and Holy Spirit, there also is found the Church which is the body of the Three."[53]

Thus the Church, by being the body of Christ, is also the body of the Spirit. The Spirit, however, is historically embodied only through the Incarnation of the Son. As Schnackers notes: "In the Logos having become man the Holy Spirit has entered into salvation history and believers thereby have access to the Father through Christ in his Spirit."[54] We can conclude,

52. De Lubac, *Méditation sur l'Eglise*, 180. My translation.

53. De Lubac, *La foi chrétienne*, 236.

54. Hubert Schnackers, *Kirche als Saksament und Mutter* (Frankfurt am Main, 1979), 93: "Im menschgewordenen Logos ist der Heilige Geist in die Heilsgeschichte eingegangen, damit die Gläubigen durch Christus in seinem Geiste Zugang zum Vater haben."

therefore, that there is a strong pneumatological element in de Lubac's Christocentric ecclesiology, but that it is subordinated to the Christological emphasis. Since his point of reference is Christ, his pneumatology is derived from the economy of salvation in a manner analogous to that by which the Church arrived at knowledge of the Trinity through the work and witness of the Son. Furthermore, since his writing is occasional, a response to specific and concrete questions, rather than an attempt at a systematic formulation of an ecclesiology, a reader must correlate the pneumatological sections in *La foi chrétienne* and *Catholicism* with the whole of his ecclesiology.

The same must be done with Trinitarian elements within his theology. We have already seen that in his theology the Church is in a relationship to the Trinity through the mediation of Jesus. This insight, in itself, represents a significant contribution to the interconnection of ecclesiology and Trinitarian theology. In other words, de Lubac's contribution is a view of the Church in its participation in the immanent Trinity, in the intra-trinitarian relations of circumincession. Contrary to his treatment of the Spirit, however, de Lubac does not explicitly relate the Church to the economic activity of the Trinity, an omission particularly evident in his discussion of the mission of the Church. Since de Lubac's work on the Church does not purport to be a systematic ecclesiology, this is not to criticize what de Lubac failed to do so much as to highlight an element requiring explicit attention were such a systematic ecclesiology to be attempted.

A third criticism of a predominantly Christocentric ecclesiology is that it tends to be ahistorical and divorced from salvation history. This criticism most often occurs when the image "body of Christ" is compared with that of "people of God." It is important to note that this supposed danger is in any case avoided when the image of the Church as the body of Christ is placed in a context of the spiritual interpretation of Scripture. It is true that the encyclical *Mystici Corporis* does not emphasize the existential historical order in its presentation of the Church as the Mystical Body of Christ in contrast to a juridical notion of the Church based on the model of human societies. The spiritual interpretation of Scripture, however, lies solidly within a synthetic view of salvation history encompassing past, present, and future as contributing to the completion of God's design for that history. Within this synthesis, the image "body of Christ" both expresses the final end of that history and is correlated

151

with the Eucharist, the sacramental means within time of accomplishing that end.

The sacraments are concrete, historical instances of God's salvific grace operative within history. As sacraments they both reveal and conceal that grace. The Church, as sacrament both signified and caused by the Eucharist, represents "really" the body of Christ in the world and yet, as sacrament, also conceals that body. De Lubac's ecclesiology, founded as it is upon the Eucharist, is a sacramental ecclesiology. Therefore it is precisely as sacrament, not as juridical institution, that the Church is the body of Christ. The full revelation of the "body of Christ," that is, members united to the head, Christ, will occur in the eschaton. Consequently the image "body of Christ" does not absolutize the Church in the present time, nor does it dehistoricize it since it is inserted into the historical order precisely as sacrament.

De Lubac's Ecclesiological Contribution

De Lubac's major contribution to ecclesiology is that through his historical study of the term *corpus mysticum* and his retrieval of the realistic symbolism intrinsic to spiritual exegesis and the Church-Eucharist relationship, he has uncovered the foundation for a eucharistic ecclesiology. This foundation permits a systematic interpretation of 1 Cor. 10:16-17:

> The cup of blessing which we bless, is it not a participation in the blood of Christ? The bread which we break, is it not a participation in the body of Christ? Because there is one bread, we who are many are one body, for we all partake of the one bread.

Such an ecclesiology is strongly Christocentric, its Christocentrism inseparable from its eucharistic emphasis since the Eucharist is the continued historical presence of Christ in the world. The identification of the Church with the Eucharist permits de Lubac to have a unique interpretation of the Church as sacrament integrally related to the typology of spiritual exegesis.

Any theory of sacramentality necessarily involves a theory of symbolic signification. In contrast to some theologians who borrow such a theory from linguistic models, de Lubac bases his on the symbolism intrinsic to the spiritual interpretation of Scripture, as is evident from this statement:

It is the same with the Eucharist as it is with the spiritual sense of Scripture, which does not eliminate the literal sense or add something else to it, but rather rounds it out and gives it fullness, revealing its depths and bringing out its objective extension. Through this "spiritual breaking" the "mystery of the Bread" is opened up, and we come to understand its ecclesial sense.[4]

4. See the texts given in *Corpus Mysticum*, pp. 82-83.[55]

Even though de Lubac wrote that the Church is a sacrament of Christ in *The Splendour of the Church* in 1953, predating later and more lengthy developments of the concept by other theologians, he never precisely developed how or with what theory of symbolic signification the Church is a sacrament. The above citation found in the same work suggests that the answer is found in a synthesis of his other works on exegesis and the term *corpus mysticum,* a suggestion borne out by this study of his work.

The contribution of such a synthesis as developed in this study of de Lubac's ecclesiology is that it places a view of the Church as the sacramental body of Christ within a context of salvation history, thus correcting a concept of the Church as a universal ideal entity. The "mystical body" in this context is the *corpus in mysterio,* not an invisible or a ghostly image of a real body, but the body mystically signified and realized by the Eucharist, i.e., the unity of the Christian community made real in an effective symbol.[56] Second, the concept of the Church as the body of Christ in its association with the eucharistic "one bread" of 1 Cor. 10:17 emphasizes the social nature of the Church. Salvation is seen as incorporation into the social unity of the body of Christ. Third, since a sacrament points to a reality beyond itself, this category permits a strong eschatological dimension in de Lubac's ecclesiology. Finally, de Lubac's theology synthesizes Christian anthropology and ecclesiology since the human person's destiny, incorporation into this unity, is engraved in his or her very nature.

De Lubac has not attempted a systematic ecclesiology. A couple of points, however, have not yet received an adequate accounting within a eucharistic theology. The first is an adequate theology of baptism. Such a

55. De Lubac, *The Splendour of the Church,* trans. Michael Mason (New York: Sheed and Ward, 1955), 112.
56. Ibid., 92.

theology needs to account for the association of non-Christians with the mystical body of Christ. As we have seen, *Lumen Gentium* affirms this association but does not indicate the theological basis for it. De Lubac does hold that it is possible for the non-baptized to be saved and thus to be incorporated into the social unity of the mystical body, but he has not developed a theology of grace to explain this possibility.

A second point that remains undeveloped in his theology is the relationship that humanity had with Christ before the Fall. If salvation consists in the restored unity of the human race in Christ, this implies a Christology and an anthropology that are mutually interrelated and preexistent. De Lubac's theology often seems to presuppose this, but does not develop it since he begins his theology with the existential order with a view to its eschatological completion.

Finally, the incorporation of a theology of the Fall into his theology is necessary in order to distinguish between membership in the human race and membership in the Mystical Body. Given freedom and the possibility of sin, the two are not coterminous. De Lubac's positive stress on unity and catholicity does not explore the implications of a failed anthropology, one that does not find its terminus in Christ.

Even though de Lubac has not attempted a complete exposition of a systematic eucharistic ecclesiology, this study of his ecclesiology has shown that what he has done possesses an organic unity and is, indeed, systematic. The double axis which provides the systematic coherence to his work consists of the principles of the spiritual interpretation of Scripture and the Eucharist. Because of the relationship between the Church and the Eucharist we can say that for him the Church does indeed represent the social embodiment of grace in the world. It is "social" since it is formed by the union of human beings who together comprise the members of the body of Christ when united with their head. The Church is "embodied" because it is a historical institution. It is also "embodied" since it is the body of Christ mystically signified by the Eucharist in covenantal union with its spouse. As body, spouse, and sacrament the Church possesses a historical incorporation. Finally, it is graced through its relationship with Christ. The Church as the anticipation of the final union of all the blessed in Christ represents the proleptic presence of the whole Christ in human history.

Bibliography of Henri de Lubac

Edgar Haulotte compiled a complete bibliography of de Lubac's writing up to and including 1963 for *L'Homme devant Dieu: mélanges offerts au Père de Lubac,* vol. III (Paris: Aubier, 1964), 347-356. The most comprehensive published bibiography is the sixty-six-page booklet, edited by H. Neufeld and M. Sales, *Bibliographie Henri de Lubac, S.J. (1925-1970)* (Einsiedeln: Johannes Verlag, 1971). For a bibliography from 1970-1990, see Neufeld and Sales, "Bibliographie Henri de Lubac, S.J., 1970 to 1990," in *Théologie dans l'Histoire,* by Henri de Lubac (Paris: Desclée, 1990), 408-437. In addition to compiling an alphabetical listing of most of de Lubac's works, I have included a bibliography of secondary literature as well as a selected supporting bibliography.

Selected Works by Henri de Lubac

Affrontements mystiques. Paris: Temoignage chrétien, 1950.
"Allégorie hellenistique et allégorie chrétienne." *Recherche de science religieuse* 47 (1959): 5-43.
"Allocution du R. P. Henri de Lubac." In *Homage au Père Auguste Valensin (1879-1953),* 19-24. Nice, 1954.
"Apologétique et théologie," *Nouvelle revue théologique* 57 (1930): 364-365.
"Das apostolische Glaubensbekenntnis." *Internationale Zeitschrift "Communio"* 4 (1975): 1-9.
"L'apport de Teilhard à la connaissance de Dieu." *Teilhard de Chardin.* Paris: Hachette, 1969.

"A propos de la conception médiévale de l'ordre surnaturel (Exchangés de vues avec J. De Blic)." *Revue du moyen age Latin* 4 (1947): 365-373.

"A propos de la formule: Diversi, sed non adversi." *Recherches de science religieuse* 39-40 (1951-1952): 27-40.

"L'Arbre cosmique." In *Mélanges Podechard,* 191-198. Lyon: Facultés catholiques, 1945.

Aspects du Bouddhism I. Paris: Seuil, 1951. [ET: *Aspects of Buddhism.* Translated by G. Lab. London and New York: Sheed and Ward, 1953.]

Aspects du Bouddhism II. Amida. Paris: Seuil, 1955.

Athéisme et sens de l'homme. Une double requête de "Gaudium et Spes." Coll. Foi Vivante 67. Paris: Cerf, 1968.

Augustinisme et théologie moderne. Coll. Théologie 63. Paris: Aubier-Montaigne, 1965. [ET: *Augustinianism and Modern Theology.* Translated by Lancelot Sheppard. New York: Herder and Herder, 1969.]

"Le bouddhisme et l'Occident moderne." *Etudes* 272 (1952): 327-346.

"Buddhist Charity and Christian Charity." *Communio* 15 (1988): 497-510.

"Can a Will Be Essentially Good?" In *The Human Person and the World of Values: A Tribute to Dietrich von Hildebrand,* ed. B. V. Schwartz, 121-131. Westport, Conn: Greenwood Press, 1960.

"Le caractère social du dogme chrétien." *Chronique sociale France* 45 (1936): 167-192, 259-283.

"Catholicism." *Bulletin de l'Association catholique chinoise de Lyon* (1932): 8-15; *Revue de l'AUCAM* (1933): 1-12.

"Catholicism." *Communio* (U.S.) 15 (1988): 234-248.

Catholicisme. Les Aspects sociaux du dogme. Coll. Unam Sanctam 2. Paris: Cerf, 1947. [ET: *Catholicism.* Translated by Lancelot C. Sheppard. New York: Longman, Green and Co., 1950; *Catholicism: Christ and the Common Destiny of Man.* San Francisco: Ignatius Press, 1988.]

"Causes de l'atténuation du sens du sacré." *Bulletin des Aumôniers de Chantiers* (August 1942).

"La charité bouddhique." *Bulletin des Facultés catholiques de Lyon* 1 (1950): 1-31.

Christian Resistance to Anti-Semitism: Memoires from 1940-1944. San Francisco: Ignatius Press, 1990.

"Christianisme incarné." *Lettres aux Aumôniers* 14 (1943): 1-5.

"Christliche Mystik in Begegnung mit den Welt religionen." In *Das Mysterium und die Mystik,* ed. J. Sudbrack, 77-110. Stuttgart: Katholisches Bibelwerk, 1974.

"The Church and Our Life." *The Life of the Spirit* 7 (1953): 539-549.

"The Church in Crisis." *Theology Digest* 17 (1969): 312-325.

"The Church in Reality." *Social Order* 3 (1953): 1161-1173.

"Claudel théologien." In *La pensée religieuse de Claudel.* Recherches et débats du

Centre catholique des intellectuels français, 65. Paris: Desclée de Brouwer, 1969.

"Le combat spirituel." *Cité nouvelle* (December 1943): 769-783.

"Le commentaire d'Origène sur Jérémie, XX." In *Mélanges J. Chaine.* Lyon: Facultés catholiques, 1950.

"Commentaire du préambule et du chapître I." In *La Révélation Divine.* Vol. I: Constitution dogmatique "Dei verbum." Coll. Unam Sanctam 70a. Paris: Cerf, 1968.

"Communauté et communion." In *Cahiers de la Communauté française,* ed. Fr. Perroux and J. Madaule. Paris: Cahiers d'Etudes communautaires, 1942.

"De l'actualité de Dieu." *Cahiers du Monde Nouveau* (October 1946).

"La conception chrétienne de l'homme." In *Semaine sociale de Paris.* Lyon: Cronique Sociale, 1948.

"*Corpus Mysticum:* Etudes sur l'origine et les premiers sens de l'expression." *Recherches de sciences religieuses* 29 (1940): 257-302, 429-480; 30 (1940): 40-80, 191-226.

Corpus Mysticum: L'Eucharistie et l'Eglise au Moyen Age. Coll. Théologie 3. Paris: Aubier-Montaigne, 1944.

"Le credo de Paul Claudel." *Choisir* 14 (1960): 9-12.

"Credo Ecclesiam." In *Sentire ecclesiam. Das Bewusstsein von der Kirche als gestaltende Kraft der Frommigkeit, Festschrift für H. Rahner,* ed. J. Daniélou, 13-16. Freiburg: Herder, 1961.

"Credo . . . Sanctorum Communionem." *International Catholic Review: Communio* 1 (1972): 18-32.

"Un curé de bourgeois, Mgr. Chevrot." *Ecclesia* 145 (1961): 145-150.

"Daniélou, Jean, Cardinal, 1905-1974 [obit]. *Internationale Katholische Zeitschrift "Communio"* 3 (1974): 472-474.

De la connaissance de Dieu. Paris: Témoignage chrétien, 1945; 2nd edition, enlarged, 1948.

"Deux Augustiniens fourvoyés: Baïus et Jansénius." *Recherches de science religieuse* 21 (1931): 422-443, 513-540.

"Deux thèses de doctorat sur Bergson." *Etudes* 217 (1933): 306-313.

Dieu se dit dans l'histoire. Coll. Foi vivante 159. Paris: Cerf, 1974.

"Le drame de l'humanisme athée." *Cité nouvelle* (May 1942): 737-756.

Le drame de l'humanisme athée. Paris: Editions Spes, 1945. [ET: *The Drama of Atheist Humanism.* Translated by Edith M. Riley. London: Sheed and Ward, 1949; Meridian Books, 1963.]

"*Duplex hominis beatitudo*"(S. Thomas la 2 ae. Q. 62, a. 1)." *Recherches de science religieuse* 35 (1948): 290-299.

L'Ecriture dans la tradition. Paris: Aubier, 1966. [ET: *The Sources of Revelation.* Translated by Luke O'Neil. New York: Herder and Herder, 1968.]

"L'Eglise dans la crise actuelle." *Nouvelle revue théologique* 91 (1969): 580-596.

L'Eglise dans la crise actuelle. Paris: Cerf, 1969.

"L'Eglise dans saint Paul." *Vie spirituelle* (May 1943): 470-483.

L'Eglise en face de la crise mondiale. Clermont-Ferrand, 1942.

"L'Eglise, Notre Mère." *Etudes* 276 (January 1953): 1-19.

Les églises particulières dans l'Eglise universelle. Suivi de: *La maternité de l'église* et d'une interview par G. Jarczyk. Paris: Aubier, 1971. [ET: *The Motherhood of the Church.* Translated by Sergia Englund. San Francisco: Ignatius Press, 1982.]

"En pensant à Dieu." *Cité nouvelle* (February 1944): 148-157.

Entretien autour de Vatican II: souvenirs et réflexions. Paris: France catholique, Editions du Cerf, 1985.

"Envergure et limites du Père Teilhard." *Choisir* 6 (1965): 19-20.

"L'Epreuve de la foi." In *P. Teilhard de Chardin: Lettres à Léontine Zanta,* ed. M. De Certeau. Paris: Desclée de Brouwer, 1965.

"Esprit et liberté dans la tradition théologique." *Bulletin de littérature ecclesiastique* 40 (1939): 121-150, 189-207.

L'éternel feminin: Etude sur un texte de Teilhard de Chardin. Suivi de: *Teilhard et notre temps.* Paris: Aubier, 1968, 1983. [ET: *The Eternal Feminine. A Study on the Poem by Teilhard de Chardin, followed by Teilhard and the Problems of Today.* Translated by René Hague. New York: Harper and Row, 1971.]

Exégèse médiévale: les quatre sens de l'Ecriture. Coll. Théologie 41 (pt. 1 and 2), 42, 59. Paris: Aubier-Montaigne, 1959, 1961, 1964.

"Exigences chrétiennes." *Masses Ouvrières* 9 (1946): 4-17.

"L'expérience de l'éternité: la 'nouvelle naissaince' selon Dostoievski." *Cité nouvelle* (October 1943): 297-330.

Explication chrétienne de notre temps. Coll. Les Lampes III. Paris: l'Orante, 1944.

"Foi, croyance, religion." *Nouvelle revue théologique* 91 (1969): 337-346.

La foi chrétienne: essai sur la structure de symbole des apôtres. 2nd edition. Paris: Aubier, 1970. [ET: *The Christian Faith: An Essay on the Structure of the Apostles' Creed.* San Francisco: Ignatius Press, 1986.]

"La foi de l'Eglise." *Christus* 46 (1965): 228-246.

"Le fondement théologique des missions." *Bibliothèque de l'Union mission du clergé de France* (1941): 3-29.

Le fondement théologique des missions. Coll. La Sphère et la Croix. Paris: Seuil, 1946.

Histoire et Esprit: L'intelligence de l'Ecriture d'après Origène. Coll. Théologie 16. Paris: Aubier-Montaigne, 1950.

"Hommage au Père Auguste Valensin (1879-1953)." In *Annales du Centre Universitaire Méditerranéen.* Vol. VII. Nice: C.U.M., 1954.

"Homo juridicus." Cahiers de notre Jeunesse (March 1943).

"Les humanistes chrétiens du XVe-XVIe siècle et l'herméneutique traditionnelle (suivi d'une discussion)." In *Ermeneutica e Tradizione*, 173-177. Rome: Istituto de Studi filosofici, 1963.

"L'idée chrétienne de l'homme et la recherche d'un homme nouveau." *Etudes* 255 (1946): 3-25, 145-169.

Images de l'abbé Monchanin. Paris: Aubier-Montaigne, 1967.

"*In Memoriam:* Le Père Huby." *Recherches de science religieuse* 35 (1948): 321-324.

Introduction and notes to *Lettres intimes à Auguste Valensin, Bruno de Solages, Henri de Lubac 1919-1955* by Pierre Teilhard de Chardin. Paris: Aubier-Montaigne, 1972.

Introduction to *Le Christianisme de Dante* by A. Valensin. Coll. Théologie 30. Paris: Aubier, 1954.

Introduction to *Dieu aime les païens* by J. Dournes. Coll. Théologie 54. Paris: Aubier, 1963.

Introduction to *Homélies sur l'Exode* by Origen. *Sources chrétiennes,* vol. 16. Paris: Cerf, 1946.

Introduction to *Homélies sur la Genèse* by Origen. *Sources chrétiennes,* vol. 7a. Paris: Cerf, 1976.

Introduction to *Je crois en Dieu* by Paul Claudel, ed. A. Du Sarment. Paris: Gaillimard, 1961.

Introduction to *Maria, Etudes sur la Sainte Vierge,* vol. VI, ed. H. du Manoir. Paris: Beauchesne, 1961.

Introduction to *Mélanges théologiques* by Yves de Montcheuil. Coll. Théologie 9. Paris: Aubier, 1946.

Introduction to *La Messe vécue* by R. Know. Paris: Spes, 1954.

Introduction to *Origène et la "Connaissance mystique"* by Henri Crouzel. Museum Lessianum, section théologique 56, Desclée de Bruxelles, 1961.

Introduction to *Rédemption* by Ch. Meurs. Lyon, 1960.

Introduction to *Saint Ignace de Loyola et la Genèse des Exercices* by Hugo Rahner. Toulouse: Apostolat de la Prière, 1948.

Introduction to *La Satisfaction vicaire, primat de la Miséricorde,* by Ph. De la Trinité. Etudes et documents 36 (1960): 2.

Introduction to *Servir dans l'Eglise. Ignace de Loyola et la Genèse des Exercices* by Hugo Rahner. Paris: Ed. de l'Epi, 1959.

"Kritik an der Kirche." *Michael* 11/2 (1953): 4.

Lettres de M. Étienne Gilson Adressées au P. Henri de Lubac et commentées par celui-ci. Paris: Cerf, 1986.

"Lettres échangées entre M. Blondel et J. Wehrlé sur la question biblique." *Bulletin de littérature ecclésiastique* 44 (1963): 117-136.

Lettres intimes de Teilhard de Chardin à August Valensin, Bruno de Solages, Henri de Lubac, André Ravier. Avant-propos et commentées par Henri de Lubac. Paris: Fayard, 1974.

"Liminaire." In *L'Eglise de Vatican II,* ed. G. Barauna, 25-31. Coll. Unam Sanctam, vol. 51b. Paris: Cerf, 1967.

La Littérature et le Spirituel, vol. I, La Mêlée littéraire, by A. Blanchet. Paris: Aubier, 1959.

"Lumen Gentium and the Fathers." In *Vatican II: An Interfaith Appraisal,* ed. John H. Miller, C.S.C., 153-175. Notre Dame: University of Notre Dame Press, 1966.

La Lumière du Christ. Coll. Le Témoignage chrétien. Le Puy: Mappus, 1941, 1942.

"La malfaisance de Rousseau." *Cité nouvelle* (June 1944): 637-645.

Preface and commentary to *Correspondance,* by M. Blondel — A. Valensin. Paris: Aubier-Montaigne, 1965.

Preface and commentary to *Correspondance* by M. Blondel — P. Teilhard de Chardin. Paris: Beauchesne, 1965.

"Marie de l'Incarnation et la Sainte Vierge." In *Maria.* Vol. III, ed. H. du Manoir, 183-204. Paris: Beauchesne, 1954.

"Meditation on the Church." In *Vatican II: An Interfaith Appraisal,* ed. John H. Miller, C.S.C., 258-266. Notre Dame: University of Notre Dame Press, 1966.

Méditation sur l'Eglise. Coll. Théologie 27. Paris: Aubier, 1953; 2nd ed. rev. and aug. [ET: *The Splendour of the Church.* Translated by Michael Mason. New York: Sheed and Ward, 1956; *The Splendor of the Church.* San Francisco: Ignatius Press, 1986.]

"Méditation sur le principe de la vie morale." *Revue apologétique* 65 (1937): 257-266.

Mémoire sur l'occasion de mes écrits. Namur: Culture et Vérité, 1989. [ET: *At the Service of the Church: Henri de Lubac Reflects on the Circumstances that Occasioned His Writings.* San Francisco: Communio Books, Ignatius Press, 1993.]

"Una messa a punto di Pére de Lubac sull'interpretazione di Teilhard de Chardin." *Testimonianze* (Firenze) 53 (1963): 193-204.

"Moehler et sa doctrine de l'Eglise." *L'Union apostolique.* October 1939.

"Le motif de la création dans *L'Être et les êtres* de Maurice Blondel." *Nouvelle revue théologique* 65 (1938): 220-225.

Le Mystère du Surnaturel. Coll. Théologie 64 (Paris: Aubier, 1965). [ET: *The Mystery of the Supernatural.* Translated by Rosemary Sheed. New York: Herder and Herder, 1967.]

"Le Mystère du Surnaturel." *Recherches de science religieuse* 36 (1949): 80-121.

"Mystique naturelle et mystique chrétienne." *Bulletin Saint Jean-Baptiste* 4 (1964): 5-21.

"The Mystique of Nietzsche." *The Month* 989 (1950): 18-37.

"Nature and Grace." In *The Word in History,* ed. T. Patrick Burke, 24-40. New York: Sheed and Ward, 1966.

"The New Man — The Marxist and the Christian View." *The Dublin Review* 442 (1948): 5-35.

"Nietzsche et Kierkegaard." *Cité nouvelle* (January 1942): 1-25.

"Nos tentations à l'égard de l'Eglise." *Revue de l'action populaire* 61 (1952): 481-498.

"Note sur saint Augustin, De. Lib. arbitrio, III, 20, 56." In *Augustinus magister.* Vol. III. Congrès International Augustinien. Paris: September 1954; *Etudes Augustiniennes,* 1955.

Notice sur la vie et les œuvres de Georges Chevrot. Institut de France, 1959.

"La notion du bien et du mal moral dans le bouddhisme." *Rythme du monde* 28 (1054): 222-243.

"La notion du bien et du mal moral dans le bouddhisme, et spécialement dans l'amidisme." In *Les Morales non-chrétiennes. Journées "Ethnologie et Chrétienté,* 52-74. Coll. Rythmes du Monde. Bruges-Paris: Abbaye de Saint-André, 1954.

"Un nouveau 'front' religieux." In *Israël et la foi chrétienne,* ed. J. Chaine, L. Richard, and F. Bonsirven, 9-40. Fribourg (Suisse): Librairie de L'Université, 1942.

"On the Death of Cardinal Daniélou." *Communio* (U.S.) 2 (1975): 93-95.

"Origène et saint Thomas d'Aquin." *Recherches de science religieuse* 36 (1949): 602-603.

"L'origine de la religion." In *Essai d'une Somme catholique contre les Sans-Dieu.* Paris: Spes, 1937. Reproduced in *Essai sur Dieu l'Homme et l'Univers,* 237-267. Published under the direction and with an introduction by B. de La Saudée. Paris: Casterman, 1937; 4th edition, Paris: La Colombe, 1957, 283-312.

"Our Temptations Concerning the Church." In *Mission and Witness: The Life of the Church,* ed. P. J. Burns. Westminster, Md.: Newman Press, 1964.

"Le paradoxe de l'homme ignoré des gentils." In *A la rencontre de Dieu; mémorial Albert Gelin,* ed. M. Jorjon et al., 397-414. Paris: X. Mappus, 1961.

"Paradoxe de la souffrance." *Promesses* 50 (1961): 22.

Paradoxe et Mystère de l'Eglise. Paris: Aubier-Montaigne, 1967. [ET: *The Church: Paradox and Mystery.* Trans. James R. Dunne. New York: Alba House, 1969.]

Paradoxes. Suivi de: *Nouveaux paradoxes.* Paris: Seuil, 1959. [ET: *(Nouveaux Paradoxes): Further Paradoxes.* Translated by Ernest Beaumont. Westminster,

Md: The Newman Press, 1958; *Paradoxes of Faith*. San Francisco: Ignatius Press, 1986.]

"The Particular Churches in the Universal Church." *Homiletic and Pastoral Review* 82 (1982): 11-17.

"Patriotisme et nationalisme." *Vie intellectuelle*. 25 January 1933, 283-300.

"Le pélerinage de Paul VI à Jérusalem 1964." *Christus* 41 (January 1964): 96-102.

La pensée religieuse du Père Teilhard de Chardin. Paris: Aubier, 1962 [ET: *The Religion of Teilhard de Chardin*. Translated by René Hague. New York: Desclee Co., 1967.]

"Le personallisme du Père Teilhard de Chardin." *Bulletin de l'Union catholique des Scientificques français* 64 (1961): 3-12.

Petit catéchèse sur La 'nature' et La 'grâce'. Paris: Communio-Fayard, 1980. [ET: *A Brief Catechesis on Nature and Grace*. Translated by Richard Arnandez. San Francisco: Ignatius Press, 1984.]

"Petrine Office and Particular Churches." *International Catholic Review: Communio* 1/2 (1972): 220-229.

Pic de la Mirandole: études et discussions. Paris: Aubier Montaigne, 1974.

"Pierre Rousselot: Petit théorie du développement du dogme." *Recherches de science religieuse* 53 (1965): 355-390.

Pierre Teilhard de Chardin: Lettres d'Egypte. Edited with a preface by Henri de Lubac. Paris: Aubier-Montaigne, 1963.

La posterité spirituelle de Joachim de Flore. Vols. I and II. Paris: Lethielleux, 1983.

"Pour le Christ et la Bible." *Vie spirituelle* (June 1942): 542-550; (September 1942): 201-212.

"Le pouvoir de l'Eglise en matière temporelle." *Revue des sciences religieuses* 12 (1932): 329-354.

Preface and notes to "Petit théorie du developpement du dogme" by Pierre Rousselot. *Recherches de science religieuse* 53/3 (1965): 355-390.

Preface to *La mystique et les mystiques* by A. Ravier. Paris: Desclée de Brouwer, 1965.

La prière du Père Teilhard de Chardin. 2nd edition. Paris: Fayard, 1968. [ET: *Teilhard de Chardin: The Man and His Meaning*. Translated by René Hague. New York: Hawthorn Books, 1965]

"La prière du Père Teilhard de Chardin." *Ecclesia* 166 (1963): 27-37.

"Le problème du développement du dogme." *Recherches de science religieuse* 35 (1948): 130-160.

"Proudhon anticlérical." *Cité nouvelle* (February 1943): 309-332.

"Proudhon contre le mythe de la Providence." In *Les Traditions socialistes françaises*. *Cahiers du Rhône*. Vol. 16, 65-89. Neuchatel: La Baconnière, 1944.

"Qu'est-ce que la mystique, Cahiers de la nouvelle journée." *Livres et Revues* 17 (1925): 405-406.

"Quid significet Ecclesiam esse mysterium?" (*Communicatio*, 26 September 1966). In *Acta Congressus Internationalis de Theologia Concilii Vaticani II,* ed. E. Dhanis/A. Schönmetzer, 25-36. Roma: Typ. polygl. Vaticanis, 26 September–1 October 1966.

Recherches dans la foi: trois études sur Origène, saint Anselme et la philosophie chrétienne. Paris: Beauchesne, 1979.

"Réflexions sur l'idée de Dieu." *Cité nouvelle* (February 1942): 339-349.

"Remarques sur l'histoire du mot 'surnaturel'." *Nouvelle revue théologique* 61 (1934): 225-249, 350-370.

La rencontre du Bouddhism et de l'Occident. Coll. Théologie 24. Paris: Aubier-Montaigne, 1952.

"La rencontre de 'superadditum' et 'supernaturales' dans la théologie médiévale." *Revue du moyen âge Latin* 1 (1945): 27-34.

"La 'res sacramenti' chez Gerhoh de Reichersberg." In *Mélanges L. Vaganay,* 35-42. Lyon: Facultés catholiques, 1948.

Résistence chrétienne à l'antisemitisme. Souvenirs 1940-1944. Paris: Feyard, 1988.

La Révélation divine. Paris: Cerf, 1968; 3rd ed. rev. and enlarged, 1983. Commentary on the Introduction and chapter one of the Dogmatic Consititution on Divine Revelation, *Dei Verbum.*

"Rôle providentiel de l'Eglise visible pour le salut des âmes." In *Actes du IIᵉ Congrès national de l'Union Missionaire du Clergé de France.* Supplément à la Revue de l'U.M.C. (1933): 37-54.

"Le sage selon Charles de Bovelles." In *Mélanges offerts à M. D. Chenu.* Paris: Vrin, 1967.

"Saint Grégoire et la grammaire." *Recherches de science religieuse* 48 (1960): 185-226.

"Saint Thomas: Compendium theologiae, c. 104." *Recherches de science religieuse* 36 (1949): 300-305.

"Les secrets arrachés aux sables de Gobi." *Etudes* 217 (1933): 641-664.

"Sens spirituel." *Recherches de science religieuse* 36 (1949): 542-576.

La spiritualité des Ursulines de l'Union romaine. Lyon: Lescuyer, 1959.

"Sur le chapître XIVᵉ du 'Proslogion' (Dieu prouvé et Dieu trouvé)." In *spicilegium Beccense. Congrès international du IXᵉ Centenaire de l'arrivée d'anselme au Bec,* 295-312. Vol. I. Paris: Vrin, 1959.

Sur les chemins de Dieu. Paris: Aubier, 1956. [ET: *The Discovery of God.* Translated by Alexander Dru. New York: P. J. Kenedy & Sons, 1960.]

"Sur la philosophie chrétienne." *Nouvelle revue théologique* 63 (1936): 225-253.

"Sur un vieux distique: La doctrine du 'quadruple sens'." In *Mélanges Cavallera,* 347-366. Toulouse: Institute Catholique, 1948.

Surnaturel. Etudes historiques. Coll. Théologie 8. Paris: Aubier, 1946.

"Teilhard de Chardin in the Context of Renewal." In *Renewal of Religious Thought*, ed. H. L. Shook. New York: Herder and Herder, 1968.

"Teilhard de Chardin in the Context of Renewal." *Communio* (U.S.) 15 (1988): 361-375.

"Teilhard de Chardin Sicht des Todes." *Dokumente* 4 (1962): 255-263.

Teilhard et notre temps. Coll. Foi vivante. Aubier, 1971.

Teilhard, missionnaire et apologiste. Toulouse: Prière et vie, 1966. [ET: *Teilhard Explained.* Translated by Anthony Buono. New York: Paulist Press, 1968.]

Teilhard posthume. Réflexions et souvenirs. Paris: Fayard, 1977.

"Témoignage de H. de Lubac." In *L'abbé Jules Monchanin*, 123. Coll. Eglise vivante. Paris: Casterman, 1960.

"Textes alexandrins et bouddhiques." *Recherches de science religieuse* 27 (1937): 336-351.

Théologie dans l'histoire. Paris: Desclée de Brouwer, 1990. 2 vols. [ET: *Theology in History.* San Francisco: Ignatius Press, 1996.]

Théologies d'occasion. Paris: Desclée de Brouwer, 1984. [ET: *Theological Fragments.* San Francisco: Ignatius Press, 1989.]

"The Total Meaning of Man and of the World: Two Interrelated Problems." *Communio* (U.S.) 17 (1990): 613-616.

"Tradition et nouveauté dans la position du problème de Dieu chez le P. Teilhard de Chardin." In *De Deo in Philosophia S. Thomae et in hodierna Philosophia* (Acta VI Congressus Thomistici Internationalis). Vol. II, 212-220. Roma: off. Libri Catholici, 1966.

Trois jésuits nous parlent: Yves de Montcheuil 1899-1944, Charles Nicolet 1897-1961, Jean Zupan 1899-1968. Paris: P. Lethielleux, 1980. [ET: *Three Jesuits Speak: Yves de Montcheuil, 1899-1944, Charles Nicolet, 1897-1961, Jean Zupan, 1899-1968.* San Francisco: Ignatius Press, 1987.]

" 'Typologie' et 'Allegorisme'." *Recherches de science religieuse* 34 (1947): 180-226.

"Unam Sanctam. Travaux théologiques sur l'Eglise." *Etudes* 232 (1937): 507-511.

"L'unité des chrétiens." *Croix de Lyon.* 30 January 1935, 1-2.

The Un-Marxian Socialist: A Study of Proudhon. New York: Hippocreme Books, 1978.

"Le VIᵉ Congrès de l'histoire des religions." *La vie Catholique.* 5 October 1935, 9.

"Versuchung eines Christen." *Michael* (January 1953): 4.

"La vie et les travaux de Mgr. Chevrot." *Documentation Catholique* 57 (1960): 1163-1176.

"Virtus proudhoniennes." *Cité nouvelle* (April 1943): 697-720.

Vocation de la France. Coll. Le Témoignage chrétien. Le Puis: Mappus, 1942.

"Witness of Christ in the Church: Hans Urs von Balthasar." Translated by H. Emery. *Communio* (U.S.) 2 (1975): 228-249.

"Zum katholischen Dialog mit Karl Barth." *Dokumente* 6 (1958): 448-454.

Selected Works on Henri de Lubac

D'Ambrosio, Marcellino. "Henri de Lubac and the Critique of Scientific Exegesis." *Communio* (U.S.) 19 (Fall 1992): 365-388.

―――. "Henri de Lubac and the Recovery of the Traditional Hermeneutic." Ph.D. dissertation, Catholic University of America, 1991.

Azria, Régine. "La Deuxième Guerre mondiale et les Juifs entre histoire et mémoire." *Archives de sciences sociales des religions* 34 (1989): 167-179.

Balthasar, Hans Urs von. "The Achievement of Henri de Lubac." *Thought* 51 (1976): 7-49.

―――. "Henri de Lubac: L'œuvre organique d'une vie." *Nouvelle revue théologique* 98 (1975): 897-913; 99 (1976): 33-59.

Balthasar, Hans Urs von and G. Chantraine. *Le Cardinal de Lubac: l'homme et son œuvre.* Paris: Lethielleux, 1983.

Beisser, Friedrich. "Die Antwort der Konkordienformel auf die Frage nach dem Verhältnis von Natur und Gnade." *Kerygma und Dogma* 26 (1980): 213-229.

Benedetti, G. "La teologia del Mistero in Henri de Lubac." In *Il Mistero del Soprannaturale* by Henri de Lubac. Italian translation, VII-LI. Bologna: Il Mulino, 1967.

―――. "La teologia del soprannaturale in Henri de Lubac." In *Agostinismo e teologia moderna* by Henri de Lubac. Italian translation, VII-XLIII. Bologna: Il Mulino, 1968.

―――. "L'antropologia cristiana nella riflessione teologica di Henri de Lubac." In *La dimensione antropologica della teologia,* ed. A. Marranzini, 439-457. Milano: Ancora, 1971.

Berranger, Olivier de. "Des paradoxes au Mystère chez J. H. Newman et H. de Lubac." *Revue des sciences philosophiques et théologiques* 78 (1994): 45-79.

Bertoldi, Francesco. "Henri de Lubac on Dei verbum." Translated by Mandy Murphy. *Communio* (U.S.) 17 (Spring 1990): 88-94.

―――. "The Religious Sense in Henri de Lubac." *Communio* (US) 16 (Spring 1989): 6-31.

Berzosa Martínez, Raúl. "La teología del sobrenatural en los escritos Henri de Lubac: Estudio histórico-teológico, 1931-1980." *Scripta Theologica* 24 (1992): 365-366. Also in *Revista Augustiniana* 32 (1991): 1277-1279.

Bird, Th. E., ed., *Modern Theologians, Christians and Jews: Introduction to the Works of Martin Buber, John Courtney Murray, Joseph Hromádka, Bernard Häring, Edward Schillebeeckx, John A. Robinson, Bernard Lonergan, John Harwood Hick, Abraham Joshua Heschel, Henri de Lubac.* London: University of Notre Dame Press; New York: Association Press, 1967.

Bouillard, Henri. "Le Père de Lubac à l'Institut." *Etudes* 209 (1958): 414-415.

Boyer, Charles. "Note sur 'le mystère du Surnaturel' du Père H. de Lubac [1965]." *Gregorianum* 48/1 (1967): 130-132.

Burke, Dennis Joseph. "The Prophetic Mission of Henri de Lubac: A Study of His Theological Anthropology and Its Function in the Renewal of Theology." Ph.D. dissertation, Catholic University, 1967.

Certeau, M. de. "Exégèse, théologie et spiritualité." *Revue d'ascétique et de mystique* 36 (1960): 357-371.

Chantraine, George. "Beyond Modernity and Postmodernity: The Thought of Henri de Lubac." *Communio* (U.S.) 17 (Summer 1990): 207-219.

Chantraine, Georges. "Cardinal Henri de Lubac (1896-1991)." *Communio* 18 (Fall 1991): 297-303.

Chapman, Mark E. "De Lubac's Catholicism through Lutheran Eyes: Appreciation, Application, Convergence." *One in Christ* 29/4 (1993): 286-301.

Ciola, Nicola. *Paradosso e mistero in Henri de Lubac.* Roma: Libreria editrice della Pontificia Universita lateranse, 1980.

Connolly, James M. *The Voices of France.* New York: The Macmillan Company, 1961.

Cuttat, Jacques A. "Fait Bouddhique et fait Chrétien selon l'œuvre du Père de Lubac." In *L'Homme devant Dieu: Mélanges offerts au Père Henri de Lubac, Perspectives D'Aujourd'hui.* Coll. Théologie 58. Paris: Aubier, 1964.

Donnelly, P. J. "The Surnaturel of P. Henri de Lubac, S.J." *Proceedings of the Catholic Theological Society of America* 3 (1948): 108-121.

Eterovic, N. *Cristianesimo e religioni secondo Henri de Lubac.* Roma: Città Nuova, 1981.

Figura, Michael. *Der Anruf der Gnade: Über die Beziehung des Menschen zu Gott nach Henri de Lubac.* Einsiedeln: Johannes Verlag, 1979.

―――. "Theologie aus der Fülle des Glaubens: Zum Tod von Henri de Lubac." *Internationale Katholische Zeitschrift "Communio"* 20/6 (1991): 540-549.

Flick, Maurizio. "Il problema della sviluppo del dogma nella teologia contemporanea." *Gregorianum* 33 (1952): 5-23.

Gilson, Etienne. *Lettres de M. Etienne Gilson adressées au P. Henri de Lubac et commentées par celui-ci.* Paris: Editions du Cerf, 1986. [ET: *Letters of Etienne Gilson to Henri de Lubac.* San Francisco: Ignatius Press, 1988.]

Gracias, Agnelo. "The Spiritual Sense of Scripture according to Henri de Lubac." S.T.D. dissertation, Gregorian University, 1975.

Granfield, Patrick. *Theologians at Work.* New York: The Macmillan Co., 1967.

Grenier, Maximilian, ed. "Henri de Lubac." *Internationale Katholische Zeitschrift "Communio"* 22/2 (1993): 99-163.

Guillet, J. "Le cardinal Henri de Lubac." *Etudes* 358 (February 1983): 280-283.

―――. "Le sens de l'Ecriture: exégèse d'autrefois, recherches d'aujourd'hui." *Recherches de science religieuse* 80 (1992): 359-372.

Haggerty, Janet. "The Centrality of Paradox in the Work of Henri de Lubac." Ph.D. dissertation, Fordham, 1987.

Haulotte, Edgar. "Bibliographie du Père Henri de Lubac." In *L'homme devant Dieu,* vol. III, 347-356. Paris: Aubier, 1964.

Henrici, Peter. "On Mystery in Philosophy." *Communio* (U.S.) 19 (Fall 1992): 354-364.

Hidber, Bruno. "Der Mensch vor Gottes Anruf der Liebe: Das Verhältnis von Gott und Mensch im Denken von Henri de Lubac." In *Historia: Memoria Futuri,* ed. R. Tremblay and D. Billy, 403-434. Roma: Editiones Academiae Alphonsianae, 1991.

Komonchak, Joseph A. "Theology and Culture at Mid-century: The Example of Henri de Lubac." *Theological Studies* 51 (1990): 579-602.

Ledure, Y. *Lectures "chrétiennes" de Nietzsche, Maurras, Papini, Scheler, de Lubac, Marcel, Mounier.* Paris: Cerf, 1984.

Léna, Marguerite. "The Sanctity of Intelligence." *Communio* 19 (Fall 1992): 342-353.

Lenk, Martin. *Von des Gottes erkenntnis: natèurliche Theologie im Werk Henri de Lubacs.* Frankfurt am Main: Knecht, 1993.

Lindsay, Austin J. "De Lubac's Images of the Church: A Study of Christianity in Dialogue." Ph.D. dissertation, Catholic University, 1974.

Llanes Maestre, Jose Luis. "La teología como saber de totalidad: en torno al proyecto teológico de Henri de Lubac." *Revista Española de Teología* 48/2 (1988): 149-192.

Maier, Eugen. *Einigung der Welt in Gott: Das Katholische bei Henri de Lubac.* Einsiedeln: Johannes Verlag, 1983.

Marthaler, Bernard L. "Henri de Lubac." In *The New Day: Catholic Theologians of the Renewal,* ed. Wm. Jerry Boney and Lawrence E. Molumby, 9-19. Richmond, Va.: John Knox Press, 1968.

McBrien, Richard. "Review of Les églises particulières dans l'Eglise universelle." *Theological Studies* 34 (March 1973): 167-168.

McKenzie, John L. "A Chapter in the History of Spiritual Exegesis: de Lubac's *Histoire et Esprit.*" *Theological Studies* 12 (1951): 365-381.

McNally, R. "Medieval Exegesis." *Theological Studies* 22 (1961): 445-454.

McPartlan, Paul. " 'You Will be Changed Into Me': Unity and Limits in de Lubac's Thought." *One in Christ* 30/1 (1994): 50-60.

———. *The Eucharist Makes the Church: Henri de Lubac and John Zizioulas in Dialogue.* Edinburgh: T & T Clark, 1993.

———. "Eucharistic Ecclesiology." *One in Christ* 22/4 (1986): 214-331.

Milbank, John. "An Essay against Secular Order." *Journal of Religious Ethics* 15 (1987): 199-224.

Moingt, Joseph, ed. "Henri de Lubac, 1896-1991." *Recherches de science religieuse* 80 (1992): 324-408.

Moltmann, Jürgen. "Christian Hope: Messianic or Transcendent: A Theological Discussion with Joachim of Fiore and Thomas Aquinas." Trans. and ed. by M. D. Meeks. *Horizons* 12 (1985): 328-348.

Mondin, Battista. "Henri de Lubac e la teologia storica." In *I grandi teologi del secolo ventesimo*. Vol. I, *I teologi cattolici*, 227-266. Turis: Boria, 1969.

Moretto, Giovanni. "Destino dell'uomo e corpo mistico: Blondel, de Lubac e il Concilio Vaticano II." *Protestantesimo* 50/2 (1995): 166-167.

Nergri, G. *P. Henri de Lubac. Una teologia spirituale*. Roma: Pontificia Università Urbaniana, 1982.

Neufeld, Karl Heinz. "Henri de Lubac S.J. als Konzilstheologe." *Theologisch-Praktische Quartalschrift* 134 (1986): 149-159.

―――. "In the Service of the Council: Bishops and Theologians at the Second Vatican Council (for Cardinal Henri de Lubac on his 90th Birthday)." Translated by R. Sway. In *Vatican II: Assessment and Perspectives*, 1, ed. R. Latourelle, 74-105. Mahwah: Paulist Press, 1996.

―――. "Die Gabe zu H. de Lubacs "Surnaturel" in Neuausgabe." *Zeitschrift für Katholische Theologie* 114/1 (1992): 59-65.

―――. "Kirche und Kardinal: Zum Kirchenbild Henri de Lubac." *Stimmen der Zeit* 203 (1985): 859-861.

―――. "Kirche zum Leben." *Zeitschrift für Katholische Theologie* 116/2 (1994): 188-192.

Neufeld, H. and M. Sales. *Bibliographie Henri de Lubac, S.J. (1925-1970)*. Einsiedeln: Johannes Verlag, 1971.

Pambrum, James. "The Presence of God: A Study into the Apologetic of Henri de Lubac." Ph.D. dissertation, University of St. Michael's College (Canada), 1979.

Parente, P. "Nuove tendenze teologiche." *L'Osservatore Romano*, 9-10 February 1942, 1.

Pelchat, Marc. *L'ecclésiologie de Henri de Lubac*. Roma: P.U.G., 1986.

―――. *L'Eglise mystère de communion: l'ecclésiologie dans l'œuvre de Henri de Lubac*. Montreal: Editions Paulines; Paris: Mediaspaul, 1988.

Perego, A. "La teologia nueva." *Ciencia y Fé* (1949): 7-30.

―――. "La nuova Teologia. Seguardo d'insieme alla luce dell'Enciclica 'Humani generis'." *Divus Thomas* 53 (1950): 436-465.

Poehlmann, H. G. "Henri de Lubac." In *Gottes Denken: Prägende evangelische und catholische Theologen der Gegenwart 12 Porträits*, 206-228. Hamburg: Reingeck, 1984.

La Potterie, Ignace de. "Die Lesung der Heiligen Schrift 'im Geist': ist die patristische Weise der Bibellesung heute möglich?" *Internationale Katholische Zeitschrift "Communio"* 15/3 (1986): 209-224.

Prévotat, Jacques. "Quatre jésuites devant le totalitarisme nazi" [G. Fessard, J. Lebreton, H. de Lubac, and H. du Passage]. In *Spiritualité, théologie et résistance,* ed. P. Bolle and J. Godel, 98-120. Grenoble: Presses universitaires de Grenoble, 1987.

Rondet, Henri. "Le mystère du surnaturel." *Recherches de science religieuse* 54/1 (1966): 69-73.

Roques. R. "Analyses et comptes rendus." *Revue de l'histoire des religions* 158 (1960): 217-219.

Russell, Ralph. "Humani generis and the 'spiritual' sense of Scripture." *Downside Review* 69/215 (1950-1951): 1-15.

Russell, William C. "Henri de Lubac." In *Modern Theologians: Christians and Jews,* ed. Thomas E. Bird, 183-199. Notre Dame: The University of Notre Dame Press, 1967.

Russo, Antonio. *Henri de Lubac: Theologia E Dogma Nella Storia: L'influsso di Blondel.* Roma: Edizioni Studium, 1990.

Sales, Michel. *Der Mensch und die Gottesidee bei Henri de Lubac.* Coll. Kriterien 46. Einsiedeln, 1978.

Sales, M. and Neufeld, K. H. *Bibliographie Henri de Lubac S.J. 1925-1974.* Einsiedeln: Johannes Verlag, 2nd ed., 1974.

Santos Hernández, Angel. "Cardenal Henri de Lubac (1896-1991): nota biobibliográfia." *Estudios Eclesiásticos* 66 (1991): 327-335.

Sauser, Ekkart. "Von Bild und Schatten: Gedanken aus Origenes und Bernard von Clairvaux." In *Für Kirche und Heimat,* ed. J. Bauer, J. Donner, H. Dopf, et al., 291-301. Wien: Herold Verlag, 1985.

Sayes, José Antonio. "La autonomía de las realidades temporales y el orden sobrenatural: A propósito de H. De Lubac y le movimiento "comunión y liberación." *Estudios Eclesiásticos* 64 (1989): 465-494.

Schindler, David L. "Christology, Public Theology, and Thomism: Henri de Lubac, Balthasar, and Murray." In *The Future of Thomism,* ed. D. Hudson and D. Moran, 247-264. Notre Dame: University of Notre Dame Press, 1992.

Schindler, David L., ed. "The Theology of Henri de Lubac: Communio at Twenty Years." *Communio* (U.S.) 19 (Fall 1992): 332-509.

Schnackers, Hubert. *Kirche als Sakrament und Mutter.* Regensburger Studien zur Theologie 22. Frankfurt am Main/Bern/Las Vegas, 1979.

Sesboüé, B. "Le surnaturel chez Henri de Lubac: un conflit autour d'une théologie." *Recherches de science religieuse* 80 (1992): 373-408.

Snellgrove, David. "Buddhist Morality." *Downside Review* 74/237 (1956): 234-253.

Sommet, J. "Catholicisme et résistance." *Recherches de science religieuse* 80 (1992): 327-344.

Sudbrack, Josef. "Die Geist-Einheit von Heilsgeheimnis und Heilserfahrung." In *Das Mysterium und die Mystik*, ed. J. Sudbrack, 9-55. Wurzburg: Echter-Verlag, 1974.

Tilliette, Xavier. "Henri de Lubac: The Legacy of a Theologian." *Communio* (U.S.) 19 (Fall 1992): 332-341.

Trapani, G. *La visione dell'uomo nel dialogo di Henri de Lubac con gli umanesimi moderni.* Roma: P.U.G., 1985.

Trethowan, Illtyd. "The Supernatural End: P. De Lubac's New Volumes [Augustinisme et théologie moderne: Le mystère du surnaturel]." *Downside Review* 84 (1966): 397-407.

Valadie, P. "Dieu présent: une entrée dans la théologie du Cardinal de Lubac." *Recherches de science religieuse* 80 (1992): 345-358.

Vanneste, Alfred. "Le mystère du surnaturel." *Ephemerides theologicae lovanienses* 44 (1968): 179-190.

————. "Saint Thomas et le problème du surnaturel." *Ephemerides theologicae lovanienses* 64/4 (1988): 348-370.

————. "La théologie du surnaturel dans les écrits de Henri de Lubac." *Ephemerides theologicae lovanienses* 69/4 (1993): 273-314.

Villain. "Un grand livre œcumenique: *Catholicisme*." In *L'homme devant Dieu*, vol. III. Coll. Théologie, vol. 58. Paris: Aubier, 1964.

Vorgrimler, Herbert. "Henri de Lubac." In *Bilan de la théologie du XX siècle*, ed. Robert Vander Gucht and Herbert Vorgrimler, vol. 2, *La théologie chrétienne: les grands courants,* 806-820. Paris: Casterman, 1970.

Wagner, Jean-Pierre. *La théologie fondamentale selon Henri de Lubac.* Coll. Cogitatio fiedi. Paris: Cerf, 1997.

Walsh, Christopher James. "Henri de Lubac and the Ecclesiology of the Postconciliar Church: An Analysis of His Later Writings (1965-1991)." Ph.D. dissertation, The Catholic University of America, 1993.

————. "De Lubac's Critique of the Postconciliar Church." *Communio* (U.S.) 19 (Fall 1992): 404-432.

Wojtowicz, Marek. "Il Compito Della Teologia Fondamentale Secondo Henri de Lubac." Th.D. dissertation, Pontificia Universitas Gregoriana, 1992.

Wood, Susan. "The Church as the Social Embodiment of Grace in the Ecclesiology of Henri de Lubac." Ph.D. dissertation, Marquette University, 1986.

————. "The Nature-grace Problematic within Henri de Lubac's Christological Paradox." *Communio* (U.S.) 19 (Fall 1992): 389-403.

Zofia, J. S. *Pznanie Boga w ujeciu Henri de Lubaca.* Lublin, Nauk: Katol. Uniw., 1973.

Selected Related Bibliography

Allo, M. B. "."Extrinsicism' et 'historicism'." *Revue thomiste* 12 (September-October 1904): 437-465.

Aubert, Roger. "Discussions récentes autour de la théologie de l'histoire," *Collectanea Mechliniensa* 18 (1948): 129-149.

————. *Le problème de l'acte de foi.* 3rd edition. Louvain: E. Warry, 1958.

————. "Ouverture au monde moderne." *Nouvelle revue théologique* 18 (1953): 161-181.

————. "Le Mysterion d'Origène." *Recherches de science religieuse* 26 (1936): 513-562; 27 (1937): 38-64.

————. "La théologie catholique au milieu du XXe siècle." *Nouvelle revue théologique* 18 (1953): 272-292.

————. "La théologie catholique devant la première moitié du XXe siècle." In *Bilan de la Théologie du XXe Siècle,* ed. Robert Vander Gucht and Herbert Vorgrimler, 423-478. Paris: Casterman, 1970.

————. *Vatican I.* Paris: Editions de l'Orante, 1964.

Balthasar, Hans Urs von. *The Glory of the Lord: A Theological Aesthetics.* Vol. I: Seeing the Form. Translated by Erasmo Leiva-Merikakis. Edited by Joseph Fessio, S.J., and John Riches. Edinburgh: T. and T. Clark, 1984. [Original: *Herrlichkeit: Eine theologische Asthetik* I: *Schau der Gestalt.* Einsiedeln: Johannes Verlag, 1961; 1967.]

————. *Liturgie cosmique.* Translated by L. Lhaumet and H.-A. Prentout. Coll. Théologie 11. Paris: Aubier, 1947.

————. *Retour au centre.* Translated by Robert Givord. Paris: Desclée de Brouwer, 1971.

Barauna, Guilherme, ed. *L'Eglise de Vatican II.* Vol. II, III. Coll. Unam Sanctam, Vol. 51b, 51c. Paris: Editions du Cerf, 1966.

Bedarida, Renee. *Les Armes de l'Esprit. Témoinage chrétien: 1941-1944.* Paris: Editions Ouvrières, 1977.

Bernards, Mattäus. "Zur Lehre von der Kirche als Sakrament." *Munchener Theologische Zeitschrift* 20 (1969): 29-54.

Besret, Bernard. *Incarnation ou eschatologie: contribution à l'histoire du vocabulaire religieux contemporain 1935-1955.* Paris: Cerf, 1964.

Blondel, M. "Histoire et dogme. Les lacunes philosophiques de l'exégèse moderne." In *La Quinzaine* 56/15 (January 1, 1904); 56/16 (February 3, 1904): 145-67, 349-73, 433-58. Reprinted in *Les premiers écrits de Maurice Blondel.* Paris, 1956, 149-228. [ET: *The Letter on Apologetics and History and Dogma.* Translated by Alexander Dru and Illtyd Trethowan, O.S.B. New York: Herder and Herder, 1967.]

————. *Exigences philosophiques du Christianisme.* Paris: Presses Universitaires de France, 1950.

Boff, Leonardo. *Die Kirche als Sakrament im Horizont der Welterfahrung.* Paderborn: Verlag Bonifacius-Druckerei, 1972.

————. *Church, Charism and Power: Liberation Theology and the Institutional Church.* Translated by John W. Diercksmeier. New York: Crossroad, 1985.

Bosworth, William. *Catholicism and Crisis in Modern France: French Catholic Groups at the Threshold of the Fifth Republic.* Princeton: Princeton University Press, 1962.

Bouillard, Henri. *Blondel and Christianity.* Translated by J. M. Sommerville. Washington: Corpus, 1969.

————. *Comprendre ce que l'on croit.* Paris: Aubier, 1971.

————. *Conversion et grâce chez S. Thomas d'Aquin.* Paris: Aubier, 1944.

————. "L'idée du surnaturel et le mystère chrétien." In *L'homme devant Dieu,* vol. III, 153-166. Coll. Théologie, vol. 58. Paris: Aubier, 1964.

————. "L'intention fondamentale de Maurice Blondel et la théologie." *Recherches de science religieuse* 36 (1949): 321-402.

Bouyer, Louis. *The Church of God.* Translated by Charles Underhill Quinn. Chicago: Franciscan Herald Press, 1982. [French original: *L'Eglise de Dieu.* Paris: Cerf, 1970.]

————. "Liturgie et exégèse spirituelle." *La Maison-Dieu* 7 (1946): 27-50.

————. "Le Renouveau des études patristiques." *La vie intellectuelle* (February 1947): 6-25.

Boyer, C. "Qu'est-ce que la théologie?" *Gregorianum* 21 (1940): 255-266.

————. "Sur un article des *Recherches de science religieuse.*" *Gregorianum* 29 (1948): 152-154.

Brown, R. E. *The Sensus Plenior of Sacred Scripture.* Baltimore: St. Mary's University, 1955.

Burghardt, Walter J. "On Early Christian Exegesis." *Theological Studies* 11 (1950): 78-116.

Carroll, Eamon R. "Mary as the New Eve." *Carmelus* 31 (1984): 6-23.

Caryl, J. "Linéaments d'une spiritualité eschatologique." *La vie intellectuelle* 78 (1947): 528-546.

Certeau, M. de. "Exégèse, théologie et spiritualité." *Revue d'ascétique et de mystique* 36 (1960): 357-371.

Chantraine. G. "Catholicité et maternité de l'Eglise." *Nouvelle revue théologique* 94 (1972): 520-536.

Charlier, Celestin. "La lecture sapientielle de la Bible." *Maison Dieu* 12 (1947): 14-52.

Chênevert, Jacques. *L'Eglise dans le commentaire d'Origène sur le Cantiques des Cantiques.* Paris: Desclée de Brouwer, 1969.

Chenu, M. D. "La position de la théologie." *Revue des sciences philosophiques et théologiques* 24 (1935): 232-57.

Congar, Yves. *Christ Our Lady and the Church: A Study in Irenic Theology.* Translated by Henry St. John, O.P. Westminster, Md.: The Newman Press, 1957.

―――. "The Church: The People of God." *Concilium.* Vol. I: Dogma. New York: Paulist Press, 1956, 11-36.

―――. "Dogme Christologique et ecclésiologie: Unité et limites d'un parallèle." In *Sainte Eglise: Etudes et approches ecclésiologiques,* 69-104. Paris: Cerf, 1963.

―――. *L'ecclésiologie du haut moyen age.* Paris: Cerf, 1968.

―――. *L'Eglise de saint Augustin à l'époque moderne.* Paris: Cerf, 1970.

―――. "L'Eglise, sacrement universel du salut." *Eglise vivante* 17 (1965): 339-355.

―――. *A History of Theology.* New York: Doubleday, 1968.

―――. *I Believe in the Holy Spirit.* Vols. I, II, III. Translated by David Smith. New York: Seabury Press, 1983.

―――. "La pensée de Moeller et l'ecclésiologie orthodoxe." *Irénikon* 12 (1935): 321-329.

―――. "Pneumatologie ou "Christomonisme." In *Ecclesia a Spiritu Sancto edocta.* Mélanges G. Philips, 41-63. Bibliotheca ephemeridum theologicarum lovaniensium 27. Gembloux, Belgium: Editions J. Duculot, 1970.

―――. *Sainte Eglise: études et approches ecclésiologiques.* Unam Sanctam 41. Paris: Cerf, 1963.

―――. "Tendances actuelle de la pensée religieuse." *Cahiers du monde nouveau* 4 (1948): 33-50.

―――. *Tradition and Traditions: An Historical and Theological Essay.* London: ET 1966.

―――. *Vrai et fausse reforme dans l'Eglise.* Paris: Cerf, 1950.

Coppens, J. "La problème du sens plenior." *Ephemerides theologicae lovanienses* 34 (1958): 5-10.

Crouzel, Henri. "L'anthropologie d'Origène: de l'arché au telos." In *Arché e Telos: L'Anthropologia di Origene e di Gregorio di Nissa,* 36-57. Studia Patristica mediolanensia 12. Atti del Colioquio Milano, 17-19 Maggio, 1979. Milano: Vita E. Pensiero, 1981.

―――. "Patrologie et renouveau patristique." In *Bilan de la Théologie du XXᵉ siècle,* eds. Robert Vander Gucht and H. Vorgrimler. Vol. 2, *La théologie chrétienne: les grands courants,* 661-683. Paris: Casterman, 1970.

―――. *Virginité et Mariage selon Origène.* Paris: Desclée de Brouwer, 1963.

Daniélou, Jean. "Christianisme et histoire." *Etudes* 255/4 (1947): 399-402.

―――. *The Development of Christian Doctrine before the Council of Nicea.* Vol. I. Translated by John A. Baker. London: Darton, Longman & Todd, 1964.

―――. "Les divers sens de l'Ecriture dans la tradition chrétienne primitive."

Analecta lovaniensia biblica et orientalia. Ser. II. Fasc. 6. Bruges-Paris: De-sclée de Brouwer, 1948: 119-126.

————. *Essai dur le Mystère de l'Histoire.* Paris: Seuil, 1953. [ET: *The Lord of History: Reflections on the Inner Meaning of History.* Translated by Nigel Abercrombie. London: Longmans, 1958.]

————. *From Shadows to Reality: Studies in the Biblical Typology of the Fathers.* Translated by Wulstan Hibberd. London: Burns & Oates, 1960.

————. "Les orientations présentes de la pensée religieuse." *Etudes* 249 (1946): 5-21.

————. *Origène.* Coll. Le génie du christianisme. Paris, 1948.

————. "Saint Irenée et les origines de la théologie de l'histoire." *Recherches de science religieuse* 34 (1947): 227-231.

Delahaye, Karl. *Ecclesia Mater chez les Pères des trois premiers siècles.* Coll. Unam Sanctam 16. Paris: Cerf, 1964.

Deman, T. "Tentatives françaises pour un renouvellement de la théologie." *Revue de l'Université d'Ottawa* 20 (1950): 129-167.

Donnelly, P. J. "On the Development of Dogma and the Supernatural." *Theological Studies* 8 (1947): 470-491, 668-699.

Dubarle, A.-M. "Le sens spirituel de l'Ecriture." *Revue des sciences philosophiques et théologiques* 31 (1947): 41-72.

Dulles, Avery. *A Church to Believe In.* New York: Crossroad, 1982.

————. *Church Membership as a Catholic and Ecumenical Problem.* 1974 Pere Marquette Theology Lecture. Milwaukee: Marquette University Theology Department, 1974.

————. *The Dimensions of the Church.* Westminster, Md.: Newman Press, 1967.

————. *A History of Apologetics.* New York: Corpus Instrumentorum,1971.

————. *Models of Revelation.* New York: Doubleday & Co., 1983.

————. *Revelation Theology: A History.* New York: Seabury Press, 1969.

————. *The Survival of Dogma.* New York: Doubleday & Co., 1971.

Dulles, Avery and Patrick Granfield. *The Church: A Bibliography.* Wilmington, Del.: Michael Glazier, 1985.

Elert, Werner. *Eucharist and Church Fellowship in the First Four Centuries.* St. Louis: Concordia Publishing House, 1966.

Falconi, C., ed. *Documents secrets du Concile, Première session.* Monaco: Editions du Rocher, 1965.

Fenton, Joseph. "The Holy Office Letter on the Necessity of the Catholic Church." *American Ecclesiastical Review* 127 (July-December 1952): 450-461.

Flesseman–van Leer, E. *Tradition and Scripture in the Early Church.* Assen, 1954.

Fouilloux, Etienne. *Les catholiques et l'unité chrétienne du XIXe au XXe siècle: itinéraires européens d'expression française.* Paris: Le Centurion, 1982.

Galvin, John J. "A Critical Survey of Modern Conceptions of Doctrinal Development." *Proceedings of the Catholic Theological Society* (fifth meeting, 1950): 45-63.

Garrigou-Lagrange, Reginald. "La nouvelle théologie où va-t-elle?" *Angelicum* 23 (July-December 1946): 126-145.

Geiselmann, Josef Rupert. "Der Einfluss der Christologie des Konzils von Chalkedon auf die Theologie Johann Adam Möhlers." In *Das Konzil von Chalkedon,* ed. A. Grillmeier and H. Bacht, vol. 3, 341-420. Würzburg, 1954.

———. "J. A. Möhler und die Entwicklung seines Kirchenbegriffs." *Theologische Quartalschrift* 112 (1931): 1-90.

———. *The Meaning of Tradition.* London: Burns & Oates, 1966.

Germond, Henri. "Dialogue théologique." *Revue de théologie et philosophie* 35 (1947): 128-133.

Goppelt, Leonard. *Typos: The Typological Interpretation of the Old Testament in the New.* Translated by Donald H. Madvig. Grand Rapids: William B. Eerdmans, 1982.

Grant, Robert McQueen. *The Letter and the Spirit.* London: SPCK, 1957.

———. *A Short History of the Interpretation of the Bible.* 2nd edition, revised and enlarged. Philadelphia: Fortress Press, 1984.

Grillmeier, Aloys. "Chapter I: Mystery of the Church" and "Chapter II: The People of God." In *Commentary on the Documents of Vatican II,* Vol. II, ed. Heribert Vorgrillmeier, 138-185. New York: Herder and Herder, 1967.

Gutiérrez, Gustavo. *A Theology of Liberation.* New York: Orbis Books, 1973.

Hamer, Jerome. *The Church Is a Communion.* Translated by Ronald Matthews. New York: Sheed and Ward, 1964.

Hanson, R. P. C. *Allegory and Event: A Study of the Sources and Significance of Origen's Interpretation of Scripture.* London: SCM Press, 1959.

International Theological Commission. *Theology, Christology, Anthropology.* Washington, D.C.: U.S. Catholic Conference, April 1983.

Jaki, P. Stanislas. *Les tendances nouvelles de l'ecclésiologie.* Roma: Casa Editrice Herder, 1957.

Keefe, Donald J. "Authority in the Church: An Essay in Historical Theology." *Communio* 7 (1980): 343-363.

———. *Thomism and the Ontological Theology of Paul Tillich.* Leiden: E. J. Brill, 1971.

Kelly, J. N. D. *Early Christian Doctrines.* New York: Harper and Row, 1978.

Kung, Hans. *The Church.* New York: Image Books, 1976.

Labourdette, M.-M. and M.-J. Nicolas. "Autour du 'Dialogue théologique'. *Revue thomiste* 47 (1947): 577-585.

Labourdette, M.-M., J. J. Nicolas, and R. L. Bruckberger. *Dialogue théologique: pièces du débat entre "la Revue Thomiste" d'une part et les R.R. P.P. de Lubac,*

Daniélou, Bouillard, Fessard, von Balthasar, S.J., d'autre part. Saint Maxime: Les Arcades, 1947.

Labourdette, M. "Les enseignements de l'Encyclique." *Revue thomiste* 50 (1950): 32-55.

————. "Fermes propos." *Revue thomiste* 47 (1947): 5-19.

————. "La théologie et ses sources." *Revue thomiste* 46 (1946): 355-371.

Lange, N. R. M. de. *Origen and the Jews.* Cambridge: Cambridge University Press, 1976.

Latourelle, Rene. *Le Christ et l'Eglise, signes du salut.* Montreal: Bellarmin, 1971.

————. *Théologie de la Révélation.* Paris: Desclée de Brouwer, 1963.

Lauriers, M. Guerard des. "La théologie historique et le développement de la théologie." *L'Année théologique* 7 (1946): 276-339.

Le Blond, J. "L'analogie de la verité, réflexions d'un philosophie sur une controverse théologique." *Recherches de sciences religieuse* 34 (1947): 129-41.

Lonergan, Bernard F. *Method in Theology.* New York: The Seabury Press, 1972.

Maritain, Jacques. *On the Church of Christ.* Translated by Joseph W. Evans. Notre Dame: Notre Dame Press, 1973. [Original: *De l'Eglise de Christ,* 1970.]

Marlé, René. *Au cœur de la crise moderniste.* Paris: Aubier, 1960.

Martelet, Gustave. *Les idées maîtresses de Vatican II.* Paris: Desclée de Brouwer, 1966.

————. "De la sacramentalité propre à l'Eglise." *Nouvelle revue théologique* 95 (1973): 25-42.

McCool, Gerald. *Catholic Theology in the Nineteenth Century: The Quest for a Unitary Method.* New York: Seabury, 1977.

McCool, Gerald A. *Catholic Theology in the Nineteenth Century.* New York: Seabury Press, 1977.

McFadden, Thomas M. "The Relationship between Nature and Grace: A Survey of 20th Century Theological Opinion." S.T.D. diss. Catholic University of America, 1963.

Mersch, Emile. *The Theology of the Mystical Body.* Translated by Cyril Vollert. St. Louis: B. Herder Book Co., 1952.

————. *The Whole Christ: The Historical Development of the Doctrine of the Mystical Body in Scripture and Tradition.* Translated by John R. Kelly. Milwaukee: The Bruce Publishing Co., 1938.

Möhler, John Adam. *Die Einheit in der Kirche.* Tubingen: H. Laupp, 1843. [French edition: *L'unité dans l'Eglise.* Paris: Editions du Cerf, 1938.]

————. *Symbolism: Doctrinal Differences between Catholics and Protestants.* New York: The Catholic Publication House, n.d.

Mooney, C. *Teilhard de Chardin and the Mystery of Christ.* New York: Harper & Row, 1966.

Moore, Dom Sebastian. "The Desire of God." *Downside Review* 65 (1947): 246-259.

Mounier, Emmanuel. "Aux avant-postes de la pensée chrétienne." *Esprit* 16 (1947): 436-444.

Mühlen, Heribert. *Der Heilige Geist als Person.* Munsterlische Beitrage zur Theologie, Heft 26. Aschendorff, 1967.

————. *Una mystica Personna.* Munich: Verlag Ferdinand Schöningh, 1967.

Murphy, Roland. "Patristic and Medieval Exegesis — Help or Hindrance?" *Catholic Biblical Quarterly* 43/4 (1981): 505-516.

Nicholas, J. N. "Le sens et la valeur en écclésiologie du parallelisme de structure entre le Christ et l'Eglise." *Angelicum* 43 (1966): 353-358.

Nicolas, M.-J. "Théologie de l'Eglise." *Revue thomiste* 46 (1946): 372-398.

Parain, Brice. "Dialogue théologique." *Le cheval du Troie* (Août-Septembre 1947): 329-339.

Philips, Gerard. *L'Eglise et son Mystère au 2ᵉ concile du Vatican: Histoire, texte et commentaire de la constitution Lumen Gentium.* Vol. 1, 2. Desclée et Cic., 1967-1968.

————. "L'Eglise sacrement et mystère." *Ephemerides théologicae lovanienses* 42 (1966): 405-414.

Pius XII. Encyclical *Humani Generis* (1950). *Acta apostolicae sedis* 42 (1950): 561-578. [ET: In *The Papal Encyclicals,* Vol. 4 (1939-1958), ed. Claudia Carlen, 175-184. Wilmington, N.C.: McGrath, 1981.]

————. "Il venerato Discorso del Sommo Pontifice alla XXIX Congregazione Generale della Compagnia di Gesu." *Osservatore Romano,* 18 September 1946.

Rahner, Karl. "The Faith Instinct." *Theological Investigations,* vol. IX, 227-241. New York: Herder and Herder, 1972.

————. "Membership of the Church." *Theological Investigations,* vol. II, 1-88. Baltimore: Helicon, 1963.

————. "Quelques réflexions sur les principes constitutionnels de l'Eglise." In *L'Episcopat et l'Eglise universelle,* ed. Yves Congar, 541-562. Coll. Unam Sanctam 39. Paris: Cerf, 1962.

Rahner, Karl and Joseph Ratzinger. *Revelation and Tradition.* New York: Herder and Herder, 1966.

Ratzinger, Joseph. *Daughter Zion.* Translated by John M. McDermott. San Francisco: Ignatius Press, 1977.

————. "Dogmatic Constitution on Divine Revelation." In *Commentary on the Documents of Vatican II,* vol. III, ed. Herbert Vorgrimler, 155-272. New York: Herder and Herder, 1969.

————. "The Ecclesiology of Vatican II." *Origins* 15/22 (November 14, 1985): 370-376.

————. *Le nouveau peuple de Dieu.* Translated by R. Givord and H. Bourboulon. Aubier, 1971.

Ratzinger, Joseph Cardinal and Hans Urs von Balthasar. *Marie, première Eglise.* Translated by Robert Givord. Montreal: Editions Paulines, 1981.

Ratzinger, Joseph Cardinal with Vittono Messori. *The Ratzinger Report.* San Francisco: Ignatius Press, 1985.

Riga, Peter. "The Ecclesiology of John Adam Möhler." *Theological Studies* 22 (1961): 563-587.

Rikhof, Herwi. *The Concept of Church: A Methodological Inquiry into the Use of Metaphors in Ecclesiology.* Shepherdstown, W.Va.: Patmos Press, 1981.

Romero, A. Esteban. "Nota bibliografica sobre la llamada 'Teologia nueva.'" *Revista Española Teologia* 9 (1949): 303-318, 527-546.

Rondet, Henri. *De Vatican I à Vatican II.* Paris: P. Lethellieux, 1959.

————. "Nouvelle Théologie." *Sacramentum Mundi,* vol. 4, 234-236. New York: Herder and Herder, 1969

Ronquette, Robert. "L'encyclique *Humani Generis.*" *Etudes* 267 (1950): 108-116.

Rousseau, O. "Théologie patristique et théologie moderne." *La vie spirituelle* 336 (1949): 70-87.

Rousselot, Pierre. "Petit théorie du développement du dogme (1909)." *Recherches de science religieuse* 53 (1965): 374-375.

————. "Les yeux de la foi." *Recherches de science religieuse* 1 (1910): 241-259, 444-475.

Scheffczyk, L. "Die Idee der Einheit von Schöpfung und Erlösung." *Theologische Quartalschrift* 140 (1960): 19-37.

Schillebeeckx, Edward. *Approches théologiques.* Vol. 3, 4. Bruxelles: Editions du CEP, 1969.

————. "The Church and Mankind." *Concilium.* Vol. I: *The Church and Mankind.* Edited by Edward Schillebeeckx. Glen Rock, N.J.: Paulist Press, 1965.

————. *Concept of Truth and Theological Renewal.* London and Sidney, 1968.

————. *Wereld en Kerk.* Holland: Uitgeverij H. Nelissen Buthoven, 1966. [ET: *World and Church.* Translated by N. D. Smith. Coll. Theological Soundings, vol. 4. New York: Sheed and Ward, 1971.]

Schoof, Mark. *A Survey of Catholic Theology 1800-1970.* Translated by N. D. Smith. New York: Paulist Press, 1970.

Semmelroth, Otto. *Die Kirche als Ursakrament.* Frankfurt am Main: Verlag Josef Knecht, 1955.

————. *Vom Sinn der Sakramente.* Frankfurt am Main: Verlag Josef Knecht, 1960.

Sheedy, C. E. "Opinions concerning Doctrinal Development." *American Ecclesiastical Review* 120 (1949): 19-32.

Smalley, Beryl. *The Study of the Bible in the Middle Ages.* New York: Philosophical Library, 1952.

Smulders, P. *The Design of Teilhard de Chardin.* New York; Westminster, Md., n.d.

―――. "L'église sacrement du salut." In *L'Eglise de Vatican II.* Vol. II, ed. G. Barauna, 313-338. Coll. Unam Sanctam 51b. Paris: Cerf, 1966.

Solages, B. de. "Autour d'une controverse." *Bulletin de littérature ecclésiastique* 48 (January-March 1947): 3-17.

―――. "Pour l'honneur de la théologie. Les contresens du Père Garrigou-Lagrange." *Bulletin de littérature ecclésiastique* 48 (Avril-Juin 1947): 64-84.

Spicq, C. "Bulletin de théologie biblique." *Revue des sciences philosophiques et théologiques* 32 (1948): 88-91.

―――. *Esquisse d'une histoire de l'exégèse latine au moyen age.* Paris: Vim, 1944.

(no author) "La théologie et ses sources: Réponse aux Etudes critique de la *Revue Thomiste* (Mai-Aug 1946)." *Recherches de science religieuse* 33 (1946): 385-401.

Thils, Gustave. *Orientations de la théologie.* Louvain: Warny, 1958.

Tillich, Paul. *Systematic Theology.* Vols. I, II, III. Chicago: University of Chicago Press, 1951, 1957, 1963.

Valeske, U. *Votum Ecclesiae.* Munich: Claudius Verlag, 1962.

Van Roo, William A. "Reflections on Karl Rahner's 'Kirche und Sakramente'." *Gregorianum* 44 (1963): 465-500.

Vollert, C. "*Humani Generis* and the Limits of Theology." *Theological Studies* 12 (1951): 3-23.

Weigel, Gustave. "The Historical Background of the Encyclical *Humani Generis.*" *Theological Studies* 12 (1951): 208-230.

Index

181